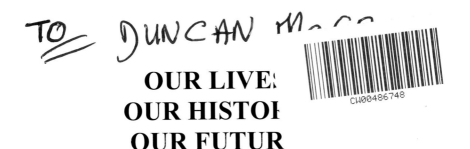

TO DUNCAN M...

OUR LIVE!
OUR HISTOI
OUR FUTUR

Written and Edited by Jim Thakoordin

In fond remembrance of Enrico Stennett 1926-2011

Copyright @ 2014 Jim Thakoordin

All Rights Reserved

Published by Jim Thakoordin

First published in 2012
Updated and reprinted October 2014

Available from Jim Thakoordin
Email: info@jimthakoordin.com
Website: www.jimthakoordin.com

Fast -Track Mail Order Tel: 01582 725726 (M) 0778 8787 310

Price £7.99 plus postage

JIM'S LATEST BOOK
714 pages 9 inches x 6 inches with over 40 photographs, published 2014. Half price £10, plus postage, directly from Jim

ALL DIFFERENT ALL EQUAL
THE STORY OF MY LIFE

Too often the vital contribution of Black workers and activists to the British trade union movement has been hidden, lost or unrecorded. This book will help set the record straight. Jim was one of a generation of leading black trade unionists who fought to put hopes, dreams and aspirations of grass roots Black workers at the heart of the agenda of the trade union movement, culminating in ground breaking campaigns for race equality.

Jim's book is important not only because we must remember our history but because it helps us learn how to shape our future. It reminds us of the importance of leadership and self organisation - as the Irish socialist James Connolly once wrote: "None so fit to break their chains as those who wear them." Above all, Jim's story provides proof that even in the most difficult of circumstances, through perseverance and solidarity, together working people can change society for the better.

Frances O'Grady
General Secretary of the Trade Union Congress

WRITTEN BY JIM THAKOORDIN

CONTENTS

PART TWO – VARIOUS ARTICLES

PART THREE – FAMOUS PEOPLE

PART FOUR – CONCLUSION

Acknowledgements

I would like to thank all the people who contributed to this book as a tribute to Enrico Stennett, including Professor Robert Moore, Professor Harry Goulbourne, Zita Holbourne and Marc Wadsworth. I am also grateful to Peter Fryer who wrote *Staying Power – The History of Black People in Britain*, published by Pluto for some research material and John Archer's Speech.

I want to use this opportunity to thank my wife Doreen for being my wife and friend for over 51 years, and my four beautiful grandchildren: Rohanie Campbell-Thakoordin; Elijah Thakoordin; Aoife Campbell-Thakoordin, and Sarah Thakoordin for their love and inspiration. My daughter Jane Thakoordin has been an important person in my life and has with her mother, Doreen Thakoordin, seen me through decades of struggles with my health and with my battles to change society through politics, trade union activism, community work and anti-racism. My daughter Jane is a special person in my life and I am delighted that we share so much in common. Doreen who has been a School Teacher almost all her working life and retired in 2005 as an Assistant Head Teacher has been a tower of strength and my best friend since I first met her in 1962, on a London Transport bus. I owe a great deal to her for my academic and other achievements. I am also grateful for the support my son Michael Thakoordin has given me. I am grateful to my parents, Mabel and Jokhan and my six sisters for their love and inspiration.

Enrico and I have known each other for many years. We worked together on his Book Buckra Massa Pickney, which he published through UPSO in 2006, ISBN: 1-84375-271-9. We had started to work on this book before he died on 7 July 2011.

With extra special thanks to my precious family.

My wife and I with our children, Michael and Jane and our four grandchildren – Elijah, Sarah and Aoife and Rohanie at the back.

About this book – by the author

This book is about black history and the importance of why we should all know where we have come from, where we are at and where we are likely to go, as history is not only about the past, it is about the present and the future as well. For Thomas Jefferson, one of the founders of the American Constitution:

> *"History by apprising [citizens] of the past will enable them to judge of the future; it will avail them of the experience of other times and other nations; it will qualify them as judges of the actions and designs of men; it will enable them to know ambition under every disguise it may assume; and knowing it, to defeat its views."*–Thomas Jefferson Notes on the State *of Virginia.*

> *History is important because we are undeniably linked to the past: we are the sum of all the events, whether they are good, bad or indifferent. "We study the past to understand the present; we understand the present to guide the future." - William Lund, because according to Fried Nietzsche: "The man who fails to learn his history is destined to repeat it." - Friedrich Nietzsche*

For too long our past has been denied to us. The involvement of the Europeans in Africa, Asia, North and South America and Australia has been significant in terms of how we perceived history and our role and status in the present world. Our history, at least the glorious parts which we have given to the world and its civilisation was either distorted, hidden or denied to us due to the European justification of imperialism, slavery, colonialism and neo-colonialism. Africa, the cradle of humankind and much of human civilisation, was re-labelled by the Europeans and black people were depicted as uncivilised, less than human beings and much inferior to the Europeans. So it was acceptable for them to conquer and enslaved our ancestors. They were captured, transported and sold into slavery and all their offspring were the owned by their masters. Tens of millions of Africans, natives of North and South America and elsewhere were forced into slavery, exploitation, miserable lives and early death.

This book has been written in order to encourage black people to look at themselves and to reflect on our past so we can understand why we are where we are, and why across Europe we are still, after slavery has been abolished nearly two hundred years ago, people are still being stereotyped as dirty, lazy, criminals, who are unwanted and unwelcomed, and therefore are forced to endure racial prejudice, discrimination, higher rates of unemployment, poor housing, low pay, harassment and bullying, institutional racism and disproportionate levels of poverty and suffering in the richest economies of Europe.

My friend Enrico Stennett provides us with a great insight of what his life was as an immigrant to Britain in 1947. Despite the fact that black people had actually discovered Europe and Britain and had lived in England before the Romans invaded Britain in AD 43 – nearly 2,000 years ago, black people in Britain are still seen as foreigners, undesirable immigrants and a liability to the state. John Archer, Marc Wadsworth and others have argued about the importance of knowing our history, and I have included a wide range of contributions from people past and present who have helped to shape our past and present and influence our future. Where ever we are, who ever we are, we take our past with us. We are what we are because of our past.

It's important for us to know of our history, because if we don't; then misunderstandings will grow faster than weeds and with that we will be unable to play the part we need to in order to secure justice, equality, fairness and respect in a world characterised by conflicts, poverty, oppression, abuse of human rights, racism and rampant capitalist greed, materialism and individualism. What we don't know we fear. What we fear we hate. Hatred is an animal born of all fears and often leads us into bloodshed, tears, destruction, and early death. That is why it is so important to study our past and make the links to the present. Learning about our past including our heritage, religion and our culture helps us and our children, to utilise our accumulated knowledge with common sense and wisdom. We often ask why so many black youths are not succeeding in this society; why are they involved in violence and anti-social behaviour including black on black murders and grievous bodily harm. Is it because they have lost their way; not feeling wanted or acceptable; alienated and under-achieved within the education system, or because of the cumulative impact of centuries of racism and oppression of black people in Europe and elsewhere.

Enrico Stennett was a role model; a historian; a friend and brother to black people around the world. He has left us with useful ideas and thoughts about the importance of black unity and respect for each other. He has explained to us the terrible outcomes when we are disunited, divided and weak. I hope you will find this book useful to you and will be able to share the thoughts of people like Enrico and others contained in this book so we can all try to use our past in a positive way to help shape our future.

I believe there is at least one important lesson we must all learn that is although we grow up in different environments and cultures we react in similar ways, and that makes us more alike than different. That is an important piece of knowledge, because instead of viewing others as total strangers, we begin to realize that we are "family". This helps us across the whole spectrum of our childhood and adult lives, because we interact with others daily, and when people can "connect" with us, we increase our chances of success in whatever we are attempting to achieve. That is a benefit that comes from understanding the roots of our and others' history and culture.

Positive gains through black unity

9

We have made progress in many areas despite the pressures of individual and institutional racism. The work that comrades like Enrico Stennett, Marc Wadsworth, Zita Holbourne, Lee Jasper, myself and countless others have done in the labour movement have paved the way for progress in many areas. We now have 27 Black members of Parliament, 45 Black people in the House of Lords – they are represented in the Cabinet and Shadow Cabinet, they are Ministers and Shadow Ministers, they are there partly because of the work we have done over the decades to increase Black representation not only in Parliament, but in every area of British life. I was a founder member of the Black Trades Union Solidarity Movement that was supported by Marc Wadsworth and others; we campaigned for equal representation in trade unions, at a time when many unions themselves were institutionally racist. We helped people like Lord Bill Morris to become General Secretary of one of the largest trade unions in Britain – the Transport & General Workers Union. Bill was appointed a Governor of the Bank of England and on the Boards of several public bodies - a long way from his humble beginnings in the Caribbean and as a labourer in England.

Black unity through Black self-organisation – the Labour Party Black Sections and the Black Socialist Society in which Marc Wadsworth and I were founder members, assisted and enabled many Black people to successfully enter Parliament. The four Black MPs elected in 1987 were all involved in and supported by the Labour Party Black Section. Keith Vaz, Bernie Grant, Diane Abbott and Paul Boetang (now Lord Boetang) were successful mainly because Black Section created the environment and provided the physical as well as the moral support which enabled them to succeed. The number of Black Parliamentarians has grown over fifteen times its size since 1987. Many of them are now stalwarts in the Conservative Party. Baroness Valerie Amos, a Black woman whose parents came to Britain from Guyana was the Leader of the House of Lords and Baroness Patricia Scotland's parents were from the Caribbean, she was the Solicitor General for the Government and the Queen.

Black people have achieved in every profession, every institution and in every aspect of British and European lives from education, science, music, politics, the media, businesses, law, medicine, the art and culture to Principals of schools, colleges and universities, Judges, multi-millionaires in businesses and some of the most influential people in Britain. They are all part of our history.

Social interactions and the influence of history

This is true not only for the individual (imagine what would have happened to you had your parents never met, or your parents had raised you with different values), but for large societies as well (how would the U.S. A, China, India or Africa would be today, for example, if the Europeans did not colonise these countries, or if the Spanish had founded and retained the colonies of North America, Asia and the Caribbean)? The future is highly unpredictable and we all have an opportunity to use our past influence to help shape the future of our own lives and environment, that of our children and future generations.

The only way we can understand who we are and how we got to be that way is by studying the past. Similarly, the only way we can understand others is by studying their past. If we don't understand what made them who they are - in terms of how they think and act - we will make all sorts of mistakes in our interactions with them. We live in a multi-cultural, multi-racial society, the culture of Britain and Europe is changing with more mixed relationships, interactions of people from different races, cultures and lifestyles. It is important that we understand these changes and compare things to what they used to be, so we can measure the impact of such changes.

Think of how you treat people differently based on how you know them. The same is true for countries when it comes to diplomacy. Our failures in Iraq were borne of a limited understanding of who they are (because we hadn't taken the time to truly study and understand their past). It was based on false assumptions and even deliberate lies and even supported by senior Black staff and politicians in the

11

American and British governments that led the war in Iraq. What a difference it would have made to fighting poverty and inequality in our world had the money spent on the Iraq war been spent in supporting the 45 million Americans in poverty, the 300 millions in poverty in Africa, or the 3.5 billion – half the worlds' population who are forced to live on less than $2 per day? This is now history, and if we do not learn from history we are likely to repeat the same mistakes. We are part of that history, whether we accept it or not.

People shape history

How important is history? We are now living in a time of rapid change, a time of progress. We prefer to define ourselves in terms of where we are going, not where we come from. Our ancestors hold no importance for us. They lived in times so different from our own that they are incapable of shedding light on our experience. Man is so much smarter now than he was even ten years ago that anything from the past is outdated and irrelevant to us. We have landed on the moon; created weapons of mass destruction; stockpiled enough weapons to destroy the world one hundred times over and have made gigantic progress in medicine, science, communications, transport and agriculture, yet there are frequent wars, famine, natural disasters, a massive amount of domestic abuse, inequality, poverty and uncertainty about the future. Therefore the past, even the relatively recent past, is important to all of us. Our ignorance of the past is not the result of a lack of information, but of indifference. We do not believe that history matters. But history does matter. According to the creator of the Ford Motor Car "history is bunk". Well this is not the case. Those who deny us the knowledge of the past are doing so for a reason – mainly to deny us the opportunity to explore alternatives.

It has been said that he who controls the past controls the future. Our view of history shapes the way we view the present, and therefore it dictates what answers we offer for existing problems. When you go into a doctor's surgery for the first time, you invariably have to fill an information sheet that asks about your medical history. Some of these forms are very detailed, asking questions that require information from rarely accessed memory banks. Why does a doctor ask these questions? The doctor is trying to construct an accurate picture of your state of health. Your health is heavily influenced by the past. Your heredity, past behaviours, past experiences are all important determinants and clues to your present condition. Whenever you return to the doctor, he or she pulls out a file which contains all the notes from past visits. This file is a history of your health. Doctors understand very clearly that the past matters. This is one of the reasons why history is very important. The past does not change, but history changes with every generation. When Black people discuss their situation whether it is about racism, politics, the economy or international issues, they need to reflect on the past.

It's the most important thing there is. The past tells you who you are. You were raised the way you are because of how your parents were raised. They were raised a certain way because that's how people were raised back then. They had no television, mobile telephones, computers, or even simple household gadgets we take for granted today, yet they brought up large families, cared for the elderly and the sick, had time for each other and frequently shared what little they had. Yet they were more content with their lot. This is unlike today's generation overwhelmed by materialism, isolated by individualism and personal greed, millions addicted to alcohol and drugs, millions addicted to pornography, gambling and recreational sex and this involves people from as young as thirteen or fourteen. Child abuse, elderly abuse and neglect and adoration of the female body have become common aspects of everyday life for many millions and this is only in a relatively small nation which constitutes the United Kingdom. This type of lifestyle and values mainly nurtured by the Americans and certain European countries such as Britain, France and Germany are actively seeking to export this atrocity to the rest of the world by market capitalism, or by force.

Even traditional societies are unable to resist such filth and degrading values due to worldwide internet and communication

13

facilities. Our thinking, lifestyles and behaviour of the future as well as our ideologies and philosophies in the future are being shaped as you are reading this book.

It's very important to reflect on our history. It's important because the past is what makes the present. We should learn to appreciate history because it lets us know about all the legendary figures that made a difference to the world in which we live today. The stories contained in this book, about the lives and times of people like Dr Martin Luther King Jr., Mahatma Ghandi, Nelson Mandela, Malcolm X, Muhammad Ali and others are important for all of us. If we choose to ignore our past, we are likely to suffer future detriment as a result. One of the many reasons why history often repeats itself is because it's one of those subjects we take for granted. This whole public fear in the West of Muslims, black liberation struggles, Iran, and Al-Qaida reminds me of the decades of the "Cold War" that the Western capitalist powers waged against the Soviet Union and their allies in order to protect themselves from socialism and real democracy which involved governance by all the people for all the people. Racism was, and is still used an instrument such as the Cold War, fear of socialism, fear of nations like Iran asserting their own independence or Muslims seeking to correct past injustices against them. It is sad to see the first Black President in the USA – the strongest and mightiest nation in the world in terms of militarism, wealth and influence broadly following the same sort of policies as his white predecessors. Enrico was very disappointed with Obama and I share his views. The Obama era has been a disappointment for the world, especially the young, the poor and disadvantaged in not only America, but the world.

The challenges facing the world today are important for Black people, especially those who are poor, or have access to less than the average income, as these are the people who are forced to pay the price for the greed and mis-management of the capitalist economies of the world mainly the USA and Europe. This is no surprise as the capitalists have built a worldwide economic, financial and political system which ensures that poorer people and poorer nations pay the price of ensuring

14

that less than ten per cent of the richest people in the world control over eighty per cent of the wealth, power and influence in the world. Now this is a subject worth exploring, and which will only make sense if you go back in history at least from the fifteenth century before slavery, colonialism and institutional racism.

"The issue today is the same as it has been throughout all history, whether man shall be allowed to govern himself or be ruled by a small elite."   -- *Thomas Jefferson*

Some interesting quotes on the importance of learning history

"Throughout history, it has been the inaction of those who could have acted; the indifference of those who should have known better; the silence of the voice of justice when it mattered most; that has made it possible for evil to triumph". Haile Selassie *(Ethiopian Statesman and Emperor of Ethiopia from 1930 to 1974, 1892-1975.*

" History will have to record that the greatest tragedy of this period of social transition was not the strident clamour of the bad people, but the appalling silence of the good people". *- Dr Martin Luther King Jr.*

"History teaches us that men and nations behave wisely once they have exhausted all other alternatives" *- Abba Eban.*

"If you want to understand today, you have to search yesterday." *- Pearl Buck*

"History is the witness that testifies to the passing of time; it illuminates reality, vitalizes memory, provides guidance in daily life, and brings us tidings of antiquity." *– Cicero*

"Only a good-for-nothing is not interested in his past." *- Sigmund Freud*

"Each age tries to form its own conception of the past. Each age writes the history of the past anew with reference to the conditions uppermost in its own time."- Frederick Jackson Turner

"Men make their own history, but they do not make it just as they please; they do not make it under circumstances chosen by themselves, but under circumstances directly found, given and transmitted from the past. The tradition of all the dead generations weighs like a nightmare on the brain of the living."- Karl Marx

"The principle office of history I take to be this: to prevent virtuous actions from being forgotten, and that evil words and deeds should fear an infamous reputation with posterity."- Tacitus

"We have the power to make this the best generation of mankind in the history of the world - or the last." -John F. Kennedy

"Few will have the greatness to bend history itself; but each of us can work to change a small portion of events, and in the total; of all those acts will be written the history of this generation." -Robert F. Kennedy

"Those who cannot remember the past are condemned to repeat it."- George Santayana

Preface

Professor Robert Moore

Enrico Stennett

Enrico Stennett's life as an immigrant in Britain epitomises the lives of the *Windrush* generation of Commonwealth immigrants. The example he set in his response to his experiences inspired young people of the following generation. Consequently in the course of a very long life Enrico influenced the outlook and careers of many people, although this is an important aspect of his life of which others have more direct experience than I.. Almost any aspect of Enrico's youth in Jamaica or his adult life in the UK could provide the basis for a compelling novel.

17

In his autobiography, in an almost casual way, Enrico reports encounters with some of the most colourful public figures of his generation ranging from Hewlett-Johnson, the 'Red Dean' of Canterbury to Josephine Baker, music hall star, holder of the Croix de Guerre and civil rights activist, to Bertrand Russell, Britain's most influential 20th century philosopher. He moved among black musicians, boxers, even the famous racing tipster 'Prince Monalulu' came within his orbit. Norman and Michael Manley were among his political acquaintances as was Alexander Bustamante, first Prime Minister of the independent Jamaica. Enrico's later opinions of some politicians' careers were not always favourable and were usually expressed in forthright and uncomplimentary terms. Early on in his time in London, when searching for somewhere to live or in his occupation refurbishing residential properties, Enrico also became acquainted with elements of a criminal underworld who were then, amongst other activities, exploiting the problems of homeless new arrivals in the city.

Enrico had many *personae*; the initially unsuccessful stowaway; 'Sugar', the spectacular dancer with whom all the girls wished to dance, agitator for African emancipation and street orator. It is possible that I first saw Enrico at Speakers' Corner in Hyde Park in the late 1950s when I used to listen to Donald Soper on Sunday afternoons, the soap-box used by Enrico and his colleagues in the *African League* **and the Coloured Workers Association of Great Britain and Northern Ireland was** next to Soper's.

Race and Identity

What I have described so far is a life containing more than enough material for a television series. But colourful as the story may be, for me it is only background to the much more serious aspects of Enrico's life. Enrico's political career began before he came to the UK. He was born into a white family of relatively wealthy owners of plantations and other businesses. He discovered at a very early age that skin colour was closely associated with social class and with social status. He was told off for holding hands with a little black girl and punished for

18

associating with unsuitable (i.e. black) companions. He saw that black people did the hardest labour and the most menial jobs, whilst white people enjoyed the benefits of that hard labour. Enrico started his education in a school that sought to impart white 'Christian' values and the history of a 'mother' country. Whilst the Tudors and Stuarts would have been taught in his school, slave rebellions would not have featured in the curriculum. But Enrico's status was even more ambiguous than he may have fully appreciated at the time and it was certainly a problem for his family. Not a 'pure' white child, was he to be educated to enable him to fill managerial or ownership roles in the family businesses? If he was, then it was doubly inappropriate that that he should associate with youngsters who would one day become servants and labourers. Enrico solved the problem for his family by striking out for the city on his own and thereafter he made his own life whilst maintaining contact with those relatives of whom he was particularly fond. Nevertheless Enrico absorbed more than many might have done from his schooling, he acquired a love of books and learning, he gained a grasp of English history and acquired some of the more admirable of the Christian virtues. Enrico nevertheless probably saw himself as a respectable and well-educated person and he really only became aware of his blackness and its meaning when he arrived in England.

To be black in Britain in the 1950s was to be regarded as less than human by many natives and openly to be denied housing, employment and access to services on the basis of that skin colour. The 'mother country' was not very maternal towards newcomers from the Caribbean. Significantly Enrico had seen himself as belonging, in part at least, to a privileged elite who, in Jamaica, looked down on 'black' people with whom Enrico was discouraged from associating. Now he found himself to be a black man, to be looked down upon and excluded from 'respectable' society. Enrico must have experienced an extreme psychological and existential shock on his arrival in the UK. Enrico's experience was a more acute version of the experience of many who came, or were invited, from the Caribbean to the 'mother country'. Most had come from the West Indies to seek employment and whilst their schooling may have led them to think of the UK as a mother country not many perhaps believed they actually *belonged* in Britain. Enrico commented that 'I did not come because I was hungry or poor, I came because I thought England was where my family belonged. They conditioned me to believe I was English.... '

Later in life Enrico experienced a similar shock, but this time the shock of return. He wished to be buried in his ancestral land and accordingly returned to Jamaica when he thought his life was nearing its end. He was returning to 'his' people and did not expect to be regarded by any Jamaicans as a privileged returnee or to be treated as 'white'. His disappointment with contemporary Jamaica was palpable and his comments upon it were touched with hints of bitterness. Like many migrants he had dreamt of returning to a society that no longer existed. Furthermore early 21st century Jamaica was not a society to which he could readily adapt after so many years in the UK. So Enrico finally returned to North Wales, where the scenery (but not the weather) reminded him of Jamaica

If the Jamaica of Enrico's childhood and youth had changed, so had the Britain to which he returned at the end of his life. The population had become more diverse since the 1950s but black people from the Caribbean were still over-represented in the lower strata of society and over-represented amongst the unemployed and the prison population. A substantial black middle class had also emerged since the 1950s, a class which Enrico felt had largely forgotten its roots and turned its back on the less privileged section of the Caribbean population. Even 'Caribbean' was becoming a problematic label with the maturity of two British-born generations of Caribbean heritage. 'Mixed' was the most rapidly growing 'ethnic' category between the 1991 and 2001 censuses. Intermarriage had become common and elements of cultural hybridism were plain to see, especially amongst the young. The rhetoric of racism now focused on 'bogus' asylum seekers, East European migrants and, especially, Muslims. By contrast legislation against racial discrimination had been enacted and both public and commercial agencies were making strides with their equalities policies – not least because the minority populations were recognised both as potential customers and employees. Nevertheless black people were still dying at the hands of the police or in custody while the criminal justice system was conspicuously failing many black victims of crime. Soon after he arrived in Britain Enrico attended the funeral of Kelso Cochrane. Forty years later Steven Lawrence was murdered by racists and some of the gang that killed him were convicted after extensive campaigning, only 19 years later. Had he lived a little longer Enrico could have attended the funeral of Mark Duggan, an unarmed black youth shot dead by the police. So much had changed in Enrico's Britain, but little had changed.

Race and Class

Enrico was acutely aware of the reality of the impact of ideas about 'race' and he observed from an early age how one's position in society was assigned on the basis of 'race'. This worked in two ways – but two ways that were connected – firstly race or skin colour marked your social standing, the esteem in which others held you. The paler your skin, the higher your social standing, your social status. But secondly race was a feature of the economic and political structure. White people owned land and other productive resources, they were employers, magistrates and administrators who wielded economic and political power over black people. This was, of course, the problem for his family because Enrico crossed the line between white and black, between power and subordination. Position in the economic order of society – class – became increasingly salient in Enrico's thinking. He came to see 'race' as a concept developed by the upper classes to subordinate whole populations in colonial systems and to create cheap labour and a divided working class in the metropolitan societies. I never had any long conversations with Enrico on the idea of race and whenever we discussed race conflict or racial exploitation he would turn it around into a class issue. Enrico was nevertheless proud of his Jamaican heritage and recognised the importance of cultural differences, but not of 'race'. Race had no objective reality, it was simply a term to be used against people. Only by understanding the conflict between those who were wealthy and powerful and those with neither wealth nor power could we understand how the idea of race worked. For Enrico 'race' had little meaning other than a trick to subordinate colonial peoples and to divide the working classes of metropolitan societies who were themselves being increasingly economically excluded. Unemployed white people and benefits claimants were coming to occupy a social status only just above asylum seekers in the British social order of the early 21st century. But ideas of 'race' gave the lowest members of the white working class a little status – that of not being black. Unmasking the nature of this division was for Enrico one of the main political tasks of anyone working in 'race relations' in Britain. Enrico also believed that the British status system, deriving from the economic order, deflected many black people from understanding the common interests of the black population. The common interests were rooted in the class position of black people, not their 'race'. People became caught up in striving for better houses or bigger cars, some craved official recognition and Honours and thus all lost sight of the true part they played in British society.

Given his denial of the reality of race or ethnicity, how did Enrico describe himself in the 2001 census? 'Citizen of the United Kingdom', he told me, 'That's what I wrote because that's what I am'. Citizen is a powerful term to be understood in contrast to 'subject of the Crown'. Citizenship in its radical derivation asserts the equality of all people, solidarity and common interests between them. It was no surprise to Enrico that conservative administrations, both Labour and Conservative, had turned the noble idea of citizenship into a term of exclusion – something to keep people out rather than bind them together. But Enrico knew that he was a citizen in the radical sense and he regarded this as a real status rather than a spurious racial or ethnic category.

Race, Class and Colonialism

As a young man Enrico noted that the railways in Jamaica were not built for the convenience of local travellers. They had been constructed for the extraction of Jamaica's wealth. The railways ran to the seaports.

Companies from overseas operated in Jamaica to generate profits for their owners and shareholders in metropolitan countries, not to serve a local market. The population had been brought to Jamaica in servitude to work for the interests of the property-owning classes. From his reading and his work with others in anti-colonial campaigns Enrico saw how across the world colonists had taken the land from the native people, settled and farmed it, making great personal profits in metropolitan markets. Native residents could starve, be it in India or Ireland, while foodstuffs were exported to make great profits in 'home' markets. The subordination of the inhabitants, deprived or land and livelihood or reduced to miserable forms of wage-labour was often ensured through extreme brutality. In Enrico's thought, at least in his later years, colonial relations were an extension of class relations and class relations were reflections of colonial domination. They were different ways to view exploitation by the rich and powerful. They were two aspects of capitalism. Enrico developed a simple Marxist analysis which enabled him to describe and explain the relations of domination and exploitation to be found in both metropolitan countries and their colonies within a single theoretical framework. Enrico was an orator and a campaigner and this theoretical stance gave his views considerable coherence and great persuasive power, without needing close academic scrutiny.

Enrico became frustrated with the apparent passivity of the black British population and their striving for status in the British class system. He was perhaps unfairly critical of those who were full engaged in making a living and striving for their children's advancement rather than mobilising against capitalism. Enrico's ideas and his oratorical power needed a movement to carry them and to develop them into a programme. Unfortunately for Enrico there was no movement that could carry his message with its radical, broad-brush historical perspective and turn it into a manifesto around which black working class people could rally.

There are sides to Enrico's history and character that I have not seen. Plainly he was very influential in his work with young people,

23

helping many to respond constructively to the pressures and indignities of life in the UK and setting many on the 'right way'. His own experiences in his early days in the UK made him especially understanding of and sympathetic to the troubles both of those who came later and those who were born here to immigrants parents. He must have been a thorn in the side of the 'race relations industry' because of the way in which he included all forms of exploitation and inequality in his analysis of capitalism whilst working for organisations that wished to bracket 'race' off to be addressed as an issue separable from class and gender. Others will write about these aspects of his life. My view of Enrico, was formed by conversations with him in his last decade and reading drafts of his autobiography. I think there is a sense in which Enrico stands for every immigrant of the post-war period; he experienced the shock of discovering that he was black and that the Mother Country was not very welcoming. But he brought with him a range of skills and aptitudes that enabled him to survive in hostile conditions.. Later he experienced a similar trauma on returning to a home country that had changed beyond his recognition.

What sets Enrico aside is that he was one of that minority of immigrants who brought with them the experience of trade union and political organisation in the colonial setting and applied it in the UK. Most importantly he was able to theorise his experiences and create a coherent explanation of social relations in Jamaica and the UK that made them part of one economic and social structure. He had seen both sides of the coin. What he learnt in Jamaica, what he saw and experienced in the UK were all of one piece. These experiences did not embitter him but enabled him to aid and support others. Part of his heritage is the demand that we be kind to one another, but uniquely perhaps that we do not see class and race or consumption and colonialism as separate issues and that thus equipped we continue the struggle for the emancipation of humankind throughout the world.

Tribute to Enrico Stennett –
Professor Harry Goulbourne

I cannot now recall the precise time when I first met Enrico Stennett, but the general circumstances were those of the late 1980s or early 1990s. During these years, I worked at the University of Warwick, and I ran a weekly seminar that was open to both academics and the general public. My memory of the first conversation with Enrico was at the end of one of these seminars. The conversation was about serious matters pertaining to the lives of black people in Britain, and in this vein we continued to converse in subsequent years until close to his passing in 2011.

In this brief note of appreciation of the life of Enrico Stennett, I want to make two personal observations about Ricky the person, and to say something about his work for the African Caribbean and minority communities of Coventry.

First, Ricky was a true Jamaican. This was brought out by the fact that I knew him as Ricky, not Enrico. It is not unusual to know a Jamaican for most of his or her life, and never come to know the name that the parents gave and that appeared on their birth certificate. It is easy to believe that every Jamaican has a formal, proper, serious name but often only few people will be privy to this name. This is because to the wider world the name that the person goes by is different - sometimes entirely different from their given name; sometimes a derivative, as in Enrico's case. In the Jamaican tradition, Ricky's popular name reflected his personality – warm and helpful, passionate, forceful, and committed to his cause.

Second, Ricky was a Jamaican patriot, through and through. Embodying the spirit of the pioneer generation of Caribbean sojourners to Britain, in late life Ricky decamped from Coventry to what appeared to be deepest and farthest Wales. I was impressed by this move. After all, this was the display of the spirit of up and go that the offspring of Caribbean migrants no longer appear to be blessed. There is at least one generation of people of Caribbean backgrounds in Britain who will not seize the opportunities for self-improvement if this involves moving away from their comfort-zones in the big inner-cities where their parents or grand-parents settled in the 1950s and 1960s. In his retirement days, wittingly or otherwise, Ricky pointed a way for the young to improve themselves by making the United Kingdom their own, and we'd hoped to see Ricky and his beloved Mary in their rural Welsh setting.

But Ricky achieved more than this: he took the momentous step of returning to Jamaica. In conversations with him and from research I have conducted on the lives of returnees, I fully appreciate his efforts to contend with the travails of the returnee, and his decision to be yet another kind of returnee - this time back to Britain. It appears that 'there'll always be a welcome when you come home again to Wales'; and, for Ricky this was true.

There is, of course, an irony here, and it's part of the experience of migration, and particularly of the Caribbean Diaspora. A profound aspect of Caribbean spread across the North Atlantic has been the desire or dream of return - return to Africa, return to 'mother country' (England, and sometimes Scotland and Ireland, and Wales, but nearly always England), and a dream yet again to return to the Caribbean. I did not know Ricky in his active, working, years; by the time we met he was within his veil of years, retired, but had time to share his experiences and observations with me. (These I have recorded in a series of interviews with Ricky, and I trust that they've been preserved as part of his legacy). Although he and Mary had some bitter and unfortunate experience in the land of his birth, Jamaica, in his latter years, from conversations with him over the phone from Jamaica and from Wales, I had a sense that Ricky took these in his stride as power for the course. Remarkably, there was an absence of bitterness in his account as conveyed through our telephone conversations.

I want to conclude these brief remarks by paying tribute to Ricky for his invaluable support and collaboration in the production of the report I was privileged to lead in the mid 1990s, entitled *The needs of the African Caribbean community in Coventry*. This was a 9-month research and report financed by the City Council of Coventry, and which became the basis of policy for the better part of a decade in that city with respect to the Caribbean community. Ricky, along with others of his colleagues, such as Kenneth Cupid, provided invaluable grass-root support to the large research team that I led, as well as a counterbalance to the various forces in the Coventry political community with which any policy researcher has to contend.

Ricky did important work in Wolverhampton and elsewhere in Britain, and was a participant in the historic anti-colonial struggle both in Britain and Jamaica. Others will no doubt speak of his contributions in these spheres. But my tribute is to Ricky as a person and to his contribution to Coventry of which I have personal experience. I whole heartedly hail him on his way to his African, Caribbean, and European ancestors - all of whom should be recognized in the making of a complex and caring man.

Tribute to my dear husband –
Mary Ann Stennett

Enrico and Mary Stennett

Speech made by Mary in Wolverhampton, in 2012, at the first anniversary of Enrico's death.

I am very grateful to everybody who could manage to take the time to be here today to honour my dear beloved husband Henry Stennett.

Most of us are familiar with the Bible, we may recall in Mathew Chapter 18: Where Jesus said 'Where two or three are gathered together in my name, there am I in the midst of them. Mr Stennett had a wonderful spirit; I know his presence is with us all here today. I know I was blessed to have met such a wonderful human being in Enrico Stennett, and even more privileged to have spent so many years of my life with him. I will always remain eternally grateful...

28

He was a gentleman. Mr Stennett was one in a million, the likes of which we will never see again. He was a little gem. He was the most lovable man you could ever dream of meeting in your lifetime. He was a charming, sweet, adorable, gentle man with kindness in his eyes, which endeared you to him. He grew up in a bygone era in a unique privileged aristocratic upbringing in Jamaica, on the Free Mountain Estate, near Mount Horeb. The Free Mountain Estate was a large plantation, which dated back to the time of slavery; the property had been handed down through the generations of Harris, Stennetts and McKinleys.

His family had large plantations in the Parish's of St James, Trelawney and St Elizabeth, all in the County of Cornwall. Mr Stennett was able to take me to the Estate when we were there, which sadly has been left unoccupied and neglected. I was completely overcome with the size of it; it was similar to the size of an English Park. We all know we were all truly blessed to have been given the opportunity to have known him.

I can be proud to be able to stand here today knowing I did all that was humanely possible to keep my husband Henry alive, and in doing so was able to prolong his life. Even as his health was failing he still had hope, he loved life and wanted to live. He had a wonderful passion for life although he was getting older, some people as they age begin to lose their zest for living, but his passion never faltered, and if it had not been for his health problems, he would still be with us today.

Mr Stennett was born a unique person, when I met him he had already achieved so much in his life, but I was to be the person he was to spend so many years of his precious life with. I often felt inadequate to deal with the relationship I found myself in. I through circumstances as we all have done in our lives, unknowingly met such an adorable human being, just by applying for a job in an office to work as a Receptionist/Telephonist in such an unlikely place as Tottenham in North London, in 1969.

Henry Stennett was not somebody you just loved, he was somebody you adored, and I adored him.

As the years moved on I began to realise I had fallen in love with an ICON. He was a cross between, Michael Manley, Paul Robeson, Michael Foot, Tony Benn, Bertrand Russell, Martin Luther King, and Nelson Mandela, I became mesmerised by him, and started to live in awe of him, which meant it was often a very difficult relationship for me. He was a complex man, born far ahead of his time, since the society and indeed the world were so far behind.

Caring for him in every way I could in the last months of his dear life and then going through all the pain of losing him, was the worst pain I have suffered and will ever suffer for the rest of my life. I had to plan his funeral alone with no support from anyone, I have not been back to his grave, when I lost him I lost the only good friend I had in my whole life. We went to live in Jamaica when he was 80 years of age believing if his health declined I would have had support from his family and if he had died they would have taken the responsibility and burden of the funeral off me, but sadly after going all that way to live in Jamaica with him I received no support from any of them.

Henry Stennett should have had the support from so many so that he had a funeral fitting for such as the Prime Minister Michael Manley would have had in Jamaica, with all the dignitaries attending and to have been televised. It is sad in that whatever is done will never do justice to the incredible human being he was, he was deprived of the recognition he so rightly deserved, partly through the jealousy of his own people towards him because he was so gifted, and his humbleness as a person. He enjoyed a lifelong passion for ballroom and Latin dancing, but the essence of his spirit was he was a politician, from a child aged 11 years in Jamaica he spoke in Sabina Park in Kingston on behalf of the PNP, he worked in their offices as a clerk and spoke on their platforms at public meetings.

At one meeting in Sabina Park in 1942 he spoke to a crowd of thousands where he was presented on the platform as the 'Voice of

Young Jamaica'. He had to be careful where he went making sure he never found himself in areas where he could be attacked, as in the lead up to elections there were many attacks by the followers of Bustamante on many people. In the 1950's when he was married to his first wife in London, as a member of the Labour Party he was on the 'B' list as a prospective Labour Parliamentary candidate.

It is as a politician he has to be remembered, fighting racism, injustice, and the brutality of this world, he was born into that calling. His life was one of sacrifice for all who suffered at the hands of racism and injustice. One of his dreams years ago was to be the Prime Minister of Jamaica which would have been his calling but it was not to be. What mattered to him more than anything was his fight for justice and equality for all; he was a politician throughout his whole lifetime.

Many people never knew the great man in their midst who was talking to them, and many will never know how truly great he was. He brought to politics superior intellect and enormous self-confidence. Science informs us that genes and environment are the dominant factors in the shaping of the human personality. On both counts Enrico Stennett was well served. He also was blessed with an inordinate capacity for sustained physical and intellectual effort and an extraordinary sense of duty and obligation.

He touched the lives of many people; he spoke with a passion about the anguish of the poor and the dispossessed. After the funeral, Mary Harris one of Henrys cousins who live in America said to me 'Mary you moved the World for Henry and I thank you for it. If any man on this planet deserved to be loved it was him. We all have to leave this earthly life, but when Mr Stennett lost his precious life, a light went out in the world which will never shine again, and even the stars in the sky were weeping.

Beloved Enrico, thank you for being who you were.

HENRY STENNETT, BUCKRA MASSA PICKNEY, I know you are with us all here today. May your precious, sweet memories, live on forever.

31

Introduction
Jim Thakoordin

Jim Thakoordin 6 August 1943

Enrico Stennett a great Jamaican and Internationalist

Enrico Stennett was born on 9th October, 1926 in Mount Carey, close to Maroon Town, in Montego Bay, Jamaica, at that time a British Colony; some of his family from his mother's side were Plantation owners. Enrico was less than a year old when Marcus Garvey a well known supporter of Black Nationalism and Pan Africanism returned to Jamaica after serving a prison sentence in America. At the age of three he was sent to the only boarding school in his village. The school was run by two English Headmistresses for pupils whose parents could afford to pay the fees for their children's education. He was sent to this school to learn to speak fluent English and English grammar. He attended the school for four years where he gained a certificate for elocution. Because of virtue of his birth (most of his family were of British and

32

German extraction) he was sent to Cornwall College in Montego Bay for further education.

Enrico was born into a system and a community severely divided and stratified by skin colour, race, class and culture, a system which still exists to this day in various ways and to which Enrico dedicated his life to change. Before reaching his teenage years he had experienced bitter racism, hostility and suffering as a mixed-race child. Race, racism, power and prejudice surrounded him from birth, and he was determined that his adult life would be focused on freeing people from racism, exploitation, suffering and degradation.

Enrico was born into an elite class structure on his mother's side, and was a product of a mixed-race relationship, which ended with the death of his Jamaican father, before he was born. Following Enrico's birth, his white mother was ostracised and her life changed substantially for the worse. The young Enrico was, to a large extent, brought up by his relatives and one particular aunt, whom he adored all his life.

A typical home of the plantation owners where
Enrico's maternal grandparents lived

Although Enrico was born and educated in a relatively middle class family before he left for England in 1947, on the Empire Windrush, in one of the strangest journey across the Atlantic. Enrico came to London with high hopes and aspirations. He wanted to study law and to do his very best to help the poorer people in society. Enrico never lost his commitment towards fighting for the underdog. On leaving College at seventeen he was employed by the Jamaican National Party, headed by Norman Manley, as a Social Worker, looking after the problems of the membership. Enrico spoke in Sabina Park as the Voice of Young Jamaica at the age of twelve, in 1938, the year of the Sugar Company Estates Workers Strike.

The strange tale of the Empire Windrush and Enrico's journey to London

This is the first time the story has been told about how Enrico arrived on the Empire Windrush in September 1948 and not on 14 June 1948 with the 493 paid passengers and one stowaway. Enrico always insisted that he arrived nearly a year before the famous 1948 journey of the Windrush. According to the records, the Empire Windrush made only one passenger journey bringing people from Jamaica in 1948. This is very true, but the ship had made a number of previous journeys to Jamaica before it docked in Kingston en route back to England after ferrying troops back to Australia and called at a number of places including Singapore and Hong Kong. The German cruise ship built in 1930 was named Monte Rosa, until it was captured by the British in May 1945 and used to transport troops to a number of countries.

It was on one of these journeys when the Empire Windrush docked in Kingston, Jamaica. Many of the men were fed up with the racism they had endured in the armed services and after the War as civilians. Whilst the ex-servicemen were returning to Jamaica, there were many more who wanted to leave Jamaica for the "Mother County". So whilst the ship was in Kingston docks in 1947, several Jamaicans entered the ship secretly and were identified as stowaways before the ship arrived in September in 1947.

In 1948 when the ship docked in Kingston on its way back to England an advert had appeared in a Jamaican newspaper offering cheap transport on the ship for anybody who wanted to come and work in the UK. At that time, there were no immigration restrictions for citizens of one part of the British Empire moving to another part. The arrival of the Windrush naturally prompted complaints from the public and some Members of Parliament, who wanted to get rid of the black population from Britain. However, the Conservative government did pander to the public after prolonged and bitter debates about the need to control black immigration and passed the 1962 Immigration Act which denied black people from the British Commonwealth the automatic right to travel to the United and to live and work here. It was acknowledged by the Labour Party as a piece of "racist legislation" and they committed to repealing it, but they never did. In fact they implemented it during their years in government from 1964 to 1970. The new Conservative Government passed an even more restrictive Immigration Act in 1971 and Labour again opposed it, but implemented it on return to government in 1974.

The Empire Windrush 1930-1954

Enrico came to England in 1948 with the intention of studying law, but on arrival he found London to be a much different place than he had anticipated. The conditions in parts of London were so poor, and the people were not too keen to welcome a black person. Enrico had great difficulty finding suitable accommodation due to racism and lack of finance. At one time he was forced to live in derelict houses in the freezing winter. He even lived for a while in a hostel, which

35

accommodated a number of people who were destitute. The environment was so filthy, that in a short space of time his body was covered in lice he decided to burn some of his clothes.

Enrico Stennett had a rich, diverse and unique experience during his early years in his native Jamaica and his life in Britain from 1948 to 7 July 2011. He had a great variety of experiences, including racism within various political parties and even the trade union and labour movement. His personal life and experiences, struggles, successes, frustrations and disappointments, together with his love for human rights, liberty, freedom and justice entitles him to be honoured by this and future generations. Enrico not only loved his native Jamaica, but he loved and cared for all the people who struggled and suffered under colonialism. He was a great historian, who read a lot of history. He would often take me back during our discussions on slavery and colonialism to the point where Christopher Columbus arrived in Jamaica in 1494. He would refer to the Arawaks who arrived in Jamaica 843 years before Columbus and their determination to resist the European invaders to their Island. Enrico was born and brought up in a geographical area of Jamaica well known for its resistance to colonialism. Sometimes I would say to Enrico "rebellion is in your blood my brother."

Enrico – a role model for black people

Enrico's life and work inspired many people over six decades in Britain. This book which covers part of his activities and experiences will be of immense interest to people from all racial, social, cultural, religious, professional and academic backgrounds. It can be used in schools, colleges and universities as resource material for people of any age, or background. There will be something in this book that will touch the hearts and stimulate the minds of every reader. As an author of several publications on race and race relations I can highly recommend this book.

The reader will be taken through a journey full of opportunities to think and reflect, to explore their own family backgrounds and historical experiences, to laugh and to weep, as well as to be reminded of some of the key issues surrounding race, community and international relations from the cruel and oppressive days of slavery to the present. We owe a great deal to Enrico for his thoughts, actions, honesty, and commitment to fairness, justice, equality and human rights. This despite criticisms and attempts by powerful institutions and individuals to deny him his right to express himself and to secure resources for the people he cared about, especially those who have been victims of racism and oppression.

Enrico's legacy

Enrico has left us with an in-depth insight into his character and feelings, which are often shared by others from black and mixed-race backgrounds, as they are frequently rejected by white people as well as black people from different social classes and cultures. Many mixed race people have been subjected to ridicule and taunts because of their heritage. As someone who has been married to an English woman from Irish and English backgrounds for over forty nine years and has two children who are a few years short of fifty, I have some knowledge of some of the dynamics surrounding mixed relationships. In addition, two of my grandchildren have an African mother and two of my grandchildren have an Irish father. Whilst mixed relationships in the past between white and black people were simply condemned by white people and institutions, it has become quite common in the 21st century to witness mixed relationships. This is very relevant in today's society, since nearly one third of relationships in Britain are between people from African, Afro-Caribbean and Asian backgrounds and white Europeans. Whilst many aspects of mixed relationships have changed during the last fifty years, there is still a lot of adverse reaction surrounding them from within and outside family members.

Enrico's experiences in Jamaica – and especially in London – made him the person we all knew and loved. He was outstanding as a husband, father, friend and comrade. As far as I know he has never been bitter or angry, but he was concerned about the way some of the people

37

he had worked so hard to help, eventually turned against him. Before becoming a Race Equality Officer, Enrico had many other jobs and interests. He had a building business which he built up from scratch, only to see it fail because he trusted fellow Caribbeans to help him run it. He was also equally disappointed when people he helped as a Race Equality Officer and a Community Worker verbally and physically attacked him, because he was unable to meet their demands, which they themselves did very little to achieve. Enrico always put himself out to support his fellow Caribbeans and indeed the British working class. He joined the Colonial Service based in Victoria Street, London and between the years of 1950- 1956 worked under Mr Ivor De Souza as a volunteer assisting with the settlement of the newly arrived West Indians in this country. He used to meet them at Victoria Railway Station, when they arrived in from the islands with only their few meagre possessions.

Between the years of 1950-1960 he spoke in Hyde Park as this was the only voice the black people had, at the time there were no black newspapers. He spoke about the racist conditions in Britain and for the freedom of the Caribbean and Africa from colonialism. He was a popular and provocative speaker at Hyde Park Corner, during both the summer and winter months.

Enrico speaking at Hyde Park Corner in 1952

In 1948 he was the founder of an organisation in Wimbledon, London, called the 'Cosmopolitan Social Association.' The emblem of this Association created by Enrico was of a black hand shaking a white hand which was used throughout Community Relations. Through this Association he worked amongst West Indians and Africans assisting them in all social problems: locating employment through the Trade Unions, assisting new arrivals from the West Indies to find accommodation and aiding both West Indians and Africans when in trouble with the Police.

In 1951, Enrico founded 'The African League' with Mr E Brewer who became Judge Advocate in Nigeria, and Mr W Longmore of Ghana. This organization was political and social; Enrico was responsible for the protest meetings held in London, in respect of Jagan of Guyana and Ceretsi Kharna of Botswana. This organisation had branches in Liverpool, Manchester, Birmingham, Nottingham and London. He was a lecturer for this organisation, speaking to co-operative societies, Trade unions and Labour Party branches throughout the country, Trade Unions and Labour Party meetings were highly challenging as he repeatedly challenged their prejudices and stereotypical notions of the lives, history and contributions made by black people for the benefit of the British nation. He left his audience in no doubt that the British people and institutions were responsible for the many social, economic and environmental problems experienced by West Indians and Africans in Britain.

Enrico was an effective communicator, full of passion and knowledge of his subject which was to secure justice and fairness for black and working-class people the world over. He founded the first black newspaper to be printed in this country called the 'African Voice. This was a monthly paper sold to the public on street corners. His work also entailed the organization of house to house meetings in the Brixton area and other areas of London. He explained to the West Indian and African population the necessity to assimilate themselves in

39

the community, to join the Trade Union Movement, the Labour Party and to take part in all social and political activities, even though he himself was denied high office within the labour movement. He was a very active member of the Westminster Labour Party and the National Union of the Furniture Trade Operators. He was on the B list for the Parliamentary Candidacy for the Labour Party. He was one of the joint secretaries of the 'Movement for Colonial Freedom' led by Fenner Brockway, Member of Parliament in the middle 1950's.

Enrico was no friends of the Commission for Racial Equality (CRE), which was responsible for advising successive governments of race relations in Britain. He had ample evidence to show that the CRE had blocked his entry and progression within the race relations industry. I remember interviewing Enrico for a Race Relations job in Luton during the nineteen seventies. He was by far the best candidate but was rejected by the panel, because he was seen as too radical and he was not favoured by the CRE in London. He later worked in a number of local Community and Race Equality Councils in relatively junior positions, when he should have been at the forefront of managing and directing the race relations structures in Britain. I believe Enrico worked for the local CREs in Coventry, Wolverhampton, London and High Wycombe.

Commitment to fairness, justice and internationalism

His experience and commitment to fairness and justice would have made him a charismatic and lively politician or trade union leader, but the envy and petty-mindedness amongst some of the political, trade union and community leaders deprived him of the influence and power he deserved, to change our society for the betterment of everyone – black and white. For Enrico, racism whether it was supported by individuals, the establishment, white supremists, governments, faith groups or any other institution, was simply unjustified, immoral and had to be addressed. He was very clear about the role of the Christian Church, governments, monarchs, feudalist landowners, imperialists, colonists and the capitalists in seeking to use their power and influence to exploit people because of their race, class, gender or status. He

40

frequently condemned the white ruling classes for justifying the enslavement, domination, exploitation and destruction of non-white people around the world through slavery, imperialism, colonialism and capitalism. Enrico was completed opposed to the exploitation and destruction of tens of millions of black natives by Europeans and their descendants in Africa, Asia, North and South America, Australia, New Zealand, the Caribbean and elsewhere. He was fiercely opposed to wars, genocide, ethnic cleansing and exploitation.

Enrico fully understood the power and ability of institutions such as the World Bank, the International Monetary Fund, the United Nations, The North Atlantic Treaty Alliance and the European Community to maintain the imbalance and unfairness in world affairs, which invariably work against poor countries in Africa, Asia, South America and the Caribbean. He recognised the ability of the rich countries to exploit the poor countries through trading arrangements designed by the rich countries and the exploitation of raw materials, minerals, oil and other commodities through unfair trading, globalisation, foreign investment and acquisition.

Throughout his working life and during his long retirement, Enrico used every opportunity to campaign for human rights, peace and equal opportunities. His work as a Race Equality Officer in Coventry and Wolverhampton, especially with the young people, was outstanding. He was a practical, caring and organised person with a keen desire to empower people by using their knowledge, skills and abilities in a positive and united way to secure changes in their lives. Enrico was conscious that, although chattel slavery had been legally abolished in 1834, a different form of enslavement continued under the free market capitalist system. He resigned from the Communist Party, the Labour Party and the Welsh National Party for a variety of reasons including institutional racism. He was a regular speaker at Hyde Park Corner when he lived in London and he made regular speeches against colonialism, wars and exploitation of labour by capitalists.

41

Even in his last few years we would have long conversations on national and international policies and events. He was convinced that many aspects of the ideology and practice associated with white superiority still existed within the socio-economic, cultural, political and financial institutions across Europe and America. He was bitterly opposed to the war in Iraq by America, Britain and NATO, the lack of democracy within the Arab States and the protection afforded to the rulers of these feudal and reactionary regimes. He was disappointed that the United Nations with over 120 countries affiliated was so weak in protecting global values such as democracy, human rights, equality in trading relationships and improvements in the quality of life across all the five continents, without resorting to wars, occupation and exploitation. Enrico was well aware that half of the world's population were living in poverty, characterised by hunger, famine, wars, under-development, corruption, lack of basic healthcare, education, sanitation and powerlessness, whilst massive amounts of the world's resources, including food and materials, are wasted.

Enrico was a special person. His spirit will continue to shine and hopefully help to pave the way for others. He lived an honest, full and remarkable life. He was generous, forgiving, honest and brave. Those who met him will always remember him with love and respect. His concerns for his people and his native Jamaica, which he loved so much, underwent a transformation as he found it difficult to re-settle in his home town in Jamaica a couple of years before his death. He returned to Wales from Jamaica with a heavy heart, as his efforts to establish a number of businesses and create employment for unemployed Jamaicans did not materialise and he lost all his investments. His last few remaining years were spent in relatively poor health, but he still managed to inspire others and to influence people through his writings. I recommend everyone to read his book *"Buckra Massa Pickney" published in 2006, ISBN: 1-84375-271-9.* Enrico was a person of integrity, courage and foresight. He spent a lot of his own time and resources to empower young people, many of whom have benefited from his work and inspiration.

Enrico Stennett supporting young people in Coventry

He was one of our most distinguished and cherished elderly statesmen with a mountain of knowledge on black and socialist history. He kept himself informed of issues around race relations, trade unions, community cohesion and empowerment, as well as international relations, the war in Iraq, Afghanistan, the uprising in the Arab States and the government led by President Barack Obama in America up to a few days before he passed away. We had planned to meet up a few weeks before his death, to write a book together, but we were unable to meet due to both of us suffering from ill health at the time. So my brother, here is the book written by both of us.

Enrico has never sought high recognition or honours for his work, although many people have been showered with MBEs, OBEs, knighthoods and even greater honours. Enrico has shaken many trees in his time, only to see the careerists and opportunists trampled over him to harvest the fruits.

Most of those in Britain today, with honours bestowed upon them by government and other institutions, were selected because they supported the state and the socio-economic culture of Britain. A sizeable number of black people, especially amongst the aspiring and current middle classes, have lost a sense of their history, their pride in being black and their responsibility towards their race and class. No one can ever accuse Enrico of betraying his race, his class or his principles.

Enrico was married to Margaret who was born in 1923 and died in 1972. They had two children Robert Anthony Stennett and Paul Raymond Stennett. Sadly Robert has died and Paul is living in Kent with his son Nile Stennett. Enrico married for the second time to Mary Ann Stennett in 1974 and they lived together until his death on 7 July 2011.

Thank you Enrico, for giving us an opportunity to know you and to share your time, experiences, memories and love with us. You will be in our hearts forever dear friend and comrade. Enrico was put to rest in Llanrhos Cemetery, Conway Road, Llanrhos, LLANDUDNO LL30 1RN

Profile of Jim Thakoordin

Jim Thakoordin with the late Bernie Grant MP, Neville
Lawrence, Jessie Jackson, Muhammad Ali and Lord Bill Morris

Jim Thakoordin, born on a sugar plantation in Guyana (formerly British
Guiana) on 6 August, 1943, has been in the forefront of the struggle for
racial and social justice, equality, equal access to opportunities for all
within British society, since his arrival in Britain in July, 1961. Jim has
been actively involved in almost all major areas of trades union,
political and community struggles for 50 years.

Jim has always used every opportunity to promote the interest of
his race and class and to secure justice, fairness and respect for

45

everyone. He has always been passionate in his commitment to changes and has used every opportunity to challenge and shape public bodies, community groups and trade unions to make them more open, transparent, accountable and responsive to the people they serve. In doing so Jim has given cause to many people to either dislike, avoid or unite against him, due to his many challenges, interventions and holding people to account. Jim is a no nonsense person who believes in thinking outside the box even if it means creating some measure of chaos.

His adult life was shaped by his upbringing on a sugar plantation on the Coast of Demerara in Guyana where he worked as a child with his parents and sisters for poverty wages. He was very attached to his mother, who like his father was illiterate but understood the difference between rights, wrong, justice, exploitation and fairness. They were politically aware of the excesses of colonialism rule and exploitation of people by the plantation owners and foreign intervention.

Jim left school without any qualifications as he was frequently absent from school due to helping his family through working in the fields, around the home by collecting firewood, helping with the few animals and finding various ways of helping his family of eight to put food on the table. Life was very difficult as Guyana had no organised social, welfare, health or community support services. The sugar plantation was the only source of income for the overwhelming majority of the population over fourteen years old. There was no income support, unemployment benefit; disability allowances childcare allowances or rights for workers. Jim often accompanied his mother at an early age to political and trade union meetings which took place frequently as the struggle for independence from colonial rule intensified during the early 1950s. His parents were committed Marxists and strong supporters of Cheddi Jagan – a Marxist who led the struggle for an end to colonial rule and became head of the government on several occasions after independence, despite the dislike of him and his policies by the British and American establishments.

At the age of 17 Jim decided to leave Guyana for economic reasons and after a great deal of struggle his parents saved up enough for his passage to London. Jim was involved in a steep learning curve having spent his time in a village with few items of clothing, no shoes, for most of the time, the only brother amongst six sisters and in a village where everyone worked hard but was still living below the poverty line. Jim worked as a porter, within a couple of weeks after his arrival and then as a London bus conductor where he met his wife Doreen, when she boarded his bus on her way home from grammar school. It was a relationship which blossomed and it is still going after 51 years of marriage, two grown up children age 47 and 50 years and their four lovely grandchildren.

Jim moved from London after marrying Doreen and they settled in Luton, Bedfordshire, thirty miles from London. Jim worked in the post office and was elected a union convenor with the Union of Postal Workers and Secretary of the Luton Trades Union Council. He was awarded a Trades Union (TUC) Scholarship to Ruskin College, Oxford in 1974 where he studied Economics, Social and Politics. Doreen worked as a teacher and supported Jim throughout his studies. Jim went on to the University of Essex where he studied Comparative Government and Sociology. He also studied for an M.A. in Industrial Relations at the University of Warwick but left early to complete a Post-Graduate Teacher's Training Certificate at the University of London before becoming a London Regional Education and Public Relations Officer with the GMB Union, in 1978.

In 1981, Jim was elected to Bedfordshire County Council as a Labour Councillor and served on several Committees. He chaired the Education Committee, Special Needs, Employment and other key Committees for many years. He was the Labour Group's Deputy Leader on the Council for a couple of years. In 1985 Jim Chaired a Committee supported by the Greater London Council and produced a book on *"Race and Trade Unions"*. Jim was only one of three full-time paid black trade union officials in Britain and he would often challenge some of the racism and sexism within the trade union movement.

47

Jim decided to leave the GMB Union in 1987 and to work for Islington Council as a Neighbourhood Officer before leaving to become the Principal Race Equality Officer in the Planning and Economic Development Department in the London Borough of Ealing. The travelling to West London each day was too much and he successfully applied for the post of Senior National Advisor to Local Government in England and Wales, with the Local Government Management Board (LGMB) - linking Equality with Quality. Jim developed several specialist projects and courses for Chief Officers, Councillors, Departmental Heads, and other groups of workers from Chief Executives to Community Workers.

He also developed specialist courses for women, Black and disabled employees to prepare themselves for promotion and career development. One such course for aspiring Chief Executives enabled nine women – eight white and one Black woman to be successfully appointed to Chief Executive positions over a couple of years. During his work at the LGMB Jim was involved in producing several publications on various aspects of equality and quality. After leaving the LGMB Jim completed a Masters in Business Administration (MBA) at the University of Hertfordshire.

Jim left the LGMB to start his own consultancy business – 'Working for Equality' as he was heavily involved as a councillor and felt that he would be better off working for himself. Jim secured a long-term consultancy contract with Barnfield College in Luton as the Equality Manager and supported the college, the students and the community until he left in 2005. Between 1995 and 2005 Jim wrote several publications on race, racism, and community issues. His book – 'Memories of the 20th Century,' published in 2005 was well received and commented on by many people.

Since 2005 Jim had to restrict some of his activities due to problems with his health which resulted in several major operations, including a quadruple heart bypass. Jim, despite his age (69years) and his health continues to serve on several local and national organisations

48

including being a national executive member of his union – the University and College Union and President of the County Associations of Trades Councils in Bedfordshire and Buckinghamshire. He is also on the Board of the Luton Law Centre, Voluntary Action Luton and the national charity, Community Matters.

Jim continues to challenge the trades union, public bodies, community and voluntary organisations, local government, and institutions to eliminate racism from their organisations and to work towards empowering Black and white people regardless of ethnic or racial origin, gender, ability, age, class, status, sexual orientation, religion, culture or beliefs. He is not afraid to challenge institutions and to hold them accountable for their policies and practices, which deny equal access and opportunities to people disadvantaged by prejudice, discrimination and inequality. He is as much involved in class issues as he is in race, on local, national and international issues.

He has been a founder member of the Black Trade Unionist Solidarity Movement and the Labour Party Black Socialist Society. Jim has campaigned for the rights, liberties and freedom of workers in Britain and abroad.

Jim has been a County, Borough and Parish Councillor for many years. He was a parliamentary candidate for the Labour Party in Milton Keynes in 1983 and served on numerous regional and national organisations, campaigning for civil, trades union and human rights and liberties. He has been a member of the Labour Party National Policy Forum and served as a Commissioner for Education and Employment for four years, chaired by the Rt. Hon. David Blunkett MP when he was Secretary of State for Education and Employment.

Jim has also served on NHS Health Authority and Trusts as non-executive director, Social Security Appeals Tribunals, Industrial and Employment Tribunals, the Further Education Funding Council, Manpower Services Commission and other agencies. Jim has been a governor of primary and secondary schools, Dunstable and Barnfield Further Education Colleges and Cranfield and Luton Universities.

Education has been Jim's passion for many years having arrived from Guyana with no formal qualifications. After several years of studying part-time at Luton College of Higher Education and through correspondence courses with the Trades Union Congress, Jim entered Ruskin College, Oxford after winning a TUC Scholarship. After graduating from Oxford University, Jim went on to secure higher qualifications from the Universities of Essex, Warwick, London and Hertfordshire.

In 2013 Jim was awarded the TUC Badge for 50 active years within the trades union and labour movement, and he was re-elected to the National Executive of his trade union – the University and College Union (UCU) for 2 further years. He published his 13th book – "All Different All Equal – The Story of my Life in June 2014. This book containing 800 pages with over 60 photographs is available worldwide.

Jim has been married to Doreen, who retired as an Assistant Head Teacher from Challney High School for Boys, in Luton. They have two grown up children and four grandchildren ages ten to eighteen. Jim is a keen gardener, writer and a supporter of West Indian Cricket.

PART ONE

ENRICO'S LIFE

PART ONE ENRICO'S LIFE

Chapter One

Thoughts of Enrico Stennett

Taken from: Buckra Massa Pickney, published by Enrico A Stennett in Great Britain, 2006

Enrico Stennett

Over the years, my friends and associates, the people who I have worked with, and all the people who know me, have continued to encourage me to write a book based on my life. Somehow I did not think it was so important, but with the passing of time, I realise a lot of people in the West Indies – especially the younger generation and people abroad – knew little about my people and the problems which faced us in life.

What I am about to do is to take you on a journey. This journey has been a perilous life where I have been punished, not only by the world at large, but by my own family. This punishment was not for something I did wrong, nor for that matter that anyone did wrong, but for the social order that existed at the time of my birth and until today.

It has often been said in conversation by racists, and sometimes by well-meaning people, that they are not against mixed marriages, but they are sorry for the children of such marriages. Whether the conversation is between black people or white people it does not matter, the result is the same: it is the actions and the thinking of these people that cause people like myself to suffer the way we do in absolute silence. In our suffering, who do we go to for understanding? We find ourselves between the devil and the deep blue sea, in no man's land, neither black nor white: we belong nowhere.

Depending on where we are and who we are with, we have to make choices or the choices are made for us, and these choices determine who we are at that given time. Europeans have called me 'nigger', and Africans have called me 'half-breed'. Here am I, in this position, being forced to make a choice. However, the choice that I make will not make any difference to my life, society has made that choice for me, and I have been pigeon-holed into the category which binds me in life to be what I am.

Not that I object to being called a half-caste; this I accept and I prefer to be a half-caste than to be white. It is the white man who has persecuted the black man and not the other way round. Unfortunately for Africa, it is a fertile land which bears good fruit and crops of every description. Not only is it fertile, it is also rich in mineral wealth – gold, black gold (oil), diamonds, silver, iron and ore, all the commodities

53

which the world requires. This is why the people of Europe leave their destitute soil in search of wealth in Africa and elsewhere. Not satisfied with taking over the continents and countries by using violence, which was alien to the African people, they plundered and killed, and the people they did not kill they turned into slaves.

In understanding this I would rather my position in life is as one who does not belong to any of the races, especially the race that has perpetrated the most barbaric deeds. The European uses, brutalises and destroys other nations and rejects them when they are no longer of use.

In this journey I shall take you through the life and times of my parents, the European side of my family and the African side I know nothing about. I am sure my readers will agree with me: to be in between two worlds is not a good place to be.

I am the Buckra Massa Pickney. As you follow me through my life you will understand what it means. You will therefore understand the feelings of millions of others who are like me in the world today; although our upbringing may differ, the end result is the same.

In writing this book, I think of my mother and her rejection by her white relatives. I think of the way I was brought up to be a certain kind of human being, but was treated differently. And with the rejection of my mother, so was I rejected. I knew nothing of my father or his family, because of my mother's hideous, anti-social crime of sleeping with a black man.

Sometimes I feel that, coming from a country where your complexion or the pigment of your skin determines your station in life, being light skinned has made my life slightly easier than for my darker brothers and not only in Britain but also in the Caribbean. In my description of the country of my birth, with its beauty and richness, it should be rich in culture also, but we are now doing everything we can to forget some of the cultures that were forced upon us. I have struggled my way through life, and now, in my twilight years, I can only remember the saying, 'It's not the intermarriage we are against but the half-caste that such marriages bring into the world.' In short, what about the children?

During the past 20 years, we have seen an increasing number of books written by up-and-coming black authors. We have also seen many prominent white men writing books and articles on the black experience. It is now a growing tendency of many of these white personalities to align themselves with black people, working alongside them, learning as much as they can about our attitudes, our experiences, our aims and objectives in life and indeed our inherent way of thinking. This enables them to write their theses whereby they can acquire the appropriate qualifications giving them the right to be accepted by the white authorities as experts in the knowledge of black people. Since 1976, the avenue open to these people to undertake their new form of exploitation of the minds and bodies of black people is through the Community Relations Councils throughout the country.

In the early 1950s, the then Labour government foresaw the political advancement of the Afro-Caribbean people. Small black organisations had aligned themselves with left-wing groups to protest against racism and the oppression of black people in Kenya, the Gold Coast (now Ghana), Nigeria, South Africa, Rhodesia (now Zimbabwe) and throughout the world. Pressure was brought to bear upon the government by holding mass demonstrations and petitioning 10 Downing Street; we were becoming a nuisance. We were exposing the actions of the Labour Party in their oppression of the black freedom fighters and their African and Caribbean leaders. Something had to be done to destroy the aspirations of the black people on their doorstep.

About 70 Labour MPs, led by Fenner Brockway and Marcus Lipton, combined to form the Movement for Colonial Freedom, (MFCF). This organisation was designed to cream off the would-be leaders of the black organisations into the MFCF, thereby leaving the newly formed black organisations leaderless and disorientated, while the government of the day made the struggle for African independence fashionable and legitimate, but only through the Labour government itself. At the same time, the government indicated that black people were incapable of controlling their own destiny, knowing full well it was the intention of the colonial powers to use any methods they could possibly find to prevent them from doing so.

Many of the so-called leaders fell in the trap; hence they disbanded their newly formed black organisations and aligned themselves with the Labour party in every way possible. However, the MFCF did not last very long; after the Tories regained control from the Atlee government, many of the Labour MPs who were part of the MFCF no longer held office, resulting in the death of the MFCF. Once again, the black people who had deserted the small black organisations quickly reorganised themselves with some of the ex-MFCF Labour MPs, and created a new movement: the Campaign against Racial Discrimination, (CARD). It was from CARD that the commission was born. This organisation gave black people their first opportunity to link up nationwide, because, for the first time in Britain, black people were able to obtain salary-based employment and a new breed of black middle class was in the making. The community relations officers saw this new movement as a means to climb the ladder of this new factious class.

They forgot the struggle for the black masses but now concentrated on how far they could progress their own individual careers at the expense of the suffering of their own people, thereby missing a great opportunity to unite, and build a national organisation. Some were no longer interested in the struggle; rather, in their effort to crown their own glory, they trampled on black people who were junior to them in the race relations industry. They were too interested in building their own small empires, their own hierarchies within the CRCs such as, Principal Community Relations Officers (PCROs), Community Relations Officers (CROs) and Assistant Community Relations Officers (ACROs). There were also other non-commissioned officers, such as education officers, housing officers, social workers and youth workers. They discovered every way possible to enlarge what they believed was their power base, not realising these structures only

56

existed at the mercy of their white masters and that the power could be dismantled by the stroke of a pen.

I worked with the above organisations for some time, only to discover to my horror that more racism was practised within the offices of these CRCs than you would find in factories. It became a dog-eat-dog situation, as they forgot what the organisation was intended for. The CRCs have changed and the 1976 Race Relations Act has undergone various amendments, just as with the 1966 Immigration Act, but none of these amendments have helped the people the organisation was set up to help. To the contrary, we are so disjointed and divided we are no better off than when we first arrived in this country. In fact our position today is a precarious one and our unity is non-existent.

During my 15 years of employment with CRCs in various parts of Britain, from time to time I have had seconded to me graduates from universities and people from various establishments looking at race issues. They would spend their time at my desk looking at what I was doing, learning as much as they could and engaging me in conversations. As they gained my confidence, they became friendlier until I realised they were there just to gain experience to write their theses for their PhDs and other academic qualifications. When they gained their qualifications they automatically became known as experts on black people.

It is ironic that today, after many centuries of suffering the indignities and humiliations forced upon us by our so-called masters, black people are still not looked upon as capable of portraying their own suffering, therefore we accept the writings of other people, but ignore the feelings and aspirations of our black brothers.

For 400 years the black man has been used as a vehicle for exploitation, both for self-glorification and financial gain. Today, writing about black people has become a multi-million pound industry. It is accepted that a white man with second-hand knowledge, learned from our own willingness to expose our inner selves, is in a better position to obtain employment at the head of any organisation created

57

by white society, claiming to be in the interests of the black man. This ensures that the white man will always be the recognised authority, leaving the black man with little self worth and incapable of knowing himself. .

You may be asking what authority or credentials I have to think myself able to write a book reflecting the lives of black people, not only in the West Indies where I was born, but in the United States of America and in Africa. I believe it is appropriate to give some information about myself.

I was born in 1926 in a little village called Maroon Town in Jamaica; this small village is known to the British and too many older generations of Caribbean people as the centre of the Maroon rebellion. This Maroon country was in the Cockpit Mountains, situated in the Parish of St James, in the County of Cornwall.

By virtue of my birth and the standing of my family within that small community, I became aware at an early age that something was amiss. Even at that tender age I became rebellious, therefore whatever I say in my writings is guided by personal experiences gained throughout my childhood until this day. On reflection, even though some of the issues raised in this book are only vaguely remembered, I have read various pieces of literature since that time which has helped make those vague memories become clear.

Jamaica was a feudal society at the time of my birth, a society where there was master and serf, with the descendants of the white slave owners in between; they were not subject to the aforementioned divisions but found themselves in the middle, disliked by both sides while carrying out the bidding of their overall masters. It may appear strange to some of my young West Indian brothers and sisters, and young black people born in this country, to learn that it was not until my arrival in Britain in August 1947 that I first knew of racism, although I did not then understand it as such, because it was an integral part of our lives.

Negro, Nigger, Darkie, Sambo, Copper Colour, Red Skin, Quadrille, Coon, Spade, Cha Cha, Coolie, Coolie Royal, and Wogs: all these words and phrases I learnt as a child from my most religious and God-fearing white family. There were other phrases to denote the white man's supremacy over their black slaves. Here I quote two of these phrases: 'So it is with brutes and niggers, treat them kindly they rebel, But rule them with the rod of iron, then they will obey you well.' and 'God made a Nigger he made him in the Night, he made him in such a hurry he forgot to paint him white.'

With the above quotations clearly in mind I can understand why the man of colour has, over the years, come to dislike himself so much. He was made to believe by white people, from his cradle to his grave, not only that he was subhuman but also according to the Longmans book, which we read at school, he was dehumanised as a monkey. These same black people brought up the children of their white masters, sometimes by breast feeding, and cared for them. It was the indoctrination of hate and contempt for the people whom they governed and ruled with a iron hand which led these same white children to turn against the same servants who had breast fed them, cared for them and brought them up.

Depicting the life and times, the suffering and desecration of black people, their minds were conditioned to such an extent that they blindly believed in their own inferiority and believed that only the Buckra Massa and the Buckra Misses knew best. They even bowed and scraped to the white babies, while the black Nanny attended to every detail of their upbringing, leaving their European mothers to prostitute themselves in the exclusive clubs throughout the island, clubs where black people were barred.

We speak of segregation in other parts of the world, including the United States and South Africa. What worries me is the hypocrisy of it all: the British are pointing their fingers at other countries, pretending to the world they disagree with what is going on, when at the same time they are the people who are responsible for the state of affairs in the

59

world today, the hatred and contempt of one man for another. They falsely hold their heads high with a sense of dignity and pride.

Quoting Tolstoy:

> '*I sit on a man's back, choking him and making him carry me, and yet assure myself and others that I am very sorry for him and wish to ease his lot by all possible means – except by getting off his back.*' (What Then Must We Do? 1886)

We see this in our everyday life when we talk about the poor, starving people of Africa, and each year we talk about the amount of money we are giving to them. We never talk about the amount of money we are taking from them when we plunder their natural resources, or the interest charged on the money we loaned and the conditions imposed by the World Bank so that these people will remain in poverty forever.

As the son of white slave masters and black slave mothers, my ancestry goes back a long way. With my experiences here in Britain, the Caribbean and the other places to which I have travelled, I feel it is quite appropriate for me to express myself in whatever way my conscience guides me, sincerely exposing my innermost feelings so that everyone can understand. I have searched my white ancestry but, unfortunately, I am unable to discover anything about my black ancestry because I did not know my father. I understand that he was of mixed race, but he died before I was born and I did not know his family; as far as I was concerned, my father did not exist. This led me to research the side of the family I knew best, and with whom I have all my connections. This ancestry is European in its entirety: Germanic, English and Scottish dating back from Henry II, the Plantagenet line, in the eleventh century.

The name Stennett is not only uncommon in Britain but also in the Caribbean. This is because it is a translation from Stheinhart, one of my German ancestors who was a medieval knight from the time of Henry II. Stennett is in the register of Burke's Peerage, so I had little difficulty in tracing my ancestors back to Scotland, England and the Caribbean. In addition, I remember my great-grandfather and all the stories he used to tell us as children about the old country; he spoke with pride and, in a way, we too believed we were from that old country.

Therefore I stand before all my readers as someone who was born into and brought up in a world where I learned to understand both sides of the coin: the white man's inhumanity to man and the black man's acceptance of his inhumane treatment and suffering. So please read my book as I take you through a journey that few people understand. I now introduce my readers to Buckra Massa Pickney.

Chapter Two

Enrico Stennett - A lesson on black history

Enrico Stennett, addressing a meeting in Luton in 1998 to celebrate the fiftieth anniversary of the landing of the Empire Windrush in June 1948 with West Indian immigrants.

"Mr Chairman, ladies and gentlemen.

First of all, I'm asking myself why I am here. We talk about the celebration, I have very little to celebrate. I don't know about you, but I have been here for fifty-one years. I may not look like it, but I can assure you I am not lying, I have been here since 1947. So, we are talking about the 'Empire Windrush' as if this ship has a lot of significance - to me it has none. Yes, I came here in 1947 on the Empire Windrush; other people came here in 1948, so what?

Now, before I continue, I think there are certain aspects of my being in England that should interest you, especially the 'host community' as they are called. I stand here before you, brought up in the Caribbean by white people, who were partly my parents, rich white people who were in fact racist to the core. I tell you these things I learned as a child from these same people who were supposed to be my parents. Then later on, when I realised that all I had learned was completely incorrect, I became very disillusioned with myself, with my parents, and to a certain degree, with mankind.

Stereotyping Black people

As a child, brought up in a little village in Jamaica, I was meant to believe that Africans had tails. In my Longmans book, I saw Africans depicted as animals swinging from tree to tree. When I went home, I would listen to the tale of our family motto, : 'with brutes and niggers, treat them kindly they rebel, rule them with a rod of iron and they will obey you well'. How many of you have heard that? 'God made a nigger. He made him in the dark. He made him in such a hurry, he forgot to paint him white'.

A brief insight of a 'white' mentality

Now I am standing before you. That is the way I was brought up, by English people, people who came from this country, people who were slave masters and sons and daughters of slave masters. At the same time, however, I was sent to school. My teachers were two old English ladies. Of course I had to speak English properly because English was my language. I had to speak it because later on I was expected to be master of the plantation. Thank God I didn't reach there.

I decided, after leaving school, that I wanted to go to this beautiful country England, the one that they told me was Heaven and Earth. You know once upon a time, an ordinary English person could not go to Jamaica. Did you know that? No way - only the people from Harrow and Eton, only what we call the people who speak with plums

63

in their mouths. You know those people were despots. Their arrogance and the way they walked with their heads upright. We all aspire to be part and parcel of these demagogues, these human Gods. Those human Gods would not allow the ordinary English person in the Caribbean, because they were afraid that the ordinary English person would show them up for what they really were.

So when I wanted to come to England, my family said I shouldn't go there. I asked why. I was told there was gold on the streets, I wanted to be with those loving people my family told me about. They are my people. You told me so. Why should I not go? 'You would not like it', they said, and they were damn well right, but I was not supposed to know that. They did everything in their power to stop me from coming, in case I learned what I have learned.

When I arrived here, my journey was not helpful. Yes, for the first time, I was on a great big ship, but I was sick all the way across. I didn't enjoy it, I enjoyed it less still, when I arrived, because here I was, a boy of nineteen years old, arriving in a country, which I believed would embrace me as a brother. I then realised not only was I not recognised, but I was not wanted. My mother deliberately refused to have anything to do with me. I had no welcome, I had nowhere to live.

I went to the Colonial Office, 6 St. Martins Place, London and there was a man, Captain Paul Weller, this man made advances to me. I was shocked, as I did not know what homosexuality meant. This man tried to put his arms around me, and embrace me. When I pushed him away, he said to me, 'I think you should go to work in the mines, I'll try and get you into the mines'.

A unique experience

When I walked down the stairs, I met a gentleman who I'd heard about in Jamaica. All Jamaicans, at a certain time, would turn on their wireless to listen to him sing, Archie Lewis.

64

Archie Lewis sang for Geraldo of Pittsburgh. Of course the reason why Archie Lewis was there was because he was a friend of Weller. Weller said to me, 'I'm sorry. I have no-one to sign with you at the moment, you will have to wait'. You had to get a ration book, remember them? - an identity card and another coupon, because these governed your life in England - without them you could not eat or drink.

Two hours later, a tall gentleman came in, black as the ace of spades, well dressed in what I now know to be called a Saville Row suit; and Weller says to me, 'This gentleman will take you where you should go' and we walked out around the corner to the No.15 bus stop. I'll never forget this. While we were waiting for the bus, another gentleman joined him, and they start speaking a language that I didn't understand. When the bus arrived we got on the bus. I turned to this man and said, 'Pardon me sir, which one of the West Indian Islands do you come from?' This man was very indignant: 'West Indies? What are you talking about? I am an African'. I looked at him stunned, as I said, 'An African, sir? Forgive me'. From that moment on, my life changed.

From that moment, I knew who I was, and I wanted to know more about me and where I came from. I realised that I was between two worlds. I had to get on to the side of the world in which I belonged. I was rejected by those in the Caribbean that I belonged to. I was determined to fight that rejection and am still determined to fight that rejection.

Someone said not long ago, that we should forget our slave past. We all, at this moment dating back into history, have a slave past. What did Cicero say of the English, Emperor of the Great Roman Empire? 'Do not purchase your slaves from England. They're dirty, nasty, and incapable of learning. In fact, they are not fit to be of the household of Athens'. Do you know in 1947, I heard the same thing said about blacks? - that they are dirty, nasty and not fit to be among the English people. History has repeated itself time and time again.

65

We are talking about the Windrush, because we said the Windrush represents fifty years of black people coming to this country. That's not so. I wonder why we continue to falsify history; we seem to coin history to suit ourselves at a given time. We seem to use history in the interests of the people who have the power at that time. It doesn't matter how you put it, it must come back to what is real.

Black people have been in this country from the time of the Romans. I do not want to sit and give you a history lesson, because this is not the time, but I can assure you that we have been here a very long time. There was a time when we were accepted. Our failure as black people was our failure to see. When Vasco da Gama went into North Africa, they received him; they gave him gold, diamonds, all the jewellery they could take back on the ship. Take this from one King to your King. That was the biggest mistake, because once he went back to Portugal and the King saw all the gold, all the Europeans went into Africa to get what they could.

Protection racket

Britain had an empire that was boasted about, an empire where the sun never sets. Britain never had an empire at all! It ran a protection racket. When I heard about the Kray twins and the Richardson brothers, I thought yes, that's the English protection racketeers.

Britain had three types of colonies, one was the Crown colony, another was the Protectorate and the other was a mandated colony. Only the Crown colonies were real colonies because Britain fought for them and captured them. India was one, as they fought the Indians, Jamaica was one because they fought the Spaniards, the other was also a part of Spain, the Rock of Gibraltar.

All the other colonies that she had were protectorates, especially those in Africa. She would go into Africa and say that all the Europeans were coming to rob and plunder. 'Give us the power to protect', they said, the poor chief would sign that protection paper and the English flag would go up overnight. The Mandated colonies are

66

when a chief, seeing that his people were in trouble, would call Britain in and give them the mandate to protect them. This was the protection racket that Britain ran throughout the world, which Britain called her Great Empire.

When we came to this country we were citizens of the United Kingdom and colonies. We had the same rights as the people of Scotland, Ireland, and Wales, because we were an integral part of this country, being a Crown colony. My passport told me that I was a citizen of the United Kingdom and colonies, not a British subject. I didn't need a passport to come here. I have been to Scotland and Wales I didn't need a passport. Why then should I need a passport to come here?

All Blacks labelled as foreigners

The fact that I didn't need a passport to come here shows beyond any doubt that I was a part of this country. How can you migrate to your own country? I don't know, but as far as we are concerned, we have migrated.

When you go to South Africa, the English in South Africa call themselves South Africans. In the Caribbean Islands, they call themselves Jamaicans. When it suits them, they call themselves English. Now, today in England we say we have made progress. Making progress here? – impossible. If you had been here for fifty years, your children were born and bred here, yet you are still looked upon as a West Indian, a Caribbean, an African, how the hell can you make progress in a country like this?

I note that if the Englishman does not call himself English, then he calls himself Anglo, Anglo-Indian, Anglo-Caribbean, but that Anglo is denied to us completely. We have been found other names. We were 'darkie', 'sambo', but now we are 'mixed race', 'mixed heritage', anything but Anglo, that tells you that you can be here for one thousand years and you will never be one of them.

67

I have been here for fifty-one years and am wondering what the next fifty years has in store for us. As I look around Europe, I can feel the tremors coming from Europe and those tremors are the rise of nationalism once more. Do not kid yourself that it can't happen to you. The Jews thought that it could not happen to them, but it damn well did. So when you walk around the street, feeling you are settled, there are many more inner fouls around, and there will be for the next hundred years.

Colour conscious colonialists

We started with a great handicap when we arrived here, that handicap was the colour of our skin. They could see us a mile away, all of the other nations, with the exception of the Asians, didn't start with this handicap. The Italians, the Greeks, the Maltese, the Cypriots, even the Germans, whom we were told by Sir Winston Churchill that we should wipe off the face of the map. How many of you remember what Churchill did? He stood up with his hand raised and pointed at a map, saying we should repeat after him, 'Oh we are going to fight, yes man, and win this war. We are going to beat the sleepy Bosch, yes man, and win this war'.

That did not stop them siding with the Germans to fight us on the streets of London when we came here. All of a sudden, these enemies were no longer enemies. We, who fought and died in the battlefields, were the enemies.

Repatriation and the Empire Windrush

'Empire Windrush' was not a ship of immigration. Let's get the facts right; it was the first attempt of repatriation by this country in this epoch. Do you know how the Windrush went to the Caribbean? All they talked about was the Windrush coming. Yes it got there by those who came and volunteered to fight for their mother country. After the war, they were no longer needed and their mother country decided to repatriate them. Are there any R.A.F. personnel in this hall? No? A lot were repatriated back to the Caribbean because they were no longer needed.

Some of these men were promised land and money, land on which they could not work and they were never given the money. There was poverty which they could not face; most of them went to the United States of America.

Some experience in London

After a while in London I found myself cold, hungry and homeless. One day I decided to go to the police for help. I said to the policeman at the desk, 'Please sir, I'm cold, can you put me in a cell?' His reply was, 'If you want to go into a cell, break a window, I'll arrest you and you can go inside'. I said, 'I didn't come here for that' and walked back into the street.

I landed up two weeks later in a Rowton House dormitory Hostel. I was there about three nights when I felt my body being eaten away, when I took off my underclothing, the white lice were crawling like maggots, these were the kind of conditions we were faced with at the time.

I remember a funny story, I was walking up the street one day with a West Indian colleague who was a tall man, we saw a lady cleaning her windows, when she saw us coming she threw away the bucket, ran inside and closed the curtains. We stood there for almost one hour, laughing, because we could not believe that people could behave like that. We were meant to believe we were stupid, now we saw stupidity that we couldn't believe existed.

Touch a black man for luck, ever heard of that expression? These are the conditions we underwent in this country and still undergo today. Most of us have houses now, thanks to the Jews. You heard about the story of a Jewish man? He had about eight workers in his cabinet factory, they were good workers, one day he came down and found three of them sleeping. He asked why they were sleeping and they told him that they didn't sleep last night because they had nowhere to sleep.

The Jewish man said, 'Okay, I'll buy you a house, and he bought them 62 Summer Layton Road Brixton London, a three storey building that housed about twenty people. Some slept at night, and some during the day, the Jamaican man who looked after the house gave the Jewish man the rent, when the house had been paid for he handed over the house to the Jamaican. That was the way we started to buy houses in this country, with the help of the Jews.

We forget that we had to bring our children to this country, after coming here with the intention of returning, first it was three months, then six, then nine and we are still here saying we are going back.

Ladies and gentlemen, I would like to talk to you all day, but I can't. I would like to conclude in saying that what we are seeing is 30% of our children are in the prisons in England, I was a Parole Officer for the Home Office visiting the Prisons, and 25% of the asylum population is black, and 25% of people in mental institutions are black. As we are only some 6% of the entire population of Britain, then something must be damn well wrong.

Let's put it right. Thank you."

Editor's update:

Black Africans and Caribbeans in prisons

According to the Guardian Newspaper, 10 October 2010, there were more black people of African and Caribbean origins, jailed in England and Wales proportionally than in the United States. "The proportion of black people in jail in the UK was almost seven times their share of the population, whereas in the US the proportion of black prisoners is four times greater than their population share. The expression of the figures was extrapolated from the Equality and Human Rights Commission report *How Fair is Britain?"*

The report drew on a 2008 Ministry of Justice document, footnoted as the source of the EHRC statement that tated: "Black prisoners make up 15% of the prisoner population ar d this compares with 2.2% of the general population." According to various sources, about 12% of the US population is black and about 40% to 45% of the US prison population is black. In 2003, one in every 100 black adults in Britain were in prison subsequent crackdown on guns, drugs and street crime has led to an explosion in the number of prisoners from an Afro-Caribbean background, who now account for one in six of all inmates.

The report, says that ethnic minorities are "substantially over-represented in the custodial system". It suggests mary of those jailed have "mental health issues, learning disabilities, and have been in care or experienced abuse". Experts and politicians said over-representation of black men was a result of decades of racial prejudice in the criminal justice system. According to Juliet Lyon, director of the Prison Reform Trust, "We have a tendency to say we are better than the US, but we have not got prison right. We have numerous efforts to address racism in the prison system ... we have yet to get a better relationship between justice authorities and black communities. Instead we have ended up with mistrust breeding mistrust." Evidence of this damaged relationship can be found in the commission's report. On the streets, black people were subjected to what the report describes as an "excess" of 145,000 stop and searches in 2008. It notes that black people constitute less than 3% of the population, yet made up 15% of people stopped by police.

The commission found that five times more black people than white people per head of population in England and Wales are imprisoned. The ethnic minority prison population has doubled in a decade – from 11,332 in 1998 to 22,421 in 2008. Over a similar period, the overall number of prisoners rose by less than two thirds. The commission says that the total number of people behind bars accelerated in the last decade despite "a similar number of crimes being

71

reported to the police as in the early 1990s … the volume of indictable offences has fallen over this time".

A quarter of the people in prison are from an ethnic minority. Muslims now make up 12% of the prison population in England and Wales. Some on the left of the Labour Party blame its policies while in power between 1997 and 2010. Diane Abbott, who raised the alarm over the growing numbers of jailed black men as a backbencher, said she "very much regretted that the last Labour government swallowed [former home secretary] Michael Howard's line that 'prison works'." Oona King, ex-Labour MP for Bethnal Green and Bow and now a member of the House of Lords, said: "Given that my father is African American, I am very conscious of the fact that a quarter of all black men under the age of 26 are in jail. IN America we are nowhere near that in Britain, but I hope these figures will force people to reflect on the effect of the level of school exclusions, low academic achievement and increasing drug abuse on black communities. At the same time we need to develop a penal system that rehabilitates rather than just punishes."

According to Ben Bowling, professor of criminal justice at Kings College London and a former adviser to the Home Affairs Select Committee. "There was never a serious examination of the consequences of locking up a generation of young black men. The result is there are some prisons in the south east which are now virtually all black. Many are converting to Islam." The problems may start at school. The commission points out that black children are three times as likely to be permanently excluded from education. "We are reaping the effects of criminalising a community in the 1970s,"

"The question is how you break the cycle when young men experience custody. Three quarters simply re-offend. We have to intervene with families more effectively to stop kids going to prison. That means looking at school exclusions. You need to deal with issues like mental health and substance abuse. It is not enough to throw our hands in the air."

The policies implemented in the last decade mean incarceration levels in Britain are now among the highest in western Europe. England and Wales have an imprisonment rate of 155 per 100,000 and Scotland of 149 per 100,000 of the population. This contrasts with rates of less than 100 per 100,000 for most countries in Western Europe.

The criminal justice system

People from BME communities are over-represented at almost all stages of the criminal justice process, disproportionately targeted by the police, more likely to be imprisoned and more likely to be imprisoned for longer than white British people.

People from BME groups are more likely to stopped-and-searched than white British people. The disparity differs between different stop-and-search powers. In 2012, research indicated that police are 28 times more likely to use 'Section 60' stop-and-search powers (where officers do not require suspicion of having being involved in a crime) against black people than white people.

Analysis of all stop and searches in 2010-2011 indicated that black people are seven times as likely, and Asians twice as likely as white people to be stopped and searched by the police. Such practices are frequently ineffective. More than 90 per cent do not lead to an arrest. Despite being over-represented in most stages of the criminal justice process, people from BME communities are under-represented in senior positions of employment. In 2011 only 4 senior judges, out of 161, were known to be from a BME community; 1 senior civil servant out of 52, working for the National Offender Management Service (NOMS) was known to be from a BME community, and 3 per cent of the senior police officers in England and Wales were from a BME community.

In 2009/10 there were 1,386,030 arrests in England and Wales, compared to 1,429,785 in 2005/06. The overall number of arrests in this period consequently decreased and, within this, the number of people from a white group decreased. However, the number of people arrested from BME communities increased, by 5 per cent for black people and 13 per cent for Asian people. In 2009/10 black people were 3.3 times more likely to be arrested than white people. Those from a mixed ethnic group were 2.3 times more likely to be arrested than white people.

Certain BME groups are more likely than the white group to be sentenced to immediate custody for serious offences which can be tried in Crown Court (indictable offences). In 2010, 23 per cent of the white group convicted for indictable offences were sentenced to immediate custody, 27 per cent of Black people and 29 per cent of Asian people.

A study in 2011, based on an analysis of over one million court records found that black offenders were 44 per cent more likely than white offenders to be given a prison sentence for driving offences, 38 per cent more likely for public order offences or possession of a weapon and 27 per cent more likely for possession of drugs. Asian people were 19 per cent more likely than white people to be given a prison sentence for shoplifting and 41 per cent more likely for drugs offences.

BME groups are significantly over-represented in the prison system, with over 25 per cent of the overall prison population from a BME background. In 2011, Black or Black British people made up 13.4 per cent of the prison population. Asian or Asian British people made up 7.4 per cent of the prison population. White British people made up 74.3 per cent of the prison population.

In 2012, the number of children in the secure estate (young offender institutions, secure children's homes and secure training centres) was 1,596. Of these, 37 per cent were from BME communities. Between October 2011 and 2012, the overall number of children in custody decreased by 21 per cent, but the number of BME children increased by 3 per cent.

Chapter Three

Enrico Stennett - Jamaica the Land of my Birth

*Taken from: Buckra Massa Pickney, published
by Enrico A Stennett in Great Britain, 2006*

Jamaica, land of wood and water

Lying in the Caribbean Sea, all alone off the coast of Central America, is a land shaped like a turtle – the island of Jamaica. Its nearest neighbour is 90 miles away, larger but of the same beauty and splendour – the island of Cuba. On this turtle-shaped island, the Blue Mountains stretch from the eastern point of St Thomas to the Cockpit Mountains in the west. First populated by the Arawak Indians from the mainland of America, Jamaica was invaded by Spain in 1494, then fought over by many other European countries. In 1655, Britain attacked the Spanish, who had occupied the island since Columbus; this war lasted until 1660 when the Spanish vacated the island from a harbour called Runaway Bay to their stronghold in Hispaniola.

This land was named Axyma by the Caribs, meaning the land of wood and water, then Xamayca by the Spaniards, meaning the land of seven rivers. This land should be called Paradise on Earth. I want my readers to imagine they are taking a journey either by air or sea and, on the horizon, seeing the blue-green island forming in the distance, taking on the shape of the island of Shangri-La – this is what Christopher Columbus thought when he first stumbled upon it by accident in the year 1494.

Aerial View of the Blue Mountains

As morning dawns, the entire island glows, as the amber sun shines on the mountains, the hills, the valleys and the plains. As you look at the amazing sight before you, this array of colours gradually appears between the mists descending from the Blue Mountains, forming a vision of tranquil beauty, unifying itself with the clear blue sky and the dark blue sea. If you are lucky enough to approach the island between 4 and 6 a.m. when the sun is rising, you will have an experience that is impossible to forget, as it is comparable to none other. At this time, the warmth and beauty of the sun is at its best, and it beckons you to come closer and be at one with nature.

This green belt of land nestling in the bosom of the Caribbean Sea is indeed a land of paradise, with its fertile soil and its varied landscape. The picturesque beauty not only gives one a feeling of life and the joy of living, but all the luxuries which nature itself provides: its yams, sweet potatoes, cassava, breadfruit, banana, cocoa, root crops, its rivers of clean clear water, its lakes and ponds with large populations of fish of various kinds and a soil which one does not have to cultivate. The beauty of its waterfalls and clean, clear water beneath, where the people of the island swim and play, and with their calypso music formed from African rhythms, this truly is the land of paradise.

One did not need any gold or money to live on this island; before the advent of the Europeans, money was unknown. The people who inhabited this island lived by the sweat of their brow and their labour, and they called the island Axyma, which means the land of wood and water. Wood in the form of cedar, mahogany, logwood, lignum vitae and other hardwoods, were later to become Jamaica's leading export, leading to the destruction of its rain forests.

Many visitors to the island enjoy such picturesque beauty in the same way they would enjoy the landscape paintings of Constable, but to enjoy the beauty of Jamaica you need to involve yourself not only with the scenery, but with its soul, which expresses itself in its people. The late Winston Churchill once described Jamaica as the most beautiful place on earth, but in the midst of its beauty once lay the most evil and tyrannical rule that ever existed. To the people who have inhabited Jamaica for the past 400 years the beauty does not exist, as they face their everyday existence with the agony and pain rendered unto them by their so-called masters; to them the island is the Rock, symbolizing its hardship, but at the same time the strength and tenacity of its people for their sheer existence.

As a child, people like myself saw a different Jamaica: a Jamaica of riches and luxury, with a Britishness that sent out the special message of superiority, which at the same time bred hatred and division among its people. We used the shades of colour of our skin as a brand

77

to determine our station in life. As young, privileged children, we recited poems singing the praises of Britain, poems such as 'Old Ironside', 'The Cottage Was a Thatched One', and many others, as we were taught to love Britain and its green and pleasant land, where the streets were paved with gold, and milk and honey flowed. We were also taught a poem about our own beautiful island, as seen by an Englishman; this Englishman was the famous British poet, Wordsworth. Who could blame us if we all wanted to come to Britain?

Hail to Jamaica the Island of Spring
Peace on her Meadows her Radiance flings
Beauty and gladness make their land
The happiest spot on earth wide water strand.

She lies mid white foam, and blue waters at rest,
Like a maiden clasped close to her true lovers breast.
Not for the rest of her mightiest gifts
Can change Ye Jamaica, sweet island of Spring.

Small is our isle, but of beauty so rare
With her no country on earth can compare.

Most visitors to Jamaica stay for a short while, enjoying the white, sandy beaches, the luxurious hotels with their landscaped lawns, delightful flower gardens and beautiful golf courses, with the sound of calypso, mento and reggae music. The hotels stretch along the beaches from Montego Bay to Negril Point, filled with hundreds of European and American tourists, who bask themselves in the glorious sun, reflecting a lavish lifestyle where food and drink is in abundance.

This is not the real Jamaica: the visitor who ventures into the interior will find another Jamaica – a Jamaica that has many contradictions formed by its multi-racial, multi-national people.

How many visitors have ever listened to the cock crow at 4 a.m. and thereafter crowing to signal each hour of the day? How many have measured their shadow against the sun by which we all once used to tell the time of the day, as it was the only clock we had? How many visitors listen to the singing of the birds as they flutter among the trees? How many have seen the hummingbird as it hovered in its flight to gather the nectar from the flowers? How many have seen the beauty of the red flowers of the shoe-black trees, have ventured into the peace and tranquillity of the woodlands or have strolled through valleys stopping to drink the cold, clear water rising from the streams in the hills? How many have stopped to pick apples from the orchard, and fruit from the orange grove or chewed the sugar cane? How many have visited the spa springs, rivers and lakes and the hot water springs from the hills of the St Thomas Bath?

It is known that the Milk River Bath in St Ann was used by the kings and queens of England to cure various illnesses. How many know about Lovers Leap? This is where, in the time of slavery, young sweethearts, learning they were to be separated and sold to new masters, fled from the slave plantations and, while holding hands, leaped to their deaths on the rocks below, believing their spirits would be joined together in everlasting freedom from the inhuman cruelty of their slave masters.

Many people see Jamaica as a tourist resort in which they can be sure of enjoying sunshine in exquisite surroundings without mixing or associating with the indigenous people from the interior. To me such people would be better off going to the South of France or Wales, Somerset or Cornwall. From Morrant Point in the East, to Negril Point in the West, from St Ann's Bay to Portland Point, we see a land of breathtaking beauty.

This island can be compared with North Wales, Cornwall, Somerset, Dorset, and Surrey combined, only that it is more delightful in its rugged beauty; surely this is 'the green and pleasant land'? Standing on the Grand Ridge of the highest peak of the Blue Mountain, one can look across to the west for a grand view of the John Crow Mountains. This mountain is so-called because it is the home of the vultures of that name. It is said it does not matter how far the vultures fly in search of their prey, they will return to their home in the mountains.

Looking across to the northeast is the city of Kingston, the second oldest city on the island, and Jamaica's capital. The mountain ranges form the backbone of the island: the Blue Mountains, the Santa Cruz Mountains, the John Figaro Mountains, the Cockpit Mountains and the Dry Harbour Mountains. There are also the seven great rivers, from the Dry River in the East, the Rio Cobra, the Great River, the Black River, the Rio Grande, the Dunns River and the Milk River. These rivers set up a network throughout the island. There are also great underground rivers, which find their outlets in small ponds and springs all over the island. The water from these rivers is pure, cold and soft. It is said that some of these rivers contain the potential for healing the sick and infirm, the Milk River being the most famous for its healing powers.

Throughout the island there are great streams with waterfalls gushing down from immense heights, resting at the bottom in huge pools of cold clear water, forming the continuation of the river or stream. The vegetation on the island is even more diverse than in Africa, with the trees and plants of immense variety.

In the Cockpit Country you will find yucca, mahoe, cedar, tumrin, eucalyptus, ebony, logwood, lignum vitae and many other kinds of trees. Throughout the island these trees are most commonly found near the mountain ranges, but can also be found in the valleys and plains. There is also a wide variety of fruit-bearing trees, the mango tree being the most common. There are about 78 different kinds of mangoes from the East Indian mango to the common mango, each one having a different shape, colour and taste. There are the jackfruit trees, the star apple trees, the sour sap trees, the sweet sap, the guava trees, the breadfruit trees and the rose apple trees, which grow in the swamps. Trees of exquisite beauty such as the nutmeg, the pimento, the genep, the almond and cashew nut trees, grow wild throughout the island, as do the neesberries; there are also many varieties of plum trees. The ackee and the pimento are peculiar to the island of Jamaica, along with the ackee fruit. There are other trees of a poisonous variety such as the byssi and the nutmeg, although the poison does not affect humans, apart from the ackee fruit, which, if consumed before the pod is opened naturally, will kill instantly.

Citrus is one of Jamaica's main exports, most of which are cultivated, and the experiments carried out at the botanical gardens in St Andrews have resulted in many new varieties of citrus fruits. There are banana plantations covering the foothills, valleys and plains throughout the island, and also sugar cane, which can be found in large quantities.

If ever an island was blessed, this one is; the people of Jamaica do not know how lucky they are. Jamaica had many large sugar estates and hundreds of small sugar producers, producing wet sugar and ginger sugar for home consumption, and dry sugar for export. It is said the wealth of a country depends on what it produces from its soil, if this is so then Jamaica should be the richest country on earth; poverty is unjustified. The soil of Jamaica is so fertile that one does not have to plant or sow seeds – or for that matter even tend them – for them to bring forth good fruit. Any seeds that are thrown away, providing they are not consumed by the birds, will grow. One only has to eat a mango or suck an orange and throw the seeds away to find weeks later, fertile growth of the seeds.

One will note that, when the various so-called charitable organisations refer to the donations to Africa, India and elsewhere, they cannot produce emaciated pot-bellied and dying Jamaican children, so therefore we do not have to depend on these organisations to survive. There is no reason for anyone on this paradise island to go hungry.

I am sure readers will understand my reasons for describing the island and some of its produce, to prove that the paradise found by the Europeans when they came to this small island was enough; they had no need to destroy the original inhabitants of the island and import slaves

81

to work on the plantations, neither did they have to destroy all our rainforests, to export hardwood and logwood for the benefit of Britain

Please continue to follow me on my life's journey as I describe the people who inhabited the island after the British arrived. Ignoring the buccaneers, pirates and prostitutes, and the destruction of Port Royal by the earthquake in 1792, let us look at the colonial establishment, which was set up to govern the island, and how the island was governed.

The island was divided into fourteen separate parishes, starting from the east: St Thomas, Portland, St Andrew, the parish of Kingston - Jamaica's capital city, St Catherine, St Mary, St Ann's, Manchester, St Elizabeth, St James, Trelany, Westmoreland, Hanover and Clarendon.

Please note that the names of these parishes are all associated with places in Britain; even the capital Kingston is associated with Kingston upon Thames. There are places with the name Cambridge, the Malvern Hills, Malvern, Great Malvern and Little Malvern, and hundreds of names of small villages and hamlets with the same names of places you will find in Britain. There are also three counties: the county of Cornwall, the County of Middlesex and the County of Surrey. I personally could claim I am Cornish but that would be confusing to British people who would believe I am speaking of Cornwall, the county in the extreme west of England. Jamaica was divided up into fourteen parishes and given to the aristocrats from Britain, with a huge proportion given to the Church of England, with land in each parish belonging to the Crown; these lands were called Crown lands.

There was no land given to the original inhabitants of the island nor was any land owned by the slaves who were brought to the island. Only the Maroons, who had fought and won their battle against the British, were given land in the John Figaro Mountains – Acompong Town – as the result of an agreement, signed by the Chief of the Maroons, the Right Honourable Nany the Maroon Queen.

This illustration is written as an outline to my story so that my readers will understand the cause of my plight and the cause of the suffering of people like me, in a country so beautiful, in a land of plenty, and why so rich a country produced so poor a people. It also helps to illustrate the meaning of the phrase 'Buckra Massa Pickney'.

Chapter Four

Enrico Stennett – Shattered Dreams

Enrico Stennett

It was now the latter part of 1950, my life had become settled and my friends had proved to me that I could survive in England and not get myself in trouble, as many of my countrymen had. Although my two friends were classed as left-wingers and Communists, they were far from being as described; they were only decent people who sought justice. Anyone who spoke of justice at that time was an enemy of the state, according to the media, and this remains so to this day.

My friends and I had been working together for some time, trying to integrate people from the Caribbean into the trade union movement and at the same time trying to teach them to be politically aware. We soon realised we could not find anyone who had any desire to spend a long time in England; some believed that within six months to a year they would have earned enough money to return to the West Indies, therefore they had no intention or desire to enter politics. All they were interested in was to find work, to work as long as they could, for as many hours as possible, and earn enough money to return home.

They were interested in getting together socially but, as there was nowhere available, without the usual colour bar and discrimination, they were inclined to support any attempt to build some kind of entertainment, but had no intention of creating any foundation for the future. All they thought about was returning home as soon as possible to their wives and children and the close family traditions they had left behind, while the single men wanted to return to their girlfriends.

We now spent our time protesting against racism in pubs and – one of the most racist establishments of all – the Working Men's clubs, who barred all black people from their premises because they did not want them mixing with their wives and daughters. Because they were all private clubs, no action could be taken against them. This proved beyond any doubt that the bulk of racists came from the working classes, whom the media had conditioned to believe that we were sub-human and not fit to mix with them. But above all there was the fear, which had been indoctrinated in them, that we were here to take their jobs, their houses and lead the women folk astray.

It was now time for us to create a new, credible movement, as all the earlier organisations were either a one-man bands or completely ineffective. Among the student population there was the West African Student Union (WASU) and later, the West Indian Students Union at 1 Cunningham Gardens, in Earls Court. We found it very difficult to get the West Indian students to join any organisation, as they were not politically inclined. No one could speak about Africa because, according to the West Indian students, they were not African and therefore they did not want any association with the Africans. The WASU was indeed very politically active, not in England, but in their respective countries, and they were working together for the unity of

85

Africa in a pan-African federation. They were not Communists or Socialists they were strictly Nationalists.

Their argument at the time was, before you become an Internationalist, you first had to become a Nationalist, because national freedom has to be achieved before one can think of international freedom. I agreed with these sentiments because, ever since the first day I arrived in England and first met an African at the Colonial House, I had decided in my mind, although I was not black but very light skinned, I was not a white man therefore I could only be an African.

We then decided to form a movement, this time a political movement called the African League; this movement was formed for the simple reason that both the League of Coloured People and the Coloured Workers' Association of Great Britain and Northern Ireland were not taking the political agenda forward. The Coloured Workers Association held all their activities at Speakers' Corner; here, the voice of the black people could be heard.

There were not enough members of the Coloured Workers' Association even to form a proper Executive Committee – they were more or less one-man bands – so the African League became the first substantial black political organisation ever in the British Isles. The first members were mature students from the WASU, students from the West Indian Student Union, and newly arrived black people from Trinidad, Jamaica, Barbados, Montserrat and many other West Indian islands. Now we had the people who could build a true organisation, but it took two white men and myself working every weekend, come rain or shine, to build the membership. Apart from speaking in Hyde Park we spoke on Tower Hill, in Brixton, and in meetings up and down the country. Within months the African League was established, not only in England, but also in all the English-speaking African countries. Before long we were in communication with all the African leaders and were in a position to convene their meetings when they were in England.

We met many African leaders who were quite different from the leaders of today; there was no greed and no corruption. Everyone we met had one thing in common and that was the freedom of Africa at any cost. Many knew they would die in working for that freedom but it did not matter; they had reached the stage when they realised that the United Kingdom was responsible for their predicament and their low position in the world. Unfortunately for them, the leeches who had sucked their blood were working out other ways to continue sucking their blood to bleed them dry. The reason why Britain had been able to rule an Empire was because she was, and still is, a brutal country. Britain thought nothing of murdering men, women and children in cold blood in order to maintain her grip on the countries she held in ransom. Britain had always held the power to select and impose on us the quislings she wanted us to accept as our leaders, but we were no longer prepared to tolerate this; now the only leaders we would support were the leaders chosen by the people themselves.

We are quite aware that the rulers of England are so devious that, when it suits them, they can turn father against son, son against father, and wife against husband; they divide their own people, setting them at each other's throats. We witnessed the days of the unions, when the ideals of the unions were used against them by their own members, having been conditioned by the authorities and the media. If this state of affairs can still exist in England today, no wonder we have so much corruption in Africa, where tribes are set against tribes, people are set against their leaders, wars are encouraged, and battles are fought, while Britain and other European nations arm one side against the other, creating the mass blood baths which we see all over Africa today.

We also found other places to hold functions as a means of bringing our people together in an organised manner; doing this while raising funds was difficult. Our work also coincided with Afro-Caribbean and African people beginning to settle in the Summer Layton Road area of Brixton. By now there were around eight houses, owned by Jewish landlords, which had been given to black people to run, in order to ensure these people had somewhere to sleep at night. The

87

conditions that existed within these houses had to be seen to be believed, but I will do my best to describe them.

The houses were Victorian buildings, which were three and four storeys high. The main kitchen was in the back room of the ground floor or the basement, with a gas stove and gas ring on the landing, and with saucepans and plates placed on make-do shelves. Each floor would have three or four rooms, and each room would be rented out to three, four, and sometimes up to five people, with beds and bunk beds along each wall. There was nowhere to hang your clothes and the places were almost uninhabitable. The people who occupied these premises slept in the beds on a relay basis: those who were at work at night would sleep in the day, and those who were at work during the day, would sleep at night. At no time were those beds empty. There was nowhere to store food, so the residents kept it wherever they could; this encouraged rats, cockroaches, bed bugs and lice. Because of these appalling conditions, it was easy to organise the people who were living in these houses, but arrangements had to be made whereby the largest room would be used every Sunday as a meeting place for the people who lived in the surrounding houses, to help us to organise and help ourselves.

We now occupied numbers 64, 67, 63, 24 and 18 Summer Layton Road, Brixton. We did not own these properties – they were owned by Jews – but the landlords who were in charge of them were from the Caribbean. Jews bought these properties because they were the main employers of black people; they realised black people were good workers, but some of them had been falling asleep at work from sheer tiredness. When asked why they were falling asleep, despite the danger from the machines they were working, the men had explained that they had nowhere to sleep, and were sleeping in the Lyons Corner houses, various dilapidated hostels and bombed houses.

The Jews decided they would find accommodation for these people but they did not want to manage the properties, so arrangements were made for the workers to do this themselves. Houses at that time were inexpensive, so the agreement made between the West Indians, who managed them, and the Jewish owners, was that the West Indians would collect the rent and pay the owner the amount of money it had cost for the Jewish man to purchase the house. At the end of the agreement, the houses would be signed over to the man who managed the house. This was giving the West Indians their first foot on the ladder of house ownership. It was also doing something else; the eyes of the West Indian people were now open, and they quickly realised how easy it was to exploit their own people.

This was made easier because English people moved out of the area in a bid to escape living among black people. As fast as English people moved out, the houses were snapped up by West Indians. This was the birth of the 'Su Su', otherwise known as 'the Pardner', and now known as the Credit Union. People who were working would join this partnership; 10 or 15 of them would become members and each would pay a certain amount of money into the partnership each week, and that money would then be given to one individual. Depending on the amount of money paid by each person each week, the money would go towards the purchase of a house. Each week it was someone else's turn to draw the money, enabling them to put a deposit on a house, which in turn would be let out to incoming West Indians in the same pattern of four to one room; this was the basis on which the purchasing of houses was built. This was the way the exploitation was carried out.

Before long the black population of Brixton began to expand resulting in the birth of black exploitation – where black people treated other blacks with impunity, as they strived to extend their house ownership. The Jews who helped us could not have foreseen what would happen, but the black people were quick to catch on, knowing the black population was growing rapidly, with shiploads of arrivals each month commonplace. They knew all the houses they could buy would be rented, and the conditions did not matter to them. Black people then decided to branch out to other parts of London, wherever they could buy houses. As fast as they bought the houses, the white neighbours would move out, giving them the chance to buy more houses, therefore the exploitation grew.

I knew a black woman who lived at 51 Summer Layton Road in Brixton. She had houses in Effer Road, and many other roads in the Brixton and Camberwell Green areas. She became rich overnight, to the extent that she was the darling of the Tory party and, when she got married, there was coverage of her wedding in the Evening Standard for two days, praising her for the strides she had made since coming to this country. Nothing was said about how she made her money.

Apart from working in the factories black people were trying other avenues, which all verged on the 'get rich quick' mentality. There were boxers, such as the Black Carnero – a heavyweight champion of Jamaica, who took his name from Primo Carnero the Italian boxer – who had fought Joe Louis; ironically this was the man who discovered the dead bodies left by John Reginald Christie at 10 Rillington Place, Paddington. There were a lot of other boxers such as Joe Hyman and Kid Hartley, who were making their way into this society. No black boxers had been allowed to box for the Lonsdale Belt until the Turpin Brothers arrived on the scene. Randolph's elder brother Dick Turpin fought the then middleweight champion of Britain, Vince Hawkins, and beat him on three occasions. Each time they denied him the Lonsdale belt. When the British boxing authorities saw his brother Randolph, who had a punch and was in a position to bring the world middleweight title to England, the bar to the black man fighting for the Lonsdale Belt was lifted. Randolph Turpin then became the world middleweight champion, by beating the black prince 'Sugar' Ray Robinson on points. The fact he did not hold the title for more than three months was beside the point.

Following Randolph Turpin, a Trinidadian by the name of Youlandi Pompeii was the second man of colour to hold a British title; he fought Archie Moore for the world light-heavyweight championship, but lost. Following him was Alex Buxton of Watford, who held both the British middleweight and light-heavyweight titles. Then Joe

Bygrave knocked out the great Henry Cooper to become the British heavyweight champion; but of course, when Cooper is mentioned by the British, he is only remembered for the lucky punch he hit Mohammed Ali with, in the fourth round of their first fight. The fact that Cooper's manager had to throw in the towel to save him from being seriously injured in the fifth round, the round in which Ali predicted he would stop Cooper, is never mentioned. Many other black boxers fought in Britain at that time; one of the most well known, Kid Guverlon, beat Pete Waterman easily, but was robbed of the fight by the referee, which caused the crowd to riot because of the unjust verdict. In the return fight Waterman was knocked out in a few rounds, with Guverlon using his famous bowler punch.

Even in the field of boxing, black people never had a fair chance; they had to knock their opponent out to win. On some occasions, even when they did knock their opponent out, they would be disqualified for alleged low punches, as in the case of Zora Folly when he knocked out Henry Cooper. In the return bout, Folly swore he would not hit Cooper lower than the head, and Cooper was knocked out in about four rounds. A lot of black fighters at the time suffered racism in every way possible; they fought for peanuts and sometimes were robbed by their managers, as in the case of Kid Harley. They were not allowed to become British champions, only Empire champions, but nevertheless they were good fighters, and they fought to earn money to improve their lives. And what better way than to purchase houses to rent rooms to the new arrivals from the Caribbean?

As the West Indians branched out in various areas, the newspapers began their attack on the West Indian community. They were building up a climate of race hatred, talking about black people taking over, and that white people would be overrun by blacks. Each day there were articles, headlines and editorials condemning the Government for allowing black immigration to continue unabated. The only voices speaking out against all this vile propaganda were those of R.V. Mathews, myself and other members of the African League. This caused friction within the communities and especially within the all-white communities, where the estate agents found themselves unable to sell houses to black people. In certain areas, when a house was for sale and it was about to be bought by a black person, the neighbours would combine and put the money together to buy the house, in order to prevent black people from buying it. This was common at that time.

There was a case in 1949, when a West Indian gentleman was living at 7 Fernside Road, Balham; he rented a room at the top of the house from an elderly, English lady. She lived on the first floor and had white tenants living on the ground floor. This lady died and left the house to her son, who did not want it, as houses did not mean much to anyone in those days. The son offered the house first to the white tenants on the ground floor, for the measly sum of £500; the white tenants refused. So he offered it to a black tenant who was living on the top floor, and was glad to buy it. When the news went out that 7 Fernside Road, Balham was to be sold to a black man, the people of Balham decided to organise a petition and collected signatures to prevent a black man buying the house. They collected ten thousand signatures, but the council refused the petition on the grounds that the man was entitled to live where he liked, and they could do nothing to stop it.

As the population of black people increased in the areas of Brixton, Clapham Common, Kennington and Stockwell, there was an outcry led by the media about black people buying white people's houses, and this stirred up a lot of resentment against black people. What were these black people supposed to do? They were told they had no chance of even being entered on the council waiting lists, as they had to be in the country for three years before this was permissible. Even then they would have to wait for at least another three years before they were considered for a house or flat, yet they were not supposed to buy houses.

One could understand how the African League developed to become the main black organisation fighting against racism in England. At the same time, we were working with African leaders in their respective countries, co-ordinating their work and arranging their meetings, which they held in London. The African League was the voice of the black people. The newspaper campaign was so effective that at one period black people in London could not purchase any houses, so many of these houses were purchased by the white wives of black men. By this time, black men who had arrived in this country as single men were now forming liaisons with Irish women, who were also arriving in London. The fact English racists treated them alike gave them a bond, which remains strong until this day.

One could see clearly the reasons why the Captain in charge of the Colonial House in St Martin's Lane had directed all the newcomers in the late 1940s and early 1950s to the East End of London, around Cable Street and the docklands. It was a deliberate policy by the authorities to create a little ghetto in the midst of London, as it had been with Harlem in the city of New York. The black people who were now arriving in England, were not so docile and humble as the American blacks, and we were not prepared to live in ghettos. As equal people we saw ourselves as entitled to live where we liked. We did not choose ghettos in our country for the Englishman to live; they had the best of everything. Why should we settle for less? We were determined that under no circumstances would we allow ourselves to be forced to live in ghettos.

We were now moving into areas such as Westbourne Grove, Paddington, Edgware Road, Maida Vale, and many white areas around the Central London area. Some of us even had the cheek to move into the so-called middle-class reserves, such as Sloane Square, Brompton Road, Chelsea and Fulham. Now the hysteria by the media increased. The then Prime Minister, Clement Atlee, was in a dilemma. The Government wanted to appease their working-class followers, but at the same time realised the effect it would have on white people in the colonial territories. Britain also needed labour, so the Government had no alternative than to remain adamant in the face of the pressure. But we remained determined: the English workers and the so-called English middle classes could have their no-go areas, but these areas were not for

93

us. Places like King's Cross, Bermondsey, Elephant and Castle, Woolwich, and Erith in Kent, tried their best to enforce their no-go areas by using the threat of violence, and sometimes did use violence. In places like Bethnal Green, Hoxton, Hackney and Stoke Newington, black people had to be careful.

There was a time when Rigley Road, Dalston, was a no-go area for black people, even though it had always held a market there. Not only was there the hooligan element to contend with, but also the thuggish policemen, who used their uniforms as cover to carry out their racist attacks, knowing they had the law behind them. The black people's battle was not an easy one, and it still remains the same today and always will. Like other black people, I moved from one place to another. I tried to avoid confrontation and I moved to the best areas possible, like St Johns Wood, Maida Vale and Purley, areas that were uplifting, because I was determined not to be a part of what the Englishman expected me to be. I was also determined that under no circumstances would I degrade myself in any way. I have always seen myself as I saw the Englishmen in the Caribbean – as an ambassador for their people. I therefore refused to drink alcohol, smoke, gamble or do anything that would bring discredit on my fellow countrymen and myself.

I now became 'public enemy number one', speaking in Hyde Park both on the platform of the African League and the Coloured Workers Association; the audience would be filled with MI5 and MI6 personnel along, with plain-clothes policemen. I was hounded at work and on the streets; they were now trying to do everything to stop me from speaking in Hyde Park and also to prevent the progress of the African League, which was now developing at a pace that the British Government could not tolerate. I was the organising secretary and we were organising meetings everywhere in England where there was a sizeable number of black people – Liverpool, Manchester, Cardiff, Bristol, Nottingham, and other areas. The branches were not large but, because they had the support of both the Communist Party and the

Trotskyites, and also because we supported the anti- weapons organisations, the African League became a bit more than a nuisance.

I spent most of my time working in furniture factories and in some cases as a joiner in the building trade. I became skilled in all areas of woodwork, both carpentry and joinery. I had now become very active politically, speaking at trade union meetings, Labour Party branches and various halls. From 1950 to 1962 I spoke in Hyde Park every Sunday and almost every day of the week, and if I was not in Hyde Park I would be somewhere else speaking. This was the only voice we had, and although on the face of it this voice was ignored, we soon realised that by the actions of MI5 and the police, who tried to stop us from speaking, our voices were taken seriously.

It was now 1950 and I had been in England for just over three years; I was lonely and had no one apart from my girlfriend's family, and a few acquaintances around London. Some of these acquaintances were noted people – both black and white – from the English middle classes. I now lived in Strutham Ground off Victoria Street, not far from Buckingham Palace, the Houses of Parliament, Horse Guards Parade and 10 Downing Street; in fact I was in the middle of the aristocracy, but continued to work in North London. The people I associated with at the time were not only leaders from Jamaica, but people who came from outstanding backgrounds who were trying their best to keep themselves above the level of intelligence practised by the so-called host community. One of my friends at that time was Michael Manley; he was someone I had grown up with in Jamaica and, although I did not know him well, I knew his father and almost all his father's associates. He is now the Right Honourable Norman Washington Manley, the then leader of the opposition. Michael was at the London School of Economics together with Rolley Simms, who returned to Jamaica but was quickly arrested by the authorities and incarcerated for speaking about British imperialism.

What I remember most from that time is the racism, which was not called racism but the colour bar, as if the colour bar was that simple.

95

In Jamaica, we were all Christians and regular churchgoers; some of us were Catholics, but I and most of my family and friends were members of the High Church of England. It was quite obvious, as Christians in Britain, we would try to follow the kind of life we led in the Caribbean. We were living close to a large church in Warwick Avenue, Maida Vale, Paddington, a church that no longer exists today. It was the High Church of England, which we were used to, so we started to attend services there each Sunday. One Sunday, after about three months' church attendance, Albert Mckoy, Oscar Jones, Tina Borova and myself went to the church as usual. We had noticed on occasion that no one would sit beside us, but by this time we were used to being ostracised by our fellow Christians. However, what happened that day left us puzzled and bewildered and completely disillusioned.

At the end of the service, on our way out, the vicar met us at the door. 'I hope you will not mind me saying this,' he said, 'I know you are Christians because you have been coming to this church every Sunday for some time now, but please do not take offence at what I am about to say. I would like you to stop coming to this church and find another one to attend.' When we asked why he replied, 'Can't you see? You are chasing away my parishioners.' He pointed out that the congregation was dwindling week by week since we had started attending the church. Dejectedly we walked away, but deep in our hearts we knew we had no intention of attending any other church for worship in this country again. We knew the God we went to worship in that church did not go there, so why should we?

I had been engaged to be married for some time now and my fiancée and I were looking forward to getting married in that particular church, but because of our treatment we decided to change our minds about having a church wedding. This was disappointing for our friends because at that time I was the first one of us who was thinking of getting married. All my associates and friends had decided they would help us financially so we could have a big wedding, but after our treatment at the church, neither my fiancée nor my friends wanted anything to do with the church.

96

Peggy and I were finally married on 15th July 1950 at Marylebone Register Office. Until the time we married, my wife had not encountered any racism in its true sense; the only racism she encountered was when she was in the ATS. She had been invited to a serviceman's dance, and at the dance she was in the company of two of her best friends. These ladies were so-called high-bred mulattos from Jamaica, who were among the first group of women to leave Jamaica to join the RAF. While everyone was dancing, two rather dark-skinned RAF personnel entered the dance hall and, recognising that these ladies were Jamaicans, the men approached them and asked them for a dance. To Peggy's shock, her friends refused to dance with the black men. When Peggy asked them why, she was told by the women that in Jamaica these men were not fit to be their servants, at best they could only be their chauffeurs, so why should they mix with them in England, when they would not have done so in Jamaica. Peggy was annoyed at their response and their snobbery. When the next dance began, Peggy approached the black gentleman and said, 'May I have this dance, please?' She decided to snub her friends for what she thought was gross ignorance, lack of dignity and an insult to the men who were fighting the same war. Now she was about to discover there was racism in England, and the cruelty that racism contained.

When we married, my wife had booked a week's honeymoon in Hastings; she did not think it necessary to explain to anyone whom she was married to or what colour her husband was, she just booked the holiday. After a small wedding reception attended by her mother, father, sister and two friends of mine, we boarded the train to Hastings. We had paid the deposit as required by the proprietor of the bed and breakfast establishment, not expecting there would be any difficulty. On arriving in Hastings, we took a taxi to the address of the bed and breakfast, but when the landlady saw me she began to make excuses, saying the booking was a mistake and if she had known I was coloured she would not have taken the booking in the first place. She had vacancies but she had no intention of letting me stay in her establishment as she had her other clientele to think of. Our deposit was returned to us and the door was closed in our face. There was no law in force to prevent her doing what she did and there was nowhere we could complain. She did not care that we were stranded and had nowhere to go.

My wife and I decided we would try other guest houses; we left our luggage at the station and began to search together for accommodation. There were vacancies everywhere but unfortunately not for us; everywhere we went together we were turned away. It was now approaching late evening and we were deciding whether to return to London when my wife suggested we gave it one more try. This time she suggested I stay at the station with the luggage while she tried to find somewhere. She was not away long when she returned to tell me she had found somewhere, and she had paid the landlady the money in advance. We intentionally waited at the station for a while, so it would be late when we arrived at the guest house. To our surprise the lady was there to greet us, but when she saw me, the grin on her face suddenly changed, her countenance was one of sheer disappointment, 'I am very sorry.' she said, 'had I known your husband was coloured I would not have given you the room. Anyway, come in, but you will have to find somewhere else tomorrow.'

The following morning when we awoke and went downstairs to the dining room, we found there was a large dining table, which could comfortably hold about eight people, at which other guests were sitting. There was a small table in the corner where we were requested to sit. We did not mind, but to our great surprise the other guests enquired why we were sitting on our own and not with them. They spoke to the proprietor about this, who explained with embarrassment that she did not think they would like us to be sitting with them. 'Nonsense,' said one of the men, and he turned to us to ask us to join them. The landlady's face went crimson with shame and, after breakfast, she asked us to stay as long as we wanted. We didn't object. As the landlady had said we were welcome to stay, we decided to spend two weeks there – the last week in July and the first week in August – as it was the custom for factories to give holidays during those weeks.

98

I was a young man who did not believe in hanging around wasting time; I always liked to be doing something constructive with my time, and as long as I was occupied I was content. I looked around and saw a grandfather clock, in bad condition, standing in the hallway and I became curious. I knew I could repair it; not only that but I could steel-wool and pumice it down and polish it – in other words, restore it. I asked the landlord if I could restore the clock for him, but his first reaction was clear – he thought I didn't know anything about clocks. However, he agreed that I couldn't do any harm and decided I could do what I liked with it because it was just standing there as an ornament. We then discussed what materials were needed and he went out to buy them. So, in between going to the seaside, for walks on the cliffs at Hastings and in the caves, I worked on the clock. By the end of our holiday, the clock was working and keeping the correct time, I had repaired the woodwork and it shone like new. This poor gentleman could not hide his astonishment; he wanted to know where I had learned to do things like this. It was quite obvious he did not believe black people had any skills, especially one so young, and he offered to give me the money we had paid for our two weeks' stay, but I refused. I told him I had enjoyed working on the clock; I had great satisfaction restoring it and my wife had been content to watch me. He then promised me we could return each year and spend our holidays with them. For years after, I received letters from them inviting us back, and we became friends to a degree.

On our return to London, my wife did not want us to go to Randolph Avenue, Maida Vale, where I was living. She did not like the conditions that existed there, so we decided to find new accommodation. We could have gone to live with her mother and father in Merton, South West London, but we decided against this. We set out to look for new accommodation, so we went to the Clapham Common area because we noticed there were rooms to let. We liked the sound of a particular advertisement, so my wife went to visit the house while I waited with the luggage at Charing Cross station; she saw the room, which she felt was suitable, booked the accommodation and paid a month's rent in advance.

When we arrived at the house in a taxi with our suitcases, the lady saw me and became absolutely furious; she walked up to my wife, very annoyed, and said, 'How dare you bring a nigger into my house!' My wife was startled, but I was not. I was furious because of the way the woman spoke to my wife and the disrespect she showed. I lost my temper and I told her I had paid four weeks' rent and I had no intention of leaving until the four weeks were up; I started to unpack. 'After all,' I said, 'we have just fought a war for your freedom, not ours, and we helped save you from Nazi Germany, but here you are, just like the Nazis, if not worse.' During our conversation, I learned she was a South African, but to me, being white South African or white English was inseparable, which I told her. She tried to return the money to my wife but I would not allow my wife to take it, so she threw it on the floor. I ignored the money on the floor saying, 'If you want to throw away money it is up to you, but it will not be collected by us.' By this time my wife had become very upset; she had now begun to see what racism was all about – that it had no justification whatever, and was hurtful and degrading.

The front door opened and four of the biggest policemen I had ever seen arrived; the landlady had called them. Upon entering the house, without saying a word, one of the policemen approached me and grabbed me by the scruff of my neck; I was startled by their actions. 'How dare you manhandle me like this,' I protested. 'What do you think you are doing, are you a peacemaker or a troublemaker?' I added, 'Don't you want to know the circumstances?' This stopped him in his tracks; he seemed somewhat surprised, like many people, by the way I spoke, and he took his hands off me. He said that he did want to hear the circumstances, so I explained the position to him. When they heard the facts the police became sympathetic, but stated that, as the law stood, the lady had the right not to let me stay. By this time Peggy was crying and, regardless of what was to happen, she did not want to stay in that woman's house another minute. I turned to my wife and told her to take a taxi to her mother's home, because I was not leaving.

After listening to what I had to say, the police changed their attitude towards me, but although they were very sorry, it was the lady's house and if she did not want me there I had to go. He told me I could take her to court if I wanted to, but thought I would be wasting my time. I then turned to the woman and told her that, because it was late, the only place I would be able to find was a hotel in the West End. I wanted to be compensated for the money I had spent travelling to Clapham and the money I would have to spend returning to the West End at that time of night. She said that she would give any money providing I left immediately and she produced £30 and picked up my money, which she had thrown on the floor, and handed it to the police. The police officer then offered to take me back to the West End, but I refused and called a taxi. The police were sympathetic as I went on my way.

One only wonders what would have happened if I had not stood up for myself the way I did. Judging by the experiences of others, she would have thrown me out, and if I had protested I would have been charged for disturbing the peace or some other trumped-up charges. From that moment, my wife resolved to do everything in her power to work with me and fight against the type of ignorance that prevailed. When we returned to the West End we tried many hotels but, as we had expected, none would accept us. My wife and I had no alternative but to call Robert Mathews, a colleague of mine, who was living near Goodge Street off Tottenham Court Road; he could not accommodate us at his home so we had to sleep in his office on the cold floor until the next morning. We tried all day to find somewhere to live, but without success. In the end we had no alternative but to return to my wife's parents' home in Merton SW19. It was then we decided we would do everything in our power to see the end of racism and to expose the people who practised it, both here and abroad.

Because of where we were now living, I found it difficult to find employment. I had to travel from Merton across London, either to the

East End or North London, to find work in the cabinet trade. I decided to look for any kind of work I could within the South West London area. I was unemployed for about six weeks, looking for employment every day. One morning we noticed an advertisement in the local newspaper; British Rail was looking for carriage cleaners so I applied for the job. An interview was arranged, but on my arrival the stationmaster called me into his office. 'Do you know what a carriage cleaner does?' he asked. 'No,' I replied. He explained, 'It means you will have to mix with very low-class people, in fact the lowest of the low, do you want to do that?' I said,' I am sorry, but I have no choice.' 'Of course you have,' he said. 'Would you do this kind of work if you were at home?' I replied, 'But I am not at home, I am in England.' Apart from the police officer I mentioned earlier, it was the first time an Englishman had ever spoken to me with such respect. 'It does not matter where you are in the world,' he said, 'or what difficulties you may have, you should never drop your standards. I have a vacancy as a carriage cleaner, but it is not for you.' He took me into his office and asked me to sit at the desk where he gave me an aptitude test. I was not prepared for such treatment or, for that matter, the test, but I passed with flying colours.

'You came here expecting to clean carriages,' he said, 'but we want office workers and people to collect tickets at the ticket offices. I will send you somewhere where you will find a decent job.' He then gave me a letter and a travel card to the station in Woking, Surrey. 'Give this directly to the person whose name is on the letter,' he instructed, 'and you will be all right.'

The following day I took the train to Woking; it was the first time I had travelled so far to look for work. I arrived at the station at exactly 10 a.m. but the gentleman who I was sent to see was not there that day – just my luck, he had a day off – but a man who said he was his assistant, dressed in dirty overalls and wearing a cloth cap, took the letter from me and read it. He crushed the letter and threw it on the floor. 'Follow me,' he said, and took me to a cupboard, pulled out a broom and handed it to me saying, 'You have a job now, start sweeping,' pointing to the station platform. I replied, 'No thank you. I did not travel all this way to find myself sweeping railway station platforms,' and walked away. As I walked away I heard him say, 'That's all you people are fit for, sweeping the floors.' All I could think of then was the difference between these two men.

Remembering the stationmaster had told me that they wanted workers in the offices and as ticket collectors, I started to look for jobs on the railway as a ticket collector, but without success. I did have one interview where I was told my English was not good enough to be understood, and that I would have to be handling money, and therefore touching the customers' hands, which would not be appreciated. I could not understand this because my English was far superior to his; I was always accused by others of speaking like an English aristocrat. After this I decided I would travel across London to work – it did not matter how far it was.

Peggy was now expecting our first child and I knew I had responsibilities so it was vital that I found a job. I managed to find a job in New Malden, Surrey; it was with a building firm, where I operated the woodwork machines manufacturing banisters and staircases. I was quite happy as I was highly skilled in the job, but the wages as a joiner were not as much as those of a cabinetmaker.

After about three months, I returned to North London to work. I had now embarked on various other activities, all concerned with politics. Apart from the Cosmopolitan Social Society, and the League of Coloured People, I had now joined Robert Mathews in Hyde Park speaking on the platform of the Coloured Workers Association of Great Britain and Northern Ireland. I was also undertaking other activities such as protest marches; I joined the Aldermaston to London march and other marches led by various left-wing organisations, including the trade unions and the Communist Party. Other duties were required, such as picketing; I allocated picketing locations such as public houses, restaurants and other public buildings that bluntly refused to serve black people. The pubs were notorious for racism and although I did not drink, I was determined to join others picketing the pubs.

A pub that was one of the worst offenders was the Atlantic pub in Coldharbour Lane, Brixton, but there were other pubs around the SW9 area and also in Camberwell Green and Peckham, so a group of us would picket those. Amongst us would be white people from left-wing organisations, who would enter the pub, ask for a drink and would be served; then one of us would join him and order a drink, only to be told either they had no drinks or they did not serve niggers. The number of public houses in those days with the policy of exclusion was surprising; it was an irony that, after we forced the brewery to take away the franchise from the proprietor of the Atlantic public house, the Atlantic was given to a West Indian – the first West Indian proprietor to run a pub in England. The policy regarding the colour bar within the pubs in the area changed, in that they were forced to let us in, but the racism continued; when the staff had served us a drink and we had finished drinking, they would smash the glass we had just used in front of us. What these people did not realise was, the more hatred they displayed towards us, the more resolute we became in our struggle against racism.

Of course there were people who were not racist, people who were standing with us in our struggle. The funny thing was, if it were not so contradictory, these non-racist people were hated by the establishment, and in some cases classed as traitors, Communists and other unmentionable tags. We also could console ourselves with the knowledge that, at the weekends we could go and enjoy ourselves with these people who accepted us as human beings. It is a fact that most of the people who stood up for us were women – both young and old. We always believed it was because women were mothers that they understood our suffering. Irish people also had empathy with us because they also suffered various forms of discrimination, and there were some in the Labour Movement who gave us their support. As young people we did not spend all our time protesting and struggling against the odds; we did find some time to enjoy ourselves. In the midst of all the racist persecution that was taking place at the time, we could always find solace in music and dancing.

In the 1950s racism was everywhere, but it was not as institutionalised as it is today; the black people did not understand its significance. To most of us it was a big joke, especially how it operated in the dance halls. We knew the men did not want to mix with us, but we did not care to mix with them either. On the other hand the women, whether young or old, were very accommodating; we had no problems. Those were the days of the big bands, the jitterbug, the bebop, the jive, Latin American music and dancing, and the blues. I had to divide my time constructively therefore all my political activities were confined to weekdays, and my social activities to the weekends. I had realised there was no point seeking higher education at that time, to enter the profession I had originally wanted, which was law. This was not possible and I had to be realistic.

I learnt that as well as the various clubs I have mentioned there were dance halls around London, such as the Lyceum, the Streatham Locarno, the Hammersmith Palais, the Astoria, the Tottenham Royal, the Ilford Locarno and, most popular of all, the Paramount, in Tottenham Court Road. My first encounter with these dance halls was not very pleasant. In saying this I must point out that, apart from the Tottenham Royal, the Streatham Locarno, the Ilford Palais and the many small dances held in town halls around London, which were mostly frequented by the English working classes, we had no problems with the dancers at the main dance halls.

Those were the days of the dance halls. As West Indians this was the music we were accustomed to and most of us were good dancers. We had rhythm, an ear for the music and a wonderful zest to enjoy our lives. Everywhere we went we stood out, but this did not go down well with the men. The women flocked around us while the men sulked and looked at us with contempt. Every weekend, women would come from all the outlying areas of London and the Home Counties to dance halls in the West End. These young ladies were immaculately dressed, rather beautiful, and were as light as a feather when they danced.

The media was just as racist as it is today; they would turn the slightest incident into a racist headline because for them, any white woman who mixed with a coloured man would be ruined and the coloured men were here to ruin the lives of the young women. Those were the days of Lord Beaverbrook; he was today's Rupert Murdoch, even the Daily Gleaner and the Express newspaper in Jamaica were owned by him, but all his newspapers were racist to the core. They were excellent at spreading messages of hate and conditioning the minds of the British working classes, just like some of today's newspapers. They often used the words 'contamination of the British race' referring to the children who were produced by mixing black and white. They talked about the mongrelisation of Britain, and as usual the police acted accordingly for the benefit of the media. Things have not changed that much as far as the media is concerned. It was claimed by the newspapers at the time that the Paramount should be closed, because many decent white girls from the suburbs were flocking to the Paramount in order to mix with black people, which was degrading to white Britain. These media articles sometimes provoked assaults; I witnessed many of these assaults, so to avoid being involved, I always had an agreement with my girlfriends that we would leave separately and meet on the platform of Warren Street underground station.

In the main dance halls we had different problems, caused by the fact we did not conform to the English way of dancing, as we insisted on jiving and jitterbugging, while the rest continued to move around the floor in uniform fashion; they were like robots, all dancing in the same way round and round in circles. The poor Englishmen could not dance and those who tried could not let themselves go with their waltz, foxtrot, quickstep and tango. The young women did not want this regimental way of dancing, they wanted freedom, relaxation and pleasure in their dancing; the West Indians provided that, just like the black Americans had done during the war. For young ladies, out looking for excitement, this was just the tonic they needed. To young people, we were exciting, and before long all would join in, jiving and jitterbugging, to the horror of the management.

One can understand the enmity which developed, caused by sheer jealousy; this resulted in the growth of the spivs, with their dress similar to ours but with winkle-picker shoes, worn so they could use them as a weapon when they wanted to. In the dance halls at that time there were far more women than men. Each night you would find a row of women, standing in queues side by side, and leaning against the walls. Some would be there all night wanting to dance but were never asked; they were called wallflowers. Many of these women who danced with us found themselves being insulted by their men folk. Some men would deliberately ask them for the next dance but immediately after they started dancing the men would ask them why they found it necessary to dance with niggers. It was not the dance they wanted, it was to abuse the girl by telling her that she was a nigger lover, and if she danced with a nigger again she would be in trouble. These women were bullied by the white boys, who tried to prevent them from dancing with the black boys. Some of these women would be called names such as nigger lovers, whores, prostitutes and other demeaning names.

Hence, in the beginning these women would be reluctant and sometimes afraid to dance with a black man on a second occasion. Some of these girls stood up to the white boys, called their bluff, told them to go to hell and danced with black boys anyway. This sometimes caused trouble, when a girl who had just danced with a black boy would be attacked by white yobs and the blacks would go in to defend them. This state of affairs was indicative of the time and happened in all the dance halls in London. The dance halls that were out of town became out of bounds to us, as there were not many black people there; if we were caught in them we risked being knifed or badly beaten up; many times we had to fight like hell for our lives. The trouble was, the police were always on the side of those who attacked us, we were always wrong. We were supposed to allow ourselves to be attacked and injured without defending ourselves, and when we did defend ourselves

107

against someone who was injured, we would be the one who would be arrested.

The Englishmen sometimes tried to pick fights with the West Indians on the dance floor and outside the dance halls. There were no-go areas for black people, such as the Locarno in Streatham, the Hammersmith Palais, the Ilford Palais and the Tottenham Royal; they were afraid to enter these areas because on many occasions knives were used as weapons against them. The girls on their part were afraid to dance with us, because if they did they would be leaving themselves open to verbal abuse and sometimes-physical attack.

As West Indians, we did not only have to contend with the jealousy and hatred of the spivs, young police officers were just as bad. Often black people would be attacked, and instead of the police going to the assistance of those who were being attacked, they would join in, with the result that the victims would be arrested and the perpetrators allowed to go free. Black people realised that they had no protection from the police or the courts, therefore we were not prepared to stand aside and allow ourselves to be ill-treated and abused. We had to make it clear that even if we were arrested we had to fight back, and in some cases find ourselves up against the police who would assault us and in turn accuse us of assaulting them. In court the police would deliberately lie and the magistrates would believe them. Many innocent young people were sent to prison for just trying to defend themselves, both against the attackers and the police.

What worried me most at the time was that some of the younger West Indian men who had arrived in this country as seamen and stowaways could not read or write. They did not know how to cope in their new surroundings; by their actions they gave the police the excuse they wanted, and the police took full advantage of it. Work was almost impossible to find, there was no unemployment benefit and no money to live on in this strange, cold country. They were forced to live by their wits any way they could; one could say these people did not set a good example nor did they lay any positive foundation for the influx of Caribbean people to this country which was to come.

We did not walk with our heads held high with dignity and pride, we were not allowed to; instead some embarked upon a career of petty crime, such as living off the immoral earnings of prostitutes, gambling in the streets with dice, blocking Cable Street and preventing any vehicles from entering. This caused the police the aggravation of having to clear the streets of dozens of gamblers as they sat in the middle of the street playing dice and cards and sometimes fighting among themselves, especially when money was lost.

Some would open small cafés in slum areas as fronts for gambling; they used these premises as drop-in centres where they congregated from all over London. At the same time it was a place where the women 'on the game' could meet them to hand over their money. These West Indians came from many of the islands in the Caribbean, although Jamaicans were in the majority. There were also many African seamen, and their behaviour was appalling to say the least. There were also other coloured people living in the East End: Ethiopians, Somalis, Eritreans, and there were a few Egyptians, but their behaviour was completely different to that of the West Indians; they were a docile people who found mixing with West Indians difficult to cope with.

As I had never seen anything like this in the Caribbean, there was no way I wanted to be a part of what was going on. In my opinion, we had not set the right example for our countrymen to follow. We did not respect ourselves so could not expect to be respected in return. I believe our behaviour at that time has been a legacy that we have had to carry with us until this day.

The British media, in their effort to condition the minds of British people against the presence of black people in England, now that the war had ended and we were no longer wanted, took every opportunity to seize on any misdemeanour committed by young black people as an example of all blacks, regardless of where they came from.

It was never taken into consideration that black people were not all alike. In Jamaica there was the same class system as existed in England, but here in England we were all lumped together and discredited, no matter who we were.

The West Indian servicemen, who had not returned home to Jamaica after the end of the war, lived scattered around London and the outlying areas and would only come to the centre of London at weekends to attend the various dance halls. There we met West Indians who had been in this country during the war and knew their way around, but they were not doing any better. Now the war was over they could not find work, so they had to resort to devious ways of earning a living.

In the dance halls, I had extra problems; because of the fact that I was an outstanding dancer, once I started to dance the entire ballroom would stop and before long my partner and I would find ourselves in the centre of a circle, as if we were giving an exhibition, with many females jostling to cut in, just for the privilege of dancing with me. I became public enemy number one. It was ironic, in an area full of white people, you could not find one white male dancing at the Paramount. The atmosphere was electric as the big bands competed to play for us; they could really enjoy their playing, seeing black people enjoying themselves to the full, as it gave the bands more room for improvisation.

Although many people had forgotten that these men had fought in the war, we knew many who had given their lives. They had come to do a job, but now the job was done, 'Get out, you are no longer wanted,' was the attitude. Mecca dance hall proprietors quite obviously did not want any trouble within their establishments so they did all they could to prevent the disruption and the fights, which often occurred. They felt action should be taken against us to stop us coming so that their problems would be solved. The problem was, how could they stop us coming? There was no simple answer. The following tactics were used to get rid of us: no jiving, jitterbugging or bebopping was allowed. The moment any one of us started, we would be thrown out, but the women would then carry on jiving and jitterbugging among themselves; it was a lost cause.

Stronger action had to be taken. We were then prevented from entering the dance halls without partners, but the women soon caught on. They would gather in the foyer waiting for us to come along, then join the queue and buy two tickets. As we came along, whether we knew them or not, they would hand us the two tickets and we would both walk in together. Sometimes we parted when we went into the hall but this did not matter – we were in. When this did not work, the clothes you wore would come into question: zoot suits were not allowed and doormen would examine your shoes and if they thought your shoes were not clean you would be turned away. If we did not have a tie we could not enter, it did not matter how hot the night was. Of course not everyone wore a tie, so this rule did not work.

Heaven and earth was moved to keep us out of dance halls. Eventually, Mecca decided to compromise and they allowed the Paramount dance hall, in Tottenham Court Road – now called the Empire Room – to be used exclusively for jitterbugging and jiving, the kind of music loved by West Indians. Before long, it became known as the dance hall for young black men. It was believed we would go there and nowhere else so, yes, we went to the Paramount, and we were quite happy there as the women followed us, but we were not prepared to be barred from anywhere.

The Paramount was quite different in that the police carried out the racism. Every weekend, the police would gather in front of the Paramount, and there would be two or three Black Marias waiting outside near the Roebuck public house. They were there to cause trouble, make no mistake about it, because they knew young black men would be walking out arm in arm with white girls. The police had devised their own ways and means to provoke trouble. I have seen the police deliberately trip up couples who were walking together, and on other occasions insult a young girl, knowing full well her escort would jump to her defence, and before you knew it, there would be a scuffle, which sometimes resulted in a full-scale disturbance. Many of these young, black men would be arrested and chucked in the Black Marias, where trumped-up charges would be preferred against them.

The magistrates were no better, they would believe the police; it did not matter how many lies they told. A black person had no chance; they would be fined or jailed on charges such as assaulting the police or disturbing the peace. We believed at that time there was no justice, and that the entire criminal justice system was stacked against us; when we complained our complaint was ignored, we were always told we had a chip on our shoulder. But we still continued to go to various dance halls as usual.

The dance hall proprietors recognised they were fighting a losing battle, so they decided to run competitions at the Paramount to find the best dancers. These dancers would be employed by Mecca to tour the provincial dance halls outside the London area at the weekends. We would be paid to dance. This was done to introduce our style of dancing to young people, hoping this would prevent them from going to London. We were employed by Mecca to do exhibitions at their dance halls throughout the south of England. I had only to work three nights per week, Friday, Saturday and Sunday, the only proviso being I should try to find a black girl as my partner; this was impossible as there were no black girls around. In the end they agreed I could use a white partner for a trial period and it was agreed I would be paid £25 per week for my three night's work and my partner was paid £20; this was excellent money at the time.

Our dancing names were exotic, such as 'The Magic Boots', 'Rupee' and 'The Gladiator'; my nickname was Sugar, and my partner and I took all the prizes. We travelled to the suburbs of London and all over the south: Southend, Brighton, Chichester and Portsmouth, to name but a few, and all our expenses were paid. We gave exhibitions in bebop, jiving and the rumba. Everywhere we went we were well received, but the moment our exhibition was over we had to leave because the women and men all wanted their chance to dance with me and my partner. Also many managers of these establishments did not approve of a black boy's partnership with a white girl; they felt it would be an incentive to encourage white girls to mix with black boys.

After working with Mecca for two months, I was called to their offices and given an ultimatum: I must find a black partner or lose my job. There was no other alternative, so I left. When the Mecca organisation saw that women were still going to the dance halls in London, they stopped employing us for the exhibition dancing in the provinces. Although it did not last very long we enjoyed ourselves; after all, it gave us extra pocket money.

Our lives were a mixture of many things: racism, joblessness and homelessness, but we managed as best we could. We did not all succumb to the misery of the life we faced; the insults, the provocation and sometimes violent attacks. Between 1947 and 1950 there was a great influx of black people, not only aboard the Empire Windrush but also on many other ships such as the Eros, and Italian ships, bringing in hundreds of people through Europe into England. As the population of black people increased, racism became more acute.

The media had a field day; all the newspapers were racist, except for the Daily Worker, and they pandered to the racists' every whim. Dance hall proprietors and managers were no better than the police; any time there was trouble the black lads were always in the wrong, but at least the girls were not afraid to back us in any way they could.

I was personally thrown out of many dance halls and not allowed back. I was barred from the Lyceum, the Hammersmith Palais, the Wimbledon Palais, the Astoria and the Locarno. There was one dance hall in London, the Paramount, that catered for us, with our music and our style of dancing, and guess what? It was packed with women from all over London, and the areas now called Greater London, and other small villages and towns in within a 60 mile radius of London. Ultimately, all the regulations that had been imposed in other dance halls were removed. The newspapers of the day, especially the

113

Daily Mirror, were racist in every way; they led a campaign against black people and they also led a campaign against English girls who associated with us in the dance halls. They depicted them as undesirable, by classing them as loose women, prostitutes and nigger lovers, because in those days there was no Race Relations Act to abide by. Attacks on black people and their friends were open to all; we had to run the gauntlet of hate coming from all angles including the Government of the day, which was trying to appease the hunger of the racist newspapers who were whipping up racial hatred between young black and white men.

Some of the ladies who came to dance halls knew nothing about us – they came out of sheer curiosity. I remember dancing with a young lady from Dorking in Surrey who was trying to get as close to me as she possibly could; her hands were all over my back starting from my shoulders and gradually moving down to the bottom of my spine. I thought this young lady was getting a bit too frisky and her attentions were getting out of hand. When I asked her the reasons for her behaviour her reply shocked me: 'I am just feeling for your tail,' she said. When I told her I had no tail and that I was just like her or anybody else, she did not believe me; according to her, that was what she had been told by her parents and she believed them. I have known young women who had paid the ultimate penalty for their ignorance and naivety, by following men back home who then took advantage of them, sometimes even to the point of being raped. If the offences resulted in a court case, they had no leg to stand on. In one case the judge told them it was their fault as they were old enough to know better, and the men were set free. The police were determined to close The Paramount, and sadly they succeeded in the end. It is now known as The Empire Room, catering for private functions only.

The year 1949 saw many outstanding Jamaican musicians coming to Britain, such as Leroy Masters the trombonist, Roy White, Jocelyn Trott and many others who either led or were members of the leading big bands in Jamaica. These people combined together to form their own band, playing most of Stan Kenton's arrangements. Their music was far superior to that of Geraldo, Billy Cotton, Victor Sylvester, James Last, Syd Lawrence, Ken Macintosh, or any other big band at the time.

Enrico loved dancing

There was only one problem for them; although no one could dispute the quality of their music, the fact they were all black meant only the Paramount would employ them. They were forced to break up their band and join other white bands, however most of them returned to the West Indies, or went to Canada or America, and some to Europe. We also saw the arrival of Harold Holnes and Dudley Hislop, two of Jamaica's most famous stage dancers; they were equivalent to the Nicholas Brothers of America, and among the world's greats.

Other Jamaicans who tried their luck in England were the Lyons Brothers, entertainers who were white and hailed from Montego Bay; they were renowned throughout the world. Others included Bertha Berzuca, with his Jamaican Negro Ballet, also on tour in England and Lesley Hutchinson, known to English people as 'Our Hutch'. Son Batson and Arthur Codlyn were tailors who set up a shop making suits for the boys near Marble Arch. But none of these were to survive for long.

After leaving my job with Mecca I had a short spell dancing in the Bertha Berzuca Ballet, appearing in the show Tobacco Road. At the same time I had a part in a play, staged at the Wimbledon Theatre, entitled How Deep Are The Roots. This play portrayed a young black man marrying into an English family. Looking back, although I thought it was great at the time, I now feel I was a party to the promotion of the racist beliefs prevailing at the time.

Throughout all this, I continued my studies at Shoreditch Technical College, two nights per week.

I had enrolled at the Technical College in City Road, Shoreditch on a course of building, joinery, cabinetmaking and wood machining. I did not know at the time that I would study technique in furniture design, the matching of wood grain, the texture of wood and other aspects of the woodworking machinery industry. It was my desire to become a good pupil, and I wanted to learn as much as I could, although I was told it would take five years to complete my training. This did not matter, as I eventually wanted to return to Jamaica. I wanted a settled life and a trade behind me; I made the right decision.

I will never forget my feeling of despair when Bertha Berzuca was found dead, alone in a dingy, dirty little room in Paddington, with only one penny in his possession; he was given a pauper's funeral. English society had no room for black entertainers irrespective of how good they might be. I have known many black artistes who lived in this country and died in the same tragic circumstances, such as Victor Garrick, the singer and tap dancer, and Kid Hartley, the lightweight boxing champion, who died sleeping rough in the East End of London, after spending the last years of his life living as a tramp.

The belief that black people had not tried to achieve in this society is an outright lie and a great insult to the black race. Our present position springs from the fact that, the more we tried to achieve, the more pressure was applied to prevent our achievement. By the end of 1950, I had now turned my back on the world of entertainment, determined to fight against the injustices suffered by my people. First, I became a member of the Communist Party; this was easy because these were the only white people who showed any sympathy to our plight, apart from the women who mixed with us socially. We were invited to their homes and they treated us how human beings should be treated. They set the example that others failed to set.

I was quite at home in the Young Communist League, where I worked actively with others for the overthrow of imperialism in our countries. I soon realised that anyone who mixed with us, whether it be socially or in the field of politics, would be condemned and ostracised by society at large and the all-powerful newspapers. This did not affect me in the least as I continued to work towards what I believed was right.

I returned to work as a wood machinist and joined the Labour Party as well as the Communist Party, and also became an active member of the National Union of Furniture Trade Operatives (NUFTO). I also joined the Amalgamated Society of Woodworking Machinists; this was to ensure I had my say in both unions. However, these two movements had little to do with black liberation because within both unions there was racism and racist connotations.

By this time I had found work at a firm in Islington, where my study at Technical College was beginning to pay off; now I had the experience to be employed working the four cutter machine, which was an outstanding achievement for someone of my age in the trade.

My involvement with the Communist Party meant my dancing days were over; there was no longer any time for what I now considered wasted energy. Politics had become an integral part of my life. There were other places of entertainment, but these were not dance halls; they were clubs, such as the Caribbean club in the West End and the Frisco club at 33 Shepherds Market, Mayfair. These clubs were not frequented by working-class girls; their patrons were women of the elite society.

117

These clubs were there for the benefit of a different class of people, where the women would not be known as whores and prostitutes and the newspapers would not attack them; these people were the cornerstone of society and these clubs were used by titled and wealthy women as a means to gratify their own desires. The men who frequented these clubs were called studs; they were paid by the women for their services. A lot of men lived very well out of this kind of life.

In my opinion, this was not much different from what was going on in the East End of London where, as I mentioned earlier, the men were living off immoral earnings; the only difference was that the women in London were working class from poor backgrounds, while the women in the elite clubs seeking their excitement and satisfaction were from a different class in society. There were people with a colonial mentality, who saw us as their subjects from the colonies and were prepared to accept us behind closed doors; at times they patronised us in such a way that it was made clear we were subordinate to them. We were not looked upon as equals, but people who needed help and friendship at their expense.

The only area where we had a little recognition was in sport, where some famous names were representing England, names such as Arthur Wint the 400 metre runner, Macdonald Bailey the 200 meter runner, George Headley the so-called black Don Bradman and Leary Constantine the fast bowler from Trinidad. Most famous of all was the American, Joe Louis, at that time considered the greatest heavyweight-boxing champion ever, and of course there were singers who came to Britain occasionally.

These were the only black people who were considered noteworthy, but, even then, many theories were put forward in order to distinguish them from the rest of the black community. The narrow-mindedness and ignorance was such that it would have been funny, if it had not been so serious and self-destructive. You cannot destroy the creditability of one race without destroying yourself.

The British, who once boasted they had an empire on which the sun never set, did not tell the world it was an empire full of slaves and a cesspool of poverty, built upon gangsterism, slave traders, pirates of the high seas and the biggest mass murders of all time; they always tried to make out that they were angels and that all the evil they had done to the world was done in the name of Christianity and therefore justifiable. While they plundered, bullied and practised their protection rackets in Africa and other countries, they were worse than the Richard brothers and the Kray twins. They preached and practised their self-righteousness for the benefit of their fellow conspirators, and at the same time mis-educated and mis-informed the British people about other civilisations and other races. One cannot spend 400 years or more teaching people that they are superior to others, then bring these inferior people to mix with them, hoping they will change overnight, and expect love and good harmony to prevail; this is a complete fallacy.

As I lived with the people in the East End, seeing their attitudes, their way of life, low self-esteem and unhygienic standards, I realised whatever these people did to me, or whatever they thought about me, it was not their fault they had been conditioned this way. I do not expect people who have been indoctrinated in this way for so long to gain awareness overnight. We, the black people who came to this country to help our mother country in her time of need, were cast aside by a worthless mother, who rejected the children she now saw as illegitimate, and treated them with contempt.

It was now just over three years since I had come home to my mother country; over three years of sorrow, grief and pain, but this made me more determined than ever to succeed. The standards I had been brought up to accept told me that under no circumstances should I allow myself to be belittled in anyway. I had been brought up with dignity and pride in myself as a human being, not as a black monkey, which my white counterparts tried their best to convince me I was. My first reaction was to return home, but then why should I return? I would only be doing what they wanted and what was expected of me. I decided to take the most difficult route, which was to remain. I decided

119

to join any movement or organisation I could use as a vehicle to enlighten the British public about my plight, and at the same time I would do all I could to fight, not only for the freedom of the colonies, but for my right to be recognised as an equal in this country.

I had now left the East End of London for good and settled in the West End and other areas in South West London and North London. To say settled is a misnomer, as I moved address almost every week, because everywhere I lived was temporary. It takes a long time for anyone to settle in a country that does not make you feel welcome, especially when landladies were thinking about their other lodgers and what their next-door neighbours were saying about them. This was a part of life we had to experience and the battle we had to fight. At this stage in my life I had witnessed many things, and realised the people of Britain, regardless of how they were treated, cared not about themselves, but about their country and, most of all, royalty and the aristocracy. There were other things I learnt, such as the way young people were treated. Just after I arrived in England, I had nowhere to sleep at nights; I was told about two Lyons Corner Houses in the West End of London, which were open all night to the public and, provided we had the money to buy cups of coffee, we could stay all night provided we did not sleep.

It was about this time that young women between the ages of 18 and 20 years old were returning to London from different parts of the country where they had been evacuated as children, to escape the bombing of London. The young men who had been evacuated with them had been conscripted into the Army, but there was nothing for the young women to do but to return to London, only to find that many of their homes had been bombed, and their mothers and fathers killed. These young ladies had nowhere to go and, with little help on offer, they were left to their own devices. They were packed like sardines in the Lyons Corner Houses, together with young black people who had nowhere to go. We all went into the Lyons Coventry Street Corner House, at Piccadilly Circus, and the Strand Corner House, opposite Trafalgar Square, to shelter from the cold. It was a pity to see how these innocent girls were suffering. One asks why women at that time had such affinity with black people – the answer is, we were suffering in the same way.

Notes from the editor: Professor Stuart Hall - Calypso Culture

Stuart McPhail Hall, (3 February 1932 to 10 February 2014) was a Jamaican-born political and cultural theorist, sociologist and Marxist who had lived and worked in the United Kingdom since 1951. Enrico knew his countryman – Stuart Hall well, and they shared many ideas, discussions, values and commitments. They were both lifelong socialists, political activist, opponents of 'Thatcherism', anti-racist and totally committed to multiculturalism. Stuart Hall was for many years the leading Black academic, political and cultural theorist who wrote numerous books and articles; gave hundreds of lecturers addressed meetings and events in many countries across the world. He was a also a prolific broadcaster debater and contributor to media discussions on race, racism and 'Britishness.' Enrico and I attended several of his meetings over the years in London and Birmingham.

Professor Stuart Hall's comments contained in an article in the Guardian on 28 June 2002, supports much of Enrico's experience in Britain during the 1950's and 1960's in relation to the music and art. Enrico was an artist with many talents who loved music, dancing, literature and arts in general. The following paragraphs from Professor Hall's article will help to capture some of the flavour of the period soon after the arrival of the Windrush:

"Since West Indians first began to settle in Britain in large numbers after the second world war, a succession of black musics have transformed the British music scene. Ska, bluebeat and, of course, reggae were followed by rap, dance-hall, "jungle", techno and house.

But the oldest of these musical forms is the calypso - the music and lyrics associated with the Trinidad Carnival - which, according to Lloyd Bradley, became "the official sound-track of black Britain" in the 1950s and early 1960s. Calypso was the first popular music transported

121

directly from the West Indies and, in the early days, migrants from the southern Caribbean would meet to listen nostalgically to the recording of that year's winning calypso or their favourite calypsonian, and relive memories of the street marching, the costume floats and steel pan music that dominate Port of Spain in the four-day saturnalia leading up to the beginning of Lent.

However, shortly after the arrival of the first postwar contingent, calypso music about the migration experience also started to be composed and performed in Britain, about Britain. Now this nearly forgotten moment in the story of Britain's black diaspora can be recaptured in word and sound. The record label Honest John has salvaged 20 calypsos composed and recorded by calypsonians in and about London in the early 1950s and issued them as a new CD titled London Is the Place for Me.

The start of the postwar Caribbean diaspora is usually associated with the arrival of the rather dilapidated troop-ship, the SS Empire Windrush, which docked at Tilbury in June 1948. The ship had been sent to scour the Caribbean and bring back second world war volunteers who had been given temporary home leave to visit their families before returning to Britain to be demobbed. Three hundred servicemen and women from throughout the islands gathered in Jamaica for the return trip, and since the ship's capacity was 600, the extra berths were offered to anyone who wanted to emigrate and could stump up the fare of £28. No papers or visas were required since these were the innocent days when all West Indians had right of entry as legitimate British passport holders. Among those who took up the option were two of the Caribbean's most famous and best-loved calypsonians, Lord Beginner and Lord Kitchener.

Aldwyn "Lord Kitchener" Roberts , a Trinidadian and former nightclub vocalist, had worked on several of the other islands before deciding - as he told Mike and Trevor Phillips, the authors of Windrush: The Irresistible Rise of Multi-Racial Britain - that he had always wanted to visit England. Kitchener, a colourful presence on the voyage, helped to organise a concert to raise funds to pay the passage of a stowaway woman who had been discovered (there were many stowaways, some of whom dived overboard and swam to safety when the boat finally docked). As the ship neared land, Kitchener was overcome by "the wonderful feeling that I'm going to land on the mother country...touch the soil of the mother country" and was moved to compose the song that provides the title track of the collection, London Is the Place for Me.

A week later, he visited a London dance club called the Paramount where, to his surprise, he discovered many of his fellow passengers already well in place, jiving and dancing. A month later, a band led by a 22-year-old Guyanese trumpeter Rannie Hart started to play regularly in the saloon bar of the Queens Hotel in Brixton and with them, hoping to extend the popularity of calypso, was their star, Lord Kitchener. He went on to a highly successful career, playing at pubs, dance clubs, cellar bars and the semi-legal "bottle parties" of the London and Manchester underground scenes until he returned permanently to Trinidad in 1962.

Confined for some time to small clubs and dancehalls, calypso really made its breakthrough in 1950, with the triumph of the West Indies cricket team at Lords. This was a symbolic victory, and a major reversal of fortunes. The great Trinidadian historian CLR James, who wrote the best book ever written about cricket, Beyond a Boundary, had long argued that true West Indian independence and the national consciousness it required would be impossible until the West Indies had taken on the colonisers at their sacred game and mastered it sufficiently to defeat them at home in open play: 1950 was that moment. The West Indian team included three of the world's finest batsmen, but the true heroes of the game and architects of victory were the spinners, Ramadhin and Valentine.

It is difficult to believe reports that there were only 30 or 40 West Indians present at the ground, but however many there were, they made their presence felt by exuberant shouting, singing and the rattling of tin cans throughout the game, in ways that astonished the natives and transformed for ever the ethos of test cricket.

But the victory moved the calypsonian Lord Beginner, another Windrush survivor, to compose on the spot the calypso that became the anthem of the moment - Cricket, Lovely Cricket, with its telling refrain, "With those little pals of mine/ Ramadhin and Valentine"; while Kitchener himself led the march round the field and down into Piccadilly. People stared at this extraordinary sight out of windows - "I think it was the first time they'd ever seen such a thing in England," Kitchener observed. "And we're dancing Trinidad-style, like mas, and dance right down Piccadilly and...around Eros." The Caribbean ethos and style of celebration was the most commented upon aspect of the game and marks the moment when a distinctively new Caribbean spirit and rhythm first announced itself as an emergent element in the rapidly changing national culture.

The calypso, a topical song associated with Carnival, specially composed for the occasion, was much influenced by this carnivalesque tradition - a period of licensed expression, when for a time, the normal rules of everyday life are suspended, the world is turned upside-down, and the people of "the below" are granted the freedom both to revel in public and to comment on and satirise the actions and behaviour of those in authority. The calypsonian is free to comment ironically on any aspect or event of everyday life, to expose the sexual and political scandals of the politicians and the rich, to recount gossip and to scandalise the powerful without fear of redress. Political commentary, the quirks, foibles, the petty dramas and the licentious stories of everyday street life are grist to the calypsonian's mill. The calypso is the repository of that year's distilled popular knowledge and wisdom - the informal "court" before which every powerful figure fears being ultimately judged.

The essence of the successful calypso lies in capturing the event or occasion in a vivid, piquant, creole idiom. The music has a driving, springy, forward-impelled, rolling two-beat, adaptable to the rhythmic movement of the road march. The lyrics, which are strung across and accented so as to insinuate themselves be tween the bass rhythm, are driven by the sinuous lilt of Trinidadian creole speech patterns. Unlike later black British music, which has been dominated by the prevalence of almost unintelligibly deep Jamaican patois, the calypso's rhymes depend on the Trinidadian accent, but the language is otherwise well-enunciated in Caribbean standard English. Kitchener reported that, when he first began to sing in a Brixton pub, the manager fired him because he said his customers couldn't understand what "Kitch" was saying. But before the mixed audience of the Sunset Club, when Kitchener began to sing, "Kitch come go to bed/I have a small comb to scratch your head", the punters understood the sexual references well enough, and those who didn't get it had its meaning explained to them by the Caribbean customers.

These compositions represent a vibrant, piquantly observed and often hilarious running commentary on life for the newly arrived immigrant in the London of the 1950s. They crystallise the migrants' first response to the encounter with that strange object, "the English at home". They have to be seen as part and parcel of the experience that produced the West Indian novel, which emerged in London at about the same moment, with writers like VS Naipaul, George Lamming and Sam Selvon. Lamming has said that his generation (and, incidentally, mine) came as members of the individual islands and only in London discovered that they were "West Indian". CLR James, writing about another famous Trinidadian calypsonian, Sparrow, observed that, "He is in every way a genuinely West Indian artist . . . a living proof that there is a West Indian nation".

Much the same is true of the black British calypso, which began as a Trinidadian music and, in London, became the first signature music of the whole West Indian community. The calypsos of the 1950s therefore must be "read" and heard alongside books like Lonely Londoners by Sam Selvon (also a Trinidadian) as offering the most telling insights into the early days of the migrant experience. They are still overwhelmingly jaunty and positive in attitude - this is the music of

125

a minority who have travelled to a strange or strangely familiar place in search of a better life and are determined to survive and prosper. The same confidence, grit and determination are evident in the press and magazine images of immigrant families arriving during the 1950s at London railway stations.

As I have written elsewhere, "Men, women and children already battened down against the freezing weather by the ubiquitous wearing of hats. People dressed up to the nines, for 'travelling', and even more for 'arrival'. Wearing that expectant look - facing the camera, open and outward, into something they cannot yet see...a new life...'Face the music, darling, and let's make a move.' "

But the darker shadows are also already evident. Kitchener's Sweet Jamaica invites Jamaicans to reflect on their decision to leave home and family behind only to find themselves "Crying with regret/No sort of employment can they get" and to think fondly of the ackee and saltfish they have left behind in the islands where the sun shines every day. As The Mighty Terror accurately observed, "No Carnival in Britain" - but, of course, there was to be one; and the Notting Hill Carnival, which survives despite the best-engineered efforts to close it down or dampen its insurgent spirit, remains one of the few homes for indigenous calypso left in Britain.

London Is the Place for Me is a witty and joyous testament to the creative power of popular culture and a document of more innocent times. It constitutes one of the best starting points for that rich, unfinished history of the black British diaspora and its intricate interweaving with British life that remains to be written."

Chapter Five

Enrico Stennett - My Quest to be a Politician

First post 1945 black Parliamentarians

I had now embarked upon my quest to be a politician; to work with the organisations I had joined in furtherance of the struggle against oppression and racism. Furthermore, my activities within the trade union movement had begun to gain momentum. The furniture trade industry was short of labour, so I did my best to encourage the unions to accept black workers in the furniture factories; this was not difficult because of the shortage of manpower at the time. Some of these workers would start out as labourers but soon became assemblers, and in some cases wood machinists. Because of my ability to find work for new, black arrivals I was now looked upon as someone to be respected by my countrymen.

I was now beginning to become recognised by the black organisations, who felt I could be relied upon when they needed help. I went to the Church Army hostel, the Salvation Army hostels and

127

anywhere I could to find accommodation and negotiated with the supervisors of the hostels to house the new arrivals from the Caribbean. My work in the factories also took a turn for the better, as the employers and the unions would notify me when and where there were vacancies, so I could find workers to fill them. I now found myself well known and in demand, but in the midst of this, not everything was good. In those days, although employers wanted your labour, that was the only thing, they wanted. As far as other workers were concerned, they made it clear how they felt: they felt threatened by the presence of black people coming to take their jobs.

This school of thought was also prevalent within the trade union branches and amongst the trade union leaders. During much of my spare time, especially in the evenings at trade union meetings, I volunteered to give talks on the problems of Caribbean people and why other workers should have no fear of us taking their jobs. During our discussions I was surprised to realise how little they knew about us and our country's affiliation and affinity with theirs. It was quite amusing to witness some of the attitudes at work. For example, if a black man was walking along the corridor on his way to the office, and he was unfortunate enough to see one of the female office workers walking towards him, he would have to turn back because, if they crossed each other's paths and if it was noticed the woman had smiled at him, the following day he would be dismissed and no excuse would be given. In some factories it was so bad that if a woman came out of the office door and saw a black man coming along the corridor, she would return to the office to avoid him because she knew what the consequences would be.

It seemed the biggest obstacle to white men accepting black men, was the women. The excuses that were made, why white men did not like white women associating in any way with a black man, were numerous. Some I would not like to mention but other excuses were as follows: they were worried about any children being half-caste and belonging nowhere; they would not like any of their family to be black; the women would be looked upon as sluts, whores and prostitutes and they would be ostracised. These were all common, preconceived ideas.

128

I worked long hours, and in those days the more work you put in and the faster you worked, the more bonus you earned at the end of the week. As I was young, I worked very hard and did not drink alcohol, or smoke. One day I was encouraged to go to the Hackney Dog Track by a Trinidadian acquaintance, but I paid the price by losing all my wages, and whatever I did win, he borrowed and never repaid me. I never returned to the dog track ever again; I had my fill as far as gambling was concerned – it was my first and last time.

The fact I did not gamble, smoke or drink allowed me to save some money, and my ambition in those days was to own a car, so I saved up to buy one. In 1951, I bought a Morris 6, just after passing my test; it was brand new and I was very proud of it. As far as I was concerned, this was to help me get to work, to places like Ponders End, Enfield, and other outlying areas. What a mistake I made.

In those days, the only people who went to work in cars were the directors; the workers, from the foreman and chargehand down, came to work on a bicycle. Each morning you would see literally hundreds of bikes entering the bike sheds but one particular morning I broke the golden rule. I drove my car up early and parked it in the street facing the factory where everyone could see it. It was unusual to see a brand new, gleaming car parked there, and not in the directors' car park; it had not been seen before, as not many cars were parked on the street in those days. Everyone, including the management, was curious but no one asked anyone within the factory if they knew who owned the car. I knew the entire factory was looking all day to see who owned the car, but I did not realise how serious it was and what repercussions would follow.

Later that evening, I waited in the factory until 6.30 p.m. hoping everyone would have gone home, and I could drive my car away, but when I went out, I was shocked to see everyone – even the management – waiting outside to see whose car it was. I did not think it was important, so I walked over to my car and drove off. The following day I returned to work and parked the car in exactly the same place it

129

had been the previous day. I arrived at my machine and was just about to turn it on, when the foreman approached me and asked, 'Who does the car belong to?' 'It's mine,' I replied. 'Yours?' 'Yes,' I replied, 'Mine.' 'How can you afford to buy such a car?' he asked. My answer was simple, 'My friend,' I said, 'I do not drink, nor smoke, and I do not go to the dogs, and you know I am here working sometimes until 10 p.m., so I saved my money because I wanted a car.' He just looked at me and walked away; I could tell he was annoyed. The following day when I returned to work, he handed me my National Insurance card and P45, and told me I was no longer wanted; that if I could afford to buy a car like that, I could do without working there.

Buying that car was a whole new ball game. At that time not many people owned cars, worst of all, I did not know of any black people who possessed one; it seemed as if I was the only one. The car had to be insured so I was advised to go to Stockwell Road where there was an insurance broker. When I applied to insure the car I was told I would have to pay £52 per annum, fully comprehensive, which meant a pound a week. I thought that was the price anyone would pay, so I paid. The Morris 6 was a new make of car and not many had been produced; they were like the Wolesey 100/10. The Wolesey was the car the police used at the time, the only difference from the Morris was that it had a bull nose. About four weeks after I had arranged my insurance, I met someone with the same car; he was very intrigued. After we began talking about the car I asked him how much he had paid for his insurance, and when he told me he paid £8 per annum, fully comprehensive I was shocked. I immediately returned to the insurance company to find out why my premium was so high. I was told I had to pay more for the following reasons: I was coloured; I was a foreigner and foreigners are excitable and get into trouble; I did not learn to drive in this country so I did not know the rules and regulations; because I was coloured, people would deliberately damage my car, so I had to be insured against that; also I was under 23 years of age. What he did not know was that I learned to drive in London and passed my test first time in Norbury. I protested vigorously, but was told there was nothing I could do; I had to pay the full amount if I wanted to drive the car.

130

I was not satisfied so I went to see Marcus Lipton, the MP for Brixton. When I told him the circumstances, he was shocked at the difference in the amount I had been charged. He contacted the insurance company and found they had a policy that applied only to black people. A question was raised in Parliament and a new law was passed, banning this practice; all people should be charged alike where insurance was concerned. I was pleased I was the first West Indian to take up such a matter with a Member of Parliament. Something had been done to pave the way for equality and justice for all black drivers.

I was now out of a job but, because I had a car, there were plenty of jobs I could apply for. I previously had no difficulty finding jobs in the woodworking industry, but now I would travel to interviews in my car, and as soon as I stepped out of the car nobody wanted to know. In the end I had to leave my car at home and take public transport to find work. Without the car it was no longer difficult to find work. When I started work I would drive the car to within about a mile of my workplace, park the car and take a bus. Then, after leaving work at night, I would take transport back to my car and drive home.

People were very complex, if not complicated; we did not know where we stood with them and what to do for the best. If we behaved in a decent manner we would be trying to be a white man, but if we behaved badly that was what was expected of us. If we tried to mix they would shun us, and if we kept ourselves to ourselves we would be accused of not wanting to mix. It was made clear in every respect that we were not wanted in Britain.

Personally, I had additional complications, in that I spoke with an upper-class accent and my diction was correct – I could pronounce my words clearly for everyone to understand. I was often asked, 'Where did you learn to speak English like that?' or worse, 'Who are you trying to pretend you are?' I told them I could not speak any differently, because that was the way I had been taught to speak in the Caribbean. This was very difficult for people to believe; they honestly believed all black people were uncivilised savages, and that we could not read and write. To find one black person who did not meet their criteria baffled them and left them thinking. Sometimes I found my working colleagues were very patronising, kind, but at the same time, begrudging. At other times they would do anything to help me, leading me to believe I was in a different class, a class that did not work in a factory. After a while, a certain respect was shown, to the extent they would go out of their way to see I was treated correctly by my employer, as I was a member of the trade union. I also decided, rather than risk being disliked for driving a car to work, I would leave the car at home and do as others did; I found I got on a lot better. However, I had many problems with this car; when I took it for a service, the car would be in a worse condition when it was returned. In the end, the car was written off after two years because the engine was in one place and the body in another, never to be driven again.

There was one instance where I was asked to work various woodworking machines. The shop steward thought the management was taking advantage of my youth and colour, so he threatened to call a strike if I was not kept on one machine like all the other workers. At the union meeting, I had to explain that I wanted to go on all the machines because I wanted to learn as much as I could. I was still attending the Technical College, studying for a City and Guilds certificate, so the comrades agreed, if that was what I wanted, then so be it.

What worried me was the journey I had to travel to work each day. I soon learned, in my search for accommodation, that certain areas were no-go areas for black people, such as King's Cross, Oxon, Elephant and Castle, Herne Hill, Camberwell Green and the Tottenham area. Black people were always beaten up in these areas by young white thugs. Also there were areas frequented by white Americans, which I kept away from. When I left the job at Green Lane, Ilford I went to work for Harris Lebus, near the River Lee in Tottenham; at that time it was the largest furniture factory in the world. I was employed just to set the machines and walk around in a white coat all day, checking the work.

132

Now my life took a different path; I felt I had to do something to help my fellow black people and, at the same time, work towards a better understanding between black and white people. I felt I was in a position to do this because I was now beginning to become accepted by white people, who said that I was not so black after all, and black people, who saw me as working for their interests. I found it difficult to negotiate the different paths that lay before me, and the decisions I had to make. Just over three years earlier, I had been in the Caribbean dreaming of a life in the motherland where I would be happy among my people. Here I was now, in the motherland, but with a different outlook on life and new priorities. There were now so many different facets to my life, I felt my responsibilities growing day by day. These responsibilities were not only to myself but also to my compatriots, as I now considered all black people to be.

Being able to read and write enabled me to understand clearly what was happening around me, and the political consequences thereof, which an uneducated person from the Caribbean could not. The racism was so overbearing and acute that it was difficult to ignore, especially when you felt you were the odd one out. In those days, the Government and the people were not as hypocritical as they are today; it was clear where they stood. This was not the mother country as I had been brought up to believe, it was a country that only believed in the exploitation of the weak and the poor, and the subjugation of its people.

It seemed as if the people of Britain and their Government believed it was their destiny to govern and control every country in the world, in league with other European nations, and from time to time declare war on each other to prove their might in conquest; the wealth and other commodities of these countries would then be divided between them. But now black people, who once fought and died for their so-called mother country's freedom, now wanted their own freedom and liberty, to do what they liked in their own country. They had learnt enough about Britain to realise they were the ones who put the Great into Great Britain and without them Great Britain would be nothing. Our minds were not bent on revenge, as we are not a vengeful people; all we wanted was our equality to be recognised. But this was not to be; instead there was oppression of black people on every front.

The might of the so-called British Empire was about to be tested, and with the test, the true barbarous nature of Britain and her counterparts would be brought to the forefront. The 'cry for freedom' by black people started to echo throughout the four corners of the world; the fear of Britain was felt in the power of their brutality as they undertook every atrocious action possible against the onward march. But the power and determination of this onward march was so powerful, that the echo was answered with one voice – the voice of the roaring lion that had been asleep for over 400 years, but had now awoken. The Empire knew that these voices had to be silenced. So the might of the British Army was amassed in order to quash the resolve of the black people, but this time it was like the charge of the light brigade 'Cannon to the right of them, cannon to the left of them, cannon in front of them'. There were too many fronts to fight on; whatever concessions could be made were quickly made on paper, if not in reality.

The early 1950s saw the Kikuyu uprising under their leader Jomo Kenyatta of Kenya, where we saw English brutality at its worst in its effort to wipe out the people of Kenya and keep them subjugated. In the words of the young Lieutenant David Lauder, cashiered from the British Army for refusing to carry out brutalities against the natives of Kenya, 'We would round up an entire village of men, women and children, compelling them to tell us where the bandits were hiding, and when we could get no information we would line them up and we would shoot them down, even pregnant women and children. We would put wire through the ears of our captives and lead them through the jungle so they could point out their fellow conspirators. We would kill the men and cut off their right hands, wrap them, and put them in our pockets, to take back to be fingerprinted.' Lauder said, 'I had stood so close while shooting a pregnant woman in the stomach, that her blood spluttered all over me. This was the end; I could no longer stand it, I could not go on.' Villages were burnt to the ground, thousands of people were murdered in cold blood, and still the people of Kenya did not take one backward step. Tough as it was at times, they had two enemies to fight: the British soldiers and their own quislings. Kwame Nkrumah of the Gold Coast was elected president of his country while in an African prison, only to have his followers break into the prison after his election, and carry him shoulder high through the streets of Accra as they rejoiced in their freedom.

Britain has never forgotten or forgiven the fact they were defeated, and had to leave one of their most precious assets in Africa, the Gold Coast. Nkrumah was deposed while he was out of his country with the connivance of the CIA and their deadly counterpart, MI6.

Britain was not the only country faced with their colonials' struggle for freedom; there were the French in Indo-China and the fall of Dien Bien Phu; the French in North Africa and the bitter wars in Algeria, Morocco and Tunisia; the Italians had been kicked out of Libya, Ethiopia and Somalia; and the Belgian overlords were on the way out in the Congo and other territories they governed. The Portuguese were also in trouble in Mozambique, while the Dutch in South Africa, in their absolute panic, created an apartheid state, so they could rob black people of their land forever.

The people of Northern Rhodesia, Southern Rhodesia and Nyasaland were also on the move: their battle was not to be an easy one. The people of Nigeria, in their quest for independence, found their country split by Britain into four regions, which resulted in one of the most bitter wars ever fought in that country – the Biafran war – with Britain and America supplying arms to both sides, hoping to see a tribal uprising leading to the mass murder of Africans by Africans, thereby causing a famine which almost wiped out the tribes of Nigeria. In the Caribbean, there was the mobilisation of people from all the islands, supported by their counterparts in England, demanding the right to govern and control their own destiny. The Europeans, realising that their power was coming to an end, had to devise ways to make it impossible for the citizens of these countries to govern themselves,

135

resulting in globalisation, where Europeans and the people from Europe who had settled in America, slaughtered the native Americans, robbed them of their country, and now became the false leaders of the so-called free world.

If hard work made you rich - the slaves would have been the richest.

What puzzled me was that the black population of England was now growing, but there was no television to condition our minds and give us false information. The newspapers and radio did their job well; even then black people behaved as if they could not care less. They had arrived in England with the intention of spending just six months to earn enough money to return to their wives and families, as they had in Cuba, Venezuela, Panama, and on the War Manpower Commission in the United States of America. They did not see themselves remaining in England, so they did not involve themselves in any activities or build a foundation for themselves in this country, which might have hastened the departure of England from their countries. Only the African students and, to a lesser degree, the West Indian students took active parts in aligning themselves with the movement for freedom. It was a time when the American whites were active in their anti-black organisations. The Ku Klux Klan was in its heyday with the lynching of the Martinville Seven, the Trenton Six, the Mississippi Eight, and many other black people, while the raping of black women was just looked upon as sport. This did not make much difference to the unity of black people in England. But I could not sit back and allow these

136

kinds of atrocities to take place without speaking out. The murder of Julius and Ethel Rosenberg sent a shudder throughout the world; this was a Jewish couple accused of spying by the Americans and murdered in peacetime.

Lynching was quite common in America for centuries.
The Ku Klux Klan carried on lynching black Americans
Up to the 20th century. Women and boys were also lynched

In America the black people's struggle began to intensify, while in England there were only a few torchbearers, supporting the struggle of their own people: a few West African students from the West African Students Union; a few West Indian students from various parts of the West Indies; and a lot of English people who allowed themselves to become outcasts by speaking out for liberty and freedom for black people around the world. The Communist party and their newspaper, the Daily Worker, tried their best to enlighten the British public about what was going on in their name; because of this they were known as the 'enemy within', and every effort was made to discredit them. There were organisations such as the Quakers and the Co-operative Society who, to a lesser degree, helped us as much as they could, but there was no charitable source available to help us in our struggle. Nevertheless, there was the peace movement, which was very active with the Aldermaston marches, and the trade union movement, whose members would sometimes support us in our struggle. All these people were condemned by the authorities, and the media was hell-bent to bring discredit on them, so much so, that Communism became a dirty word and the Socialist Workers Party of Great Britain and Ireland were seen as reactionary by all. The branding of individuals was so common that it embraced all areas of society: there was the Red Dean of Canterbury, Doctor Hewitt Johnson, concerning whom every effort was made to turn him into a non-person; there were the Canon of St Paul's Cathedral, the Reverend Canon Collins, and Bishop Trevor Huddleston, well known for his work against apartheid in South Africa and among the poor in the East End of London; there was Bertrand Russell, a great philosopher, and Desmond Shaw, to name but a few.

My wife, Peggy, had no political views; she was just a nice person, unaware of what was going on. I was busy being involved in the trade union movement, the Communist Party and the Labour movement as a whole. I later resigned from the Communist Party, because I did not want to associate myself with their policy of opposition to the Hungarian uprising, and joined the Labour Party. In the Labour Party I was looked upon as a left-winger, and to the Communist Party I was a Trotskyite. This did not bother me; all that concerned me was my struggle against tyranny. My work with the trade union movement had helped me to help my people in many different ways; I could get their support in meetings to organise demonstrations and to raise funds for helping movements abroad. I could also meet the various leaders coming to England from Africa and the West Indies, and organise meetings in Trafalgar Square, where Cheddi Jagan, Seretse Khama, Ezequa Awalowa, Amin Occono, Sebaca Alowa, Topawala, and many more African leaders would be main speakers, putting their case forward to the British public.

I was constantly harassed by the police, MI5 and MI6; I was actually told I was a danger to the establishment. I did not see why; after all I was only a young man fighting for survival. My friends were few and far between, in fact my only true friend was my wife Margaret.

138

She was the only one I could talk to when I needed some understanding. My Jewish friend, whom I mentioned earlier, was the editor for the Watford Recorder; he was not a Communist but he was a humanist. Being an avid reader he knew what was going on, and we became very good friends and started to work together; we decided we would do whatever we could to unite black people, and build a strong organisation. We decided that, because black people were afraid of politics, we would form an organisation that would bring them together socially.

We invited the following people to form a committee: my friend, S. Laird Freeman; E. Davidson; W.F. Bayley; S.J. Stacey; L. Cousins; B. Lindsey; J. Pettigrew; my wife Margaret Stennett, and myself. The committee consisted of two white people and the rest were black. This organisation was entitled the Cosmopolitan Social Club and we designed an application form for people seeking. The emblem of the club was a white hand shaking a black hand, and was created by my wife and myself. The Commission for Racial Equality has since used this emblem, symbolising unity and friendship between all races.

The club's temporary office was the home of my wife's parents, 9 Mill Road, Merton, London SW19. The first meeting was held on the 24th November 1950; an Executive Committee was created and on that day I was elected the General Secretary. There were many obstacles placed in the way of this organisation's development. It was very hard work travelling around week after week, sometimes with six inches of snow lying on the ground, holding meetings and trying to boost the membership; it was a slow process. At the same time we were trying to find venues to hold our dances and other entertainment; this proved to be difficult as, in those days, West Indian people were excluded from almost everywhere.

But it was not long before we started our activities, which were mostly dancing, with admission fees at three shillings and sixpence. In addition, we embarked on other activities whereby we could teach our people what was happening politically, and how to join a trade union.

Since joining the union I had discovered that they carried a lot of power. If I could pack the branch meetings with a lot of black members we could actually form the policies of the Labour Party, and could therefore make changes in our favour. The meetings I attended very seldom had a quorum, but when there was, important decisions were made; these decisions were sent to branches of the Labour Party, and from there they would sometimes become official Labour policy.

We did have some form of support from organisations such as the Co-operative Societies and the Quakers (the Society of Friends), and sometimes we would hold our dances at the London School of Printing, near Waterloo. The dances never made any profit. The executive members would club together to pay the band and the rent for the hall. In the end it was decided not only were we wasting our time but we were wasting our money as well. Unfortunately, the Cosmopolitan Social Club, through lack of support from the West Indian people, was not able to succeed with its aims and objectives, and therefore became defunct.

So we had our chances to change things for the better, but black people were not interested – they were defeatists. They were happy-go-lucky and all they wanted to do was to enjoy themselves in whatever way they could; instead of helping the people who were trying to help them, both white and black, they were constantly discrediting themselves and leaving themselves open to abuse by the system and the police.

The corruption in countries like Nigeria, which is said to be the most corrupt country in Africa, is not new; corruption has existed in Europe for centuries. Was it not corruption which led to slavery, a trade which saw millions of people taken away from their homeland, brutalised, dehumanised, and trampled beneath the dust, as they sweated on the sugar plantations, the cotton fields and the banana plantations, to make Britain rich? Such brutality could only be achieved through evil and corruption. How dare the British, the Europeans and the so-called Euro-Americans accuse any other nation of being corrupt? This is sheer fallacy and hypocrisy. We know that lies and hypocrisy are now called diplomacy, and the British boast they are the world's greatest diplomats. Which is why they always point their finger at other people, and in doing so, they hope no one will point at them; now we are pointing back.

Many people – both black and white – who have witnessed me writing this book, have warned me the book will not be printed. When I asked why, their answer was that I have been too frank. They admit everything I write is the truth, but they maintain that no one likes the truth, especially when it is directed against them. As a person of African descent, I feel compelled to write as I see it, regardless of the consequences. If publishers refuse to publish my book, it is because they do not want to be exposed for what they really are.

As black people, living in London in the 1950s, our eyes were opened; we understood the reasons for our predicament and our suffering and the loss of our self-respect. We were now determined to discover all the devious methods that had been used against us. At first we were baffled; we asked ourselves how a small country off the coast of Europe, not much bigger than a postage stamp, could rule, govern, and control almost two-thirds of the world's surface. Was it because they were super-intelligent as they made themselves out to be? Living among them we quickly found the answers; their brutality was unmatched by any nation before or since. Now it was our duty to ourselves to learn and absorb as much as we could of the English psyche. Most of their existence depended on psychological warfare, but although we learned so much we still had a long way to go before we could become as devious as them. We pray we will never become the cruel barbarians they have prided themselves on being.

I was now living in England: it had been my choice, as I came here against the wishes of my people. I was aware I was not wanted but I had nowhere else to go. Even if I returned to Jamaica I would still be living in a part of England, only I would not have been privy to the knowledge and understanding that I was now having at first hand. At

141

first it was my intention to become academically qualified, like other West Indians of my class. You must understand that, in the Caribbean, we are educated in accordance to the role that we can play in society. Wherever you have people governed by law you have to have lawyers and barristers. This profession is used not only to condition the people but as a means of oppression and control. In the colonies we were encouraged to become lawyers, so law became my first priority. Also, the workers or slaves must be kept fit, so they can undertake everyday tasks, especially in the field of manual labour; hence we were also encouraged to be doctors. These were the two main professions open to us.

You will notice that people from the Caribbean or Africa never became scientists, engineers, shipbuilders or any profession that could help them build their country, only professions that could be used to confine us and stop us from thinking or creating any form of industry, which would enable us to survive. Even our raw materials were exported, to be processed in England, to give work to the British. It was not uncommon for all Caribbean students in England to be studying for degrees in law and medicine. When I applied to a university, I was told although I had a Senior Cambridge Certificate – the equivalent of six A levels – and a Junior Cambridge Certificate – eight O levels – I could not be accepted. No one told me about Ruskin College, an Oxford college that specialises in providing educational opportunities for adults with few or no qualifications, not even the trade union movement. I was told, even though my qualification came from Cambridge, it was a special qualification designed for the colonies only, and had no value in England. I then applied to the Probation Service, but I received no reply, hence woodwork was the only field open to me. If I wanted to survive, I was condemned to the factory.

As time passed, there were many other young people from the Caribbean arriving in England, some of whom had attended the same college as I had – Cornwall College in Montego Bay – or Kings College, Kingston, and other colleges throughout the Caribbean. Some of these men were extremely gifted, and educated to a very high standard. They also tried for university places but were turned down. A friend of mine, a distant relative who came from one of the elite families in Jamaica, was studying law with his father's firm before he came to this country; he was much lighter skinned than I, and extremely intelligent. His great ambition was to be a banker, so he applied to every bank in London for a junior position. At that time, such positions paid only £5 per week, but every application he made was turned down, because he had been honest and proud enough to say what country he came from. In the end, this young man ended up working as a labourer, sweeping the factory floor. For him, this was the last straw; he was admitted to a mental institution and his parents had to come to England to take him home.

My wife's parents were lovely people who had no race hatred, and behaved as good Christian people ought to behave, although they did not pretend to be practising Christians. Peggy worked as a dress designer for Harrods of Knightsbridge, and spent all her spare time helping me in the things I wanted to achieve. Her parents also supported me, together with my two English friends who worked with me. This kept me sane, as I came to realise it was not the English people who were evil, but those who governed and controlled them. Any hatred I might have had for English people was diluted as I gained intelligence and understanding; I realised not all English people were bad and not all black people were good.

Chapter Six

Enrico Stennett - Farewell to Jamaica

Explaining the tragedy of the conditions on the Island of Jamaica

Rampant crime, violence and anti-social behaviour

144

Because of fear along with the cold climate many old West Indians would love to return to their respective islands, these islands especially Jamaica would be the beneficiary of the returnees. Many have homes to sell which are valued at hundreds of thousands of pounds and with their pensions could change the entire situation in Jamaica. They would bring a new way of life, a lot of money back to the Island and would help in every way towards the progress and uplifting of the island, but alas because of the stupidity and ignorance, lack of education, lack of discipline, the island has become so corrupt that the river is muddy from the head of the stream to the bottom of the sea.

The Government is corrupt, the Police are corrupt and 90% of the population live within that corruption and have become so corrupt themselves that no one who is not corrupt would be able to survive.

I was one of those people who wanted to lay my bones in the land of my birth, so at the age of 80 years my wife and I decided we should try to escape the cold and go to a warm climate. I am one of four brothers; two have since departed this world I hope to a better place, leaving my younger brother in Jamaica. My wife and I had made many trips to Jamaica since 1985. Because we were chaperoned we did not fully understand the situation there. We took a long time before we came to the conclusion we would return to Jamaica.

My return was discussed with my brother who said I did not have to build a home or buy one, he had a lovely home with only him and his wife in occupation. It was suggested as brothers we could live together as we were both getting old and that both wives got on alright, we could live together for the rest of our lives. It was stated we did not have to pay rent, that we could share all expenses therefore making life easier for him and for us.

We sold our property and made all arrangements for our return convincing ourselves it was the right thing to do, but right from the outset things started going wrong.

145

We had just sold our property and made all arrangements for the transfer of the money and personal effects, but we were told when we arrived in Jamaica my brother and his wife would be leaving for the United States as their daughter was having their first child, and they were going to support her and would be away for 6 months.

When we did arrive the arrangements were made and we realised it was not one which would last. We were living miles into the mountains completely on our own, left at the mercy of one of their sons and his wife who we never saw, unless we were prepared to pay him to come and see us. He was supposed to collect only the bills connected with the house. He had different ideas. He would tell us the money required was in £s, when we enquired after a while we discovered the bills we were paying were sometimes four times the amount we should pay.

We realised our position was very vulnerable. I contacted my brother in the States only to discover he was angry about the book I wrote covering my life story. There are chapters which he disapproved of because it affected our childhood, and his attitude was I would not be welcome at his house unless I was prepared to be controlled by him.

We had no alternative than to completely change our plans. I had family in other parts of the island but had very little help from them. The problem was all they wanted was money. They were not talking pounds they talked in hundreds and thousands.

My wife and I began to feel as if we were money trees where they could come and pick the money off the trees daily. We discovered everywhere we went there were demands from the Government for money, some which could not be explained. For example I was sent to one office for returnees, where I had to pay £400. When I asked what for I was told by the attendant he did not know and did not see why we should pay it, but it was the law.

I was lucky to escape without paying a fortune at the Customs because I met a decent customs Officer who thought we were celebrities after looking at one of my books I wrote, he welcomed us back to Jamaica.

I was shocked to be looked upon as a white man and was called white people by the Police and whitey by the children. It took me back to when I first came to England I was called Blackie, Darkie, Sambo all different names. In England I was a black man, here in Jamaica I was a white man. I was never accepted as a black person even by my darker brother, because I was from England, I was a multi-millionaire in their terms and we were easy prey to everyone who came along.

I had to travel from Kingston to Montego Bay so I had to buy a car. The car I brought was a Nissan Cefiro I had to pay 3 million Jamaican dollars for it. I was surprised when I was told that 1.2 million dollars of the money I paid was in taxes.

When my wife and I were travelling through the island our eyes were opened to the corruption of the Police. We were stopped on petty excuses either we were driving too fast or our stop light was faulty, any excuse they could find. They would tell us what they could do, they could put our car in the Compound leaving us in the street, or they could give us a ticket: they would calculate how much we would have to pay to redeem the car from the Compound to pay the fine to the Court. They asked us if we thought it was worth it all that problem. They said there is an easier way out. Just give us 5,000 Jamaican dollars and go on your way. It took us time before we caught onto what was happening.

This happened on many occasions. At one point we needed the help of the Police. I had bought a Farm and was having problems with the people stealing all the crops; I paid to have crops planted such as Pumpkin, Cassava, Corn and others. When the time came for me to reap, everything would be reaped and I had nothing. My pigs would be killed on the spot and what was not killed would be stolen, even when I had the pigs killed myself to be sold to the butchers. After they received the carcass of the pigs they would refuse to hand over the money. I started having to take them to Court, and soon discovered there was no one I could trust, not even my own family.

When I asked the Police for help to remove a man living on my property I was told bluntly they would help but it would cost me. When I asked what it would cost I was told 4 crates of beer. I went to the Off Licence and had 4 crates put into my car but I took them back to the Police Station. In view of everybody the four crates of beer were taken from the car. That was not the end. Two Policemen accompanied me to the Farm and they were determined to get the men off the farm. This took some time, in the end with threats from the Police the men decided to leave.

I was happy until one Policeman told me he wanted gas money. Gas means petrol for the car. 'Isn't it a Police car?' I said. 'Yes' he replied 'but it is us who put the men off your farm and we want the gas for the car'. I refused to give him the money in front of the people who gathered around, because I was afraid he would arrest me for bribery as they would have done in England. 'Don't talk nonsense said the Policeman, drive up the street and we will follow you, which we proceeded to do. When we were out of sight of the farm we stopped. I was told '5,000 Jamaican dollars would do.' I paid the money, because by this time I began to become afraid of the police myself. After paying them the money one of the Officers said to me 'now you are protected we will protect your farm by going up there every day to see these men do not return.'

'Thank you' I said and we parted company.

The Farm was 10 acres of land which I leased, we had our own family land in Katadupa over 100 acres, but it was almost in wilderness. I had spent over 2 million dollars clearing the land for cultivation and building a Pig Pen. It was my intention to help my family develop the property but the main road leading to the farm was in such a bad condition it was impossible for an ordinary car to travel on it. It was almost impossible to carry the materials such as sand, cement, and steel

148

for the construction, over three lorries loaded with materials broke down. In the end the stores refused to deliver the goods.

My family wanting to see the development of the farm started to use my money to build the roads which was impossible; many tons of sand and cement were wasted when the lorries were abandoned. I had cultivated many crops on the farm including short term crops, such as peppers, tomatoes, cabbages I also planted an acre of yams. This cost a lot of money because I had to pay labour costs which were more than I would have paid in England. The people were so crooked they would agree to do certain work either by measurement or price. They would start working and demand money immediately; they would demand money as they went along. You would find that half way through the work you have paid more than half the money which was agreed. They would stop working with excuses they did not know the ground was so hard or there was so much work.

They would find every way possible knowing you have to continue by demanding more if I wanted the work done, for more money than which the job was originally agreed on at 50,000 Jamaican dollars, which would end up 150,000 Jamaican dollars. You were constantly bled, but when the crops were ready for harvest, there would be nothing to harvest. All the crops would be harvested by people who watch you when you plant, but they reap.

In one case over 250 heads of yam were planted. When we went to reap all the yam hills were empty. I have met farmers who have land lying wasting and bluntly refused to do any farming because of being afraid of the thieves and murderers. I have known friends of mine who have had their house built; they have had to sleep on the site night and day to prevent the material from being stolen.

One cannot walk the streets in peace, there are beggars every inch of the way some act as if we owe them money, and you have to be careful when saying no. Every day you wake up there is murder in the Parishes especially the Parish of St James. A small country like Jamaica has the largest murder rate in the world per capita. You were

149

not safe walking, driving, or even in your own home. You have heard of people being murdered in their own homes and dumped in rubbish heaps.

The government is not respected because they have lost credibility the power and the will to govern. While I was in Jamaica, Police were killed and their heads put on a stake and exhibited showing the criminals had more power than the Police. The Police themselves believed they were the people in authority and could do just what they like. Some of the Police would buy taxis and give them to young people to drive, stating how much they expect to earn in a day. So you have. hundreds of taxis on the streets driving so recklessly and with such speed causing a lot of death, they had to do so as they had to make the money the Police demanded per day.

People can commit the most vicious crimes and cannot be tried in a Court of Law because of intimidation. Witnesses to cases would be found dead in some cases their families would be threatened, removing all the authority from the criminal justice system. One judge told me she knew many murders had come before her, but no evidence was prepared by the Police, sometimes the Police themselves do not attend Court proceedings for the trial. So the Court has no alternative than to release the prisoners. All of the Police Stations run their own Drinking Bars throughout the island. I have met clients in the Police Station Bars where I had to not only buy the client a drink but the Police.

What country in the world can tolerate such behaviour? This is an island in anarchy an island which has no respect for authority, no respect for life, without dignity and pride as a people, a lost island. An island, unless some drastic change on behalf of the leaders takes place, is going to be one which will destroy itself. The people are lazy they do not want to help themselves all they want to do is live off each other.

I love Jamaica but what I see happening to that little island is beyond belief. The population is growing so fast there are thousands of children going to school; you may be travelling through villages you believe would be a place where few people could live, until the school day is over you can count hundreds of young children mostly girls.

A few boys among them behave so badly that strangers are afraid to be near them. Sex and perverseness has become the order of the day, the reggae and rock music blaring out night and day without any respect for other people. It can make one feel you are living in the jungle among wild animals and not human beings.

I went to Jamaica with £200,000 I spent two and half years there and was just able to return to England with enough money to give us a new start. Families, strangers, people you know and those you do not know, there is no difference. I am afraid for Jamaica. It cannot feed the population which exists now, but the rate of population growth doubles every 10 years. Soon they will have no land to cultivate or nothing to eat. The Government will no longer be able to borrow large sums of money, which they are not in a position to repay.

The Politicians know the precarious position which confronts Jamaica; most of them have their homes in Miami and elsewhere in the United States, ready to run when they no longer can control the people. One has got to consider in this day and age all nations seek to be educated, it's a priority that the children are brought up with dignity and pride in themselves and respect for those around them.

These politicians over the years since so called independence have set out to mislead, mis-educate and misgovern the people of Jamaica; hence we have an illiteracy rate of about 90%. The few who are educated do not use their education to help their brothers but use it to get as much money as they can in preparation for their departure, as they will do if Jamaica continues on the downward slope as it is.

I may return to Jamaica but I can assure you it will only be for a week or so because I am used to freedom not to live in fear, while all the time I spent in Jamaica I was living in constant fear.

151

I no longer want my bones to be laid in my native land because it's a land I no longer know, it's a strange place and I was a stranger. I know a lot of quite wealthy people who would give anything to return to their country especially during the winter and they are getting old, but they are so afraid for their lives some would not even venture to go there on holiday.
Jamaica I weep for thee!

Editor's notes:

Enrico and his wife Mary arrived in Jamaica for a new start in December 2006, having sold their property in Wales and transported all their belongings to Jamaica to spend the rest of their lives. Sadly, due to numerous problems and disappointments in Jamaica they decided to return to Wales, in England in July 2009, when Enrico was age 83.

Enrico was never the same person again. His illness worsened and his health deteriorated during the last two years of his life. He was in many ways a very disappointed person, but never bitter. He visited me in Luton in 2010 and we spent a couple of days together. We talked for hours and we visited some places and friends. I remember sending him back home with almost a boot full of food and fruit, such as vegetables, kidney beans, rice, cooking oil, sweet potatoes, yams and mangoes.

I knew he was struggling and we discussed a whole range of options with him. I wanted him to move nearer to his friends in Wolverhampton, Coventry or Luton. He informed me that his wife wanted them to remain in Wales and living so close to the sea was quite healthy. He also wanted to be near the hospital that had treated him for his kidneys and other medical conditions for a number of years. Enrico was very concerned about his health and that he did not have a great deal of time left for him to do a few more things such as us writing another book.

The couple of days I spent with Enrico was most enjoyable, but also sad. I could see he was not eating well, not enough to sustain himself in good health. We embraced each other and bid each other farewell before he set off in his car. I led the way to the entry to the M1 motorway, junction 10   and returned home in tears, thinking I may never see my good friend again.

We kept in regular contact with each other at least on a weekly basis. We discussed current affairs, history, international relations, racism, and government policies. He was totally against the austerity measures imposed on working class people by the coalition government.

During 2011 Enrico's health deteriorated further and he spent time in hospital. He was very popular with the staff and they did their best for him. He praised the National Health Service no end. He returned home to his flat, as he was totally against going into a care home. Enrico was always lively and well informed. Mary took care of Enrico until he went back to hospital. We had a number of conversations and he informed me that he wanted to see me within a couple of weeks otherwise it would be too late. I had another serious operation in November 2010, after a quadruple heart bypass in 2009 and my own health took a turn for the worse in 2011.

I had serious difficulty walking during the first six months of 2011, and I regularly felt anxious and in a state of panic. I was unable to drive or travel long distances on my own. I kept in contact with Mary and Enrico until he was unable to communicate with me. Mary informed me of Enrico's death. Enrico wanted to be buried in Wolverhampton near his friends and the place where he last worked. Unfortunately, despite several attempts and pleadings with Wolverhampton Council and the local Cemetery Management, I was unable to secure a place for him to rest in peace in Wolverhampton. The cost was in excess of £6,000 and no one wanted to share the cost with me.

I attended the funeral of this great man along with 100 or so, other people from Wolverhampton, Coventry, Wales, London and elsewhere. I made a speech in the small welcoming village church,

153

kissed his coffin and wished him peace. It was a very sad day for many of us. Enrico was very concerned about young people and equal rights for women and he would have been so pleased to see so many young women at the funeral, who took their turns to use the spades and help to refill the spot where the coffin was laid.

We returned to a function room at a local public house and many speeches were made by friends. Mary was too upset to speak. I made a commitment to organise a Memorial Event for Enrico in Wolverhampton a year later to commemorate the memories and work of this friend and brother. And here we are today. I have kept this promise to my dear friend.

Chapter Seven

Enrico Stennett and Jim Thakoordin –
Short Essays on Race and Racism

History would have been kinder to black people if Hannibal had not turned back from the gates of Rome

Stolen images from Africa

History is supposed to be the record based upon what really occurred at a given time in the evolution of mankind. Although history takes many forms the end results are always the same, embracing the life of man, animals and plants. The historians recalled history as they saw it in their mind's eye. At the same time it is always noted that the historian in his reflection of history at any given time will always coin such history to suit the writer and his nationality.

True history has been mis-represented by many historians mostly by design, in some cases by ignorance. The fact remains that all the noted historians have seemed quite able to take out of context the historical process of mankind and conveniently presented themselves, their race and the country of their origin as being the creator and the contributor to the entire well-being of man. This misappropriation of man's fundamental heritage was designed for the purpose of influencing generations to come that they only were responsible for all that was good and progressive in that epoch.

The Europeans have tried to convince the world that they were the forerunners of civilised thinking, the forerunners of mechanization, and the only nations capable of advancement, hence when they speak of other continents or countries outside the ambit of Europe they speak of dark and uncivilised land. For example, Africa is called the Dark Continent, Asia the wild continent, Australia a continent of cannibals, America, the continent of the unknown. All this seems to emphasise their inherent belief in their superior wisdom, therefore conditioning the minds of man that all of mankind who did not find its roots in Europe are of an inferior infrastructure. This conditioning has influenced man's thinking to such an extent that even the victims sometimes become convinced of their inferiority. The true facts of history state the civilized and advanced thinking did not come from Europe but from the continent of Africa, Asia and America.

These continents and civilizations are roughly 10,000 years older than any of the European civilizations. As late as 7,000 B.C. the British Isles was so remote and its people so backward they were living in caves painting themselves blue. They were known as the Blue foots.

Yet today these Blue foots tried to convince the world they are the forerunners of civilization and the upholder of all that is good and just. The most important question is, when Hannibal of Carthage crossed the Alps with his army of 10,000 soldiers and 5,000 elephants and marched onto the gates of Rome, had he torn the gate down instead of turning back would not history be coined in a different way, the Europeans would be in the position of the black people today.

Asians and Africans have been travelling throughout Europe for thousands of years, bartering their goods with Europeans. These Asians

156

and Africans were always friendly people. They did not take with them any arms in their travel as it was not their intention to capture, imprison and enslave the inhabitants of Europe. They brought with them news of the outside world and trinkets made of gold, silver, copper and ivory, often as free gifts to their newly acquired friends in each land where they ventured. Sometimes these trinkets were used as a peace offering as a means to prevent confrontations from the many barbaric races and tribes they encountered.

Centuries of Black presence in Britain

Britain has always been a mixed society made up of immigrants. If we go far enough back into history, we could argue that everyone who lives in Britain today had his or her origins elsewhere. From the Bronze Age and the Neolithic migrants who travelled to North West Europe 40,000 years ago, to the various armies including the Romans, Saxons, Vikings, and Normans, to the waves of immigrants and refugees from France, Ireland, Russia, Eastern Europe, Africa, Asia, and the Caribbean; the fact is that most people in Britain today are either immigrants or descendants of immigrants. It is correct to say that at some time in European history all the inhabitants were people with black and brown skins. Black people actually discovered Europe long before it was populated by people with white skins, blond hair and blue eyes.

Europeans, especially Britain, given its long colonial past, including its involvement in the Trans-Atlantic slave trade involving Africans for centuries, has benefited from immigration and ethnic diversity throughout its history in all areas of social, economic, cultural, scientific, and recreational activities. Each group of immigrants has helped to enrich the life and progression of British society. I was very interested in the historical insight into the presence of Black people in Britain, their backgrounds and experience, the way in which they have been portrayed, and the contributions that they have made to British society over the centuries and, in particular, over the last 400 years.

157

Most people know about the Black and Asian immigrants who arrived in Britain during or after the Second World War (1939-1945), which began in Europe and claimed the lives of over 20 million people.

Very few people are aware of the fact that there were Black people before 400 AD. Septimus Severus, a Romanised African commander, who became the Emperor of Rome in 193 AD, led many Roman soldiers into Britain. He arrived in Britain in 196 AD and was stationed in York. Among the Roman soldiers stationed in Britain were hundreds of Negroes who, under the command of Severus, "restored the Hadrian Wall and helped to save Britain from the barbarians" (from Roman Britain, by R. G. Collingwood, pp. 38-9). Some historians believe that black people were present in Britain even earlier than this.

What is certain, however, is that Black people had established sizeable permanent settlements in parts of Britain by the late 16th Century. In 1555, it was reported that, "the five Africans who visited England were stared at very hard indeed by local inhabitants ... along with the 250 elephant tusks, 36 casks of maleguetta pepper, and over 400 pounds of 22 carat gold [from their country]" (from Staying Power, The History of Black People in Britain, by Peter Fryer, p.7). These Africans were slaves brought to England by John Locke when he returned from Guinea. He educated them and trained them to act as interpreters for traders. Africans were brought to Britain when British merchants and explorers journeyed into Africa with imperialistic and colonial ambitions. Sir John Hawkins, who was among the first Englishmen to benefit from the lucrative triangular trade in slaves, took at least 300 Africans from the Guinea Coast. These Africans were either captured by his men or sold to him and transported to Haiti and the Dominican Republic.

Hawkins sold his cargo of men to the Spaniards for £10,000 worth of pearls, hides, sugar, and ginger. Having realised a profit of some 12 per cent on the venture, Hawkins was financed by Queen Elizabeth I to make a second slave-hunting journey in 1564 on the 600-

ton vessel, The Jesus of Lubeck, and a crew of 300 men. Hawkins' coat of arms included a portrayal of three black men shackled with slave collars and another black man bound with rope.

During the decades following Hawkins' journeys to Africa, many more slave traders and merchants set sail from Plymouth to engage in the triangular trade. As a consequence, many Black people were brought to Britain to be sold as slaves or servants. The growing population of Black people in Britain caused considerable concern among some people, prompting Queen Elizabeth I to sign an order to repatriate Black people. On 11 August 1596, the Queen's Privy Council instructed the Lord Mayor of London and the sheriffs of other towns that:

> *"Her Majesty understanding that there are late divers blackamoors brought into the realme, of which kind there are already too manie, considering how God hath blessed this land with great immense of people of our owne nation ... those kinds of people should be sent forth of the lande."*

The Queen's attempt to rid England of Black people did not succeed. In 1601, she issued a further proclamation in which she declared:

> *"[The Queen is] highly discontented to understand the great numbers of Negars and Blackamoores which are crept into this realm ... who are fostered and relieved here to the great annoyance of her own people that want relief which these people consume as also for that the most of them are infidels, having no understanding of Christ or his Gospel. The Queen had therefore given 'especial commandment that the said kind of people should be banished and discharged out of the Her Majesty's dominions."*

This mindset has remained with the British people over the centuries even though the overwhelming majority of the non-white population in Britain were born here. .

The Hypocritical Meaning of the Word Democracy

The word DEMOCRACY is one of the most misused words ever to exist according to the English dictionary the meaning of democracy which is a form of government for the people by the will of the majority of the people (based on conception of the equality of man). Let's analyze these words and think about them clearly. If this is so what country in the world that we know of in this day and age practices democracy.

Studying the world today and what is happening in the various countries who profess to be practicing democracy, leads me to believe their meaning of democracy is based on lies and distortion.

It is said you can fool some of the people some of the time, a great many people can be fooled and are fooled, but there are millions of people who are not fooled by the fictitious democracies practised by the two party states. In the first place a country has to be united for its common good where all the people who live within that country should be on equal terms, where no one has to go to bed hungry or no one has to die because they cannot afford to be looked after by the medical profession.

This so called democracy has succeeded in dividing the world into two camps the possessed and dis-possessed. All democracies seem to have a two party state and nothing of substance in between. These two parties stand predominant, misleading the people instead of leading them, when they do lead them it is to self destruction. The two large so called democracies who boast that the entire world should be like them are nothing but criminals, thieves and vagabonds. They have nothing to offer the people of the world but their greed deception, and corruption.

Let's take one country as an example, the United States a country of over 300 million people where the Statue of liberty stands claiming that all men were born equal and should be equal. They also claim they are the most god-fearing and religious people in the Christian world, they proudly claim America is Gods country. Some God! One third of its people are living in conditions which exist in the so called third world. These people do not know the meaning of democracy. What is democracy doing for them? In my view democracy spells hypocrisy where lies have become truth, and the truth has been discarded, where the so called leaders of the people do not act on behalf of the people, but only a small section of the people, the wealthy who gained their wealth through exploitation, extortion and robbery, whereas the majority of the people have no power in their democracy to do anything to right what is wrong.

One will note in the United States of America when there is a so called democratic election, one third of the people do not bother to vote, and millions of black people had been denied the vote for centuries. When elections do take place once every 4 years, people are not compelled by any law to vote. They do so if they wish and 90 per cent of these people do not know what they are voting for, after sifting through the lies and half lies by the politicians and those who have gifts of manipulation, they find themselves in a quandary where it does not matter whether they vote or not because it does not make any difference to them. Both parties have the same policies and the same principle and the leadership of these two parties is designed to maintain the status quo, where the rich will be richer still and the poor will be poorer still.

How many Wars has America been involved in, in the past five decades or more with her fellow gangsters supporting her? Who fights these Wars? The people who died on the battle field are not the rich and powerful, who are in their clubs, brothels or any place where they can gain their pleasure at the expense of the poor.

The poor have purposely been kept poor, the world has enough for everyone but in a democracy one man can have billions. He can own three, four, five houses, while the poor sleep by the wayside in shacks while they scrounge for a morsel of bread. In this democracy of ours one can often see dogs sleeping in luxurious beds, having caviar and the best of food available, while human beings suffer in the gutter.

How many people have been slaughtered burnt alive by Napalm bombs, flame throwers that burn people alive. How many people have been killed by uranium depleted bombs that strip the flesh from their bones by bombers flying five miles in the sky pushing their buttons that lay eggs of mass destruction, killing men, women and children, who have done no harm, but in some cases fighting to share a loaf of bread thrown to them by the rich and powerful.

We always seem to talk about our soldiers and praise them with false praises. We make them heroes for doing our bidding as they continue to murder people who are flesh and blood like us, while we make our excuse that these people who have died are only collateral damage.

The Churches of America who profess to be Christians who believe in God only believe in their own God not the Universal God. Their God will bless the soldiers who are sent out to murder innocent people, and the religious maniacs support these murders without question. None of these countries where America has been involved had declared war on America; on the contrary these countries have no power to declare these wars, neither Vietnam, Korea, and even little Grenada, a small island in the West Indies.

America believes she has the power to dictate to the world what the world should be, like her. If there is a God then he would not like to see mankind of any description become like America, a nation of thieves and vagabonds. One must not forget America like Australia was first populated by white criminals sent in exile to these countries. Later on it was the people who suffered religious persecution who ran away to America to become the founding fathers of present day

162

America. To do so they had to exterminate an entire nation who had not the guns or the desire to fight back. Even when they did fight back they were slaughtered by the use of the Gatling-gun by the thousands. The few who were left were placed in reservations in their own country, while the criminals from Europe moved in to take over. It is these people who want to rule the world. God forbid that this should be so.

In the countries which claim to be democratic one will note most of the leaders belong to the legal profession, in America the attorneys, in England the solicitors and barristers. They are there along with the rich people. Lets take the American House of Representative; no poor person could afford to be a Senator, in England, in the Conservative party almost the entire cabinet has always been multi-millionaires, as the saying goes, everything is tied up in neat parcels - not to be opened by the working classes.

Native Australians condemned to ethnic cleansing and genocide, that took the lives of tens of millions of native since Europeans invaded the continent.

163

Until the mid-60s, indigenous Australians came under the Flora And Fauna Act, which classified them as animals, not human beings. This also meant that killing an indigenous Australian meant you were not killing a human being, but an animal.

To this day, Australia breaks every code of the Geneva Convention when it comes to indigenous Australians and their human rights. The "public housing" that the government has given them are one-bedroom shacks with no running water, no electricity and no gas, that entire families are forced to live in. These shacks are in communities in the outback, as far away from "civilised" society as possible. Out of sight, out of mind."

There have been two great Wars, one 1914-1918 and the other 1939-1945. There were Wars before such as the Crimean War where millions of people perished, and the last War saw 17 million people die in one country alone; that country is Russia. There have been millions who died in England and Germany and other countries in Europe. There were hundreds and thousands of African and Caribbean people who died also, but we do not mention them because they are not important, after all who are they, nobody! We were told the last War would be the end of Wars, but then we did not cater for the New Imperial Power which was in the making. Since the last War one cannot even in his wildest dreams count the number of people who have perished.

The gangsters of the world seem to gang up against the weak and the dis-possessed. We are in an age where our entire life depends on one commodity more precious than gold, diamonds or any other precious stone; we have built a society where without it we cannot survive. Without oil to keep us warm in the cold countries we will freeze to death by the thousands. Without oil the rich are unable to fly around in their private jets prostituting the World, neither will they be able to run their big cars, neither will they be in a position to fly their planes around the world exploiting the poor.

164

Victims of European colonialism

Where would it be possible for mankind to fly their jets and bombers across the world to destroy nations and people, just as they did in Iraq, where thousands of people were slaughtered on the first night by the British and American invasion? It speaks for itself, where Iraq was concerned its leaders had to be removed so the oil multi millionaires could get hold of the Iraqi oil.

What about the pipeline which has been built through Afghanistan to exploit the oil from the Bearing Sea near Russia. Mankind should be ashamed we know the lies which came from the lips of the then President of the United States and his cronies all oil multi-millionaires and the then Prime Minister of England who told lies about weapons of mass destruction, and how eager they were to convince the world that all our lives were at stake if they did not do what they had to do.

The United Nations are not much better. After all, they are stationed in America, supported by America and dictated to by America. As the President of America said at the time. "To hell with the United Nations we Americans have the power, and we do just what we want. After all we are capable of wiping the leaders of Iraq off the earth". In doing so, divide the people of Iraq to be at logger heads with each other while they go in for their plunder.

The world knows these two individuals, Blair and Bush should be tried by the Human Rights Commission just like other leaders who have committed mass murders, but know the leaders of America and Britain believe they are untouchable they can do what they want, and get away with it.

The Election of a black president to the United States does not change anything. This man does not see himself as a black man, he sees himself as an American and in so doing forgets the past and sometimes ignores the plight of black people. His main aims and objective is to maintain the might of America. Nothing has changed although the Election was fought for the need to change.

Here in Great Britain we are now facing a new government, which is equally warmongering, as demonstrated in their attacks on Libya with the French, on a mission to replace the Gaddafi regime. The supported the rebels and with their superior military strength they replaced the Gaddafi regime in the most brutal colonial fashion. The previous British Prime Minister and American President, who were responsible for the lies and the mass murder of the Iraq people, are still running around free. The world knows about their guilt, and as I said before, they believe they are untouchable.

At the time the opposition Parties in Britain and America, did nothing to stop the lies and distortion although they were quite aware of what was going on. Now they are running for election in America and all that has happened has been forgotten overnight apart from Afghanistan, while the leaders of the Tory Party and the American President are once again beginning to spout their lies, misinformation and promises to engage in a war with Iran, if it fails to desist from becoming a nuclear power. They are also keen to protect their Israeli and Arab allies in the Middle East.

Prime Minister Cameron and his coalition government have carried out a series of vicious assaults on the working class people of this country, including severe cuts in living standards, cuts in benefits and pensions, increasing the retirement age, privatising parts of the

166

National Health Service and cutting its budget, reducing spending on education and training, allowing prices to increase well above inflation and implementing a whole range of legislation to take away the gains so bitterly fought for by working class people over many decades. His government is doing all this whilst protecting the rich and the powerful financial and business interests. As a result the rich is getting richer and the poor, poorer. Black people are amongst the most severely affected people with massive increase in unemployment, poverty and drop in living standards.

The Tories are determined to turn the clock back for working class people. They are ideologically driven in all they do. Attacking the NHS is a serious assault on the sick, disabled and the poor who cannot afford private medical care. It is noted on one hand he is saying one thing to the public and on the other in private he is putting forward his real intention, once again to deprive the working classes of some of the few good thing, which have happened to them over the last 65 years, such as the NHS, the welfare state, employment rights and equal access to further and higher education. The government is determined to destroy the public sector and services and to hand much of their provisions over to the private sector. Putting profits before people and greed before need.

The present management and service delivery system is not working. We need greater accountability, higher standards and better value for the vast sum of money that is going into the National Health Service. The coalition government led by Conservative Prime Minister, David Cameron and Nick Clegg, the Deputy Prime Minister from the Liberal Democrats have made a serious mistake by passing a Health and Care Bill that will create a two tier NHS. It will privatise much of our NHS service; create longer waiting lists and poorer service for the less well-off that need free and easily accessible healthcare. I believe the poor and the elderly will suffer most from this legislation passed in the Care Bill in 2012. Cuts by central government year on year in the welfare state, grants to local government and others measures resulting in the elderly being hospitalised and cared for in Care Homes instead of living

167

in their own homes, is unacceptable in a very rich country. Far too many elderly people are living in fear, poverty, cold and damp conditions and are subjected to premature death through no fault of their own. On many occasions their homes are being sold to pay for their care, which are often identified as inadequate and expensive. we have been active campaigners for free and accessible quality health care and will continue to do so as long as we live.

Sadly hospitals still have a lot to learn judging by the following quote:

> *"In the twenty first century most doctors and nurses still haven't got much of a clue about the quality of care we're providing, the effect we have on you, what happens to you after you're discharged, whether we've made your life better or worse or even if we've killed or cured you. We operate and consult in a vacuum, with virtually no feedback, just muddling through and hoping for the best." Dr Phil Hammond, 2002. Trust me, I'm a doctor. Metro Publishing, London*
> *"Many trust board members cannot be sure that their hospital is operating within the law." Audit Commission, 2009 (Taking in on trust)*

All three main political parties have now messed about with our greatest asset – the NHS. We cannot trust our politicians with our NHS. It is our NHS and we must be prepared to defend it. I would never be alive now without the NHS.

There is a saying, 'If life was a thing money could buy, the rich would live and the poor would die'.

The people of these countries are so conditioned deep down they become as corrupt as their leaders, which is why they support the corrupt practice of racism and all the evil which goes with it and the lies and distortions which rule the world.

How Britain and America Helped to Destroy the Island of Jamaica

168

Jamaicans have often been told by England how lucky we are to be British. How Britain has civilised us and built our country from an island that did not exist, to an island of rich and prosperous people. The commercialisation, the education, and other progress could only be made through colonisation.

Let's examine the illusion of the above statement. In the first place the masses of black people living in Jamaica at the time of my birth were either semi-illiterate or completely illiterate. The great majority could not read or write and had no trade or profession. There was development which took place in Jamaica, such as the Railway which ran from the Dockland of the city of Kingston and wound its way through the interior of the 14 parishes. This railway system was not built for the purpose of helping the people to travel from one part of the island to the other, but solely to bleed the country of all its wealth. All the products of Jamaica were drained daily from the interior to the Docklands to be shipped to the Mother country, not for the benefit of the people, but to make the Mother country rich and powerful.

The English people who lived in Jamaica were like Tin Pot gods, they did not mix with the black people, they were the bosses who walked around with their head held high full of arrogance and pomposity with the essence of superiority, as if they were super human beings.

Many black people believed the white man was God, and was born to rule. These poor black people accepted their treatment, believing this was their station in life, and that God made them to serve. They saw no other kind of life than one of serving the white man and accepting the white man's superiority. This inferiority complex was embedded in the minds of the people, so deep that until this day it is almost impossible to eradicate. In this belief lay the basis for recognition and acceptance that everything which was white was pure and good, and everything which was black was evil. The black man looking at himself in the mirror saw himself as ugly and devil like.

169

The Bible reinforces this belief in all its texts referring to the Nubians and the Nubian King Nimrod who built the tower of Babel. The Bible also refers to Sem, Ham and Jephat and the black people according to the Bible are Hamites, the black man being the sons of Ham are cursed. The black man was also made to be hewers of wood and drawers of water. Believing in the Bible the way they do, inferiority is bound to be a part of their psyche. The only doctrine the black man was forced to accept was Christianity, and they took the Bible literally and believed in every word.

The non-white people were graded as one would grade commodities. There were the Mulattoes, the Sambos, the Brown Skin, the Copper Colour, the Negritta, and the Negrilla and at the bottom of the pile, the Nigger. In other words we belonged to a system which was based on the shade colour of one's skin, the lighter skin you were the higher position you had in life and the black skin was at the bottom of the pile. This has been embedded within us for centuries from time of slavery and beyond. It is also rooted within our psyche that physiologically we find it difficult to eradicate, wherever we may be. Surely this was an attempt by the white man namely the English to bring about the complete destruction of a people, not to help them as they pretended to do.

Until today it has become so deep rooted within us, that it makes unity among us impossible. I would like to quote Tolstoy: 'I sat on a man's back with my hand closely around his neck, squeezing him and choking him to death, yet I pretend to the man and all the world that I am doing everything to relieve his burden accept getting off his back."

During slavery the slaves were forbidden to speak their own language based on what country in Africa they were from. They were punished, whipped and brutalised and forced to speak a language which they could not comprehend. Without a language of their own it was impossible for them to be educated. These people had to invent some type of language similar to the English language which is called Creole, Patois, or broken English. There is no such language as Jamaican

170

today, we are told the University of Jamaica is insisting on making Creole a recognised language. This is a fallacy, no other country in the world speaks the language which is spoken by the ignorant masses of Jamaica and therefore such a language should never be recognised internationally. There is no seat of learning in any part of the world where one could go to gain a diploma in Creole or Patios, which would be recognised, therefore anyone who advocates the teachings of the present Creole language to the people of Jamaica, is misleading the people.

We must realise whether we like it or not the English language is our Mother Tongue, unless we have the full command of the only viable language which is open to us as a small nation, there is no possible way we will be able to progress, and take our rightful place in the world society at large.

The slave masters did not correct the speaking of Patois or Creole providing the slaves could understand orders which were given to them. The language they spoke did not matter apart from when the masters believed the slaves were using a language that they the masters did not understand. Afraid of the revolt by the slaves against the yoke of oppression, the masters were quite content to allow the slaves to use broken English. This language is called Creole or Patois whichever you prefer to call it. Creole and Patios are still the main language used by the poor and uneducated people of Jamaica. This prevented progress educationally as far as the masses were concerned.

Creole is not a recognised language, neither is Patois and to write in any of these languages is almost impossible. It is impossible for the ordinary man and woman from a poor background in the Caribbean much more the masses to be educated in a language they do not understand.

When schools were finally opened to the black people it was for those black people who have made some progress after 200 years of so called freedom from slavery, these black people were in a small minority. It was dictated that the black people could only follow a

171

certain profession which was either Law or Medicine, it was important that now slavery was abolished black people were educated to a certain degree and with a specific purpose in mind. The doctors were there to maintain the good health of the workers in the interest of Britain, and the lawyers were there to maintain and uphold the British law which governed and controlled the people.

Now that Slavery was abolished the British occupation of Jamaica was becoming less economical with the constant demands of the workers for a small share of the produce yielded by their labour. The Police Force now became the biggest employer with the head of the Police and all Officers imported from England to control the people. This also applied to the medical services. Most doctors were of English origin, even in the small towns and villages the doctors were white English men. Also the Legal Profession the dispenser of Justice. The political institutions such as the House of Representatives that governed Jamaica before Universal Adult Suffrage, did not represent the black people it represented the interests of Britain. This consisted of mainly white people with a few black people who had become land owners who maintained the rule of law as operated at the time.

A hundred years after slavery was abolished there were no schools where black people could attend. The few schools that were established throughout the island were for the benefit of the English settlers' children and not for the black people. There were no hospitals in the small towns and villages throughout the island, and there was no means of sanitation as can still be seen by the stinking galleys that still carry human waste openly in the City of Kingston and Montego Bay. There was the establishment of some commercialism. These establishments were created not for the people of Jamaica but for commerce in respect of the English people who lived in Jamaica and for their bosses and associates in England.

Yes there was the Centre of Administration where the Administrator General was English, the Kingston and St Andrew Co-operation headed by English civil servants, the United Fruit Company which was governed and controlled by England, the Banks (including Barclays Bank) where all Bank Managers and their staff were white people, in these offices no black people were employed.

There were also the stores in King Street Kingston where not one of the assistants working in these stores was black. The black man was excluded from every commercial institution which existed, and was relegated to be labourers toiling on the plantations for Tate and Lyle and the Banana producers. There was no compulsory education for the black children especially those who lived in the far reaches of urban areas of the various parishes.

Yes there were schools of a sort in the 19th century, but the Catholic Church administered these Schools whose teachers were mainly Nuns. Even Boys Town and Alpha Cottage the Correction Centres which helped many black youngsters were established and run by Nuns. There were no Colleges catering for the poor, and few black children were able to acquire the Senior and Junior Cambridge Certificate which would advance them to further education.

The Jamaican people were deliberately denied any form of progression which could help them to establish themselves as a Nation. They were always deemed to be incapable of learning as far as England was concerned. Our Mother Country did not envisage the day when they would not possess and control us, therefore there was no need for us to be educated neither was there any need for us to speak the only language which was forced onto us.

As Jamaicans we must realise without a language we have no culture and without a culture we have no past present or future, which is why our so-called Governments are finding it difficult to govern our country in our interest because through lack of education we are ungovernable. The religious dogma which originated in Rome namely Christianity and the Bible was used as a means of mis-education and control. In the time of Slavery the Slaves only had one day off from their forced labour which was in the name of Christianity where they

173

could go to the Churches of their White Masters to worship their White Masters God.

The depiction of Michelangelo in the image of Christ and his disciples were pictures of all Europeans also the Angels of the Heaven. Everything which was good and pure was white as the driven snow, and to obey your Masters you had to be good and obedient. Therefore the 10 Commandments were embedded in your mind so deep within, you had no other alternative than to be good and obey your Masters, because by obeying your Masters you are doing the Will of God. On the other hand, Lucifer/Satan were depicted as the evil one black and devil like, who lived in a hot place called Hell. Unless you obeyed the Will of the White God then the black Satan or Devil will be your Master, and Hell will be your lot.

This kind of conditioning of the minds of the black people had become so effective, even until today the black people are killing each other all over the world because of their hatred for each other.

At the same time the religious fanaticism within them is so great, they are afraid to question their original indoctrination lest they be condemned where their soul will be thrown into the bottomless pit at the battle of Armageddon.

The Black people must realise it is about time they awoke from the spell which has been cast upon them, the spell which has divided them which prevents them from uniting as a people, the spell which casts such hatred in them from one to another, unless they respect themselves, they cannot demand the respect of others. You must respect yourself to demand respect, and among black people such respect does not exist. When our masters finally realised they had no other alternative but to leave the island they devised other ways to control us.

It was now a new period, Britain had realised that the tools they used throughout the centuries for the exploitation of the people were now becoming useless. There was nothing they could do which would

174

stem the determination of the workers supported by the new middle class in their fight to be liberated. Guns, batons and brute force could no longer hold the people back. The weapon of divide and rule was no longer effective. It was obvious although the masses wanted independence, they were not equipped and no attempt was made to prepare them for such an independence. A way out had to be found, hence it was agreed that our masters would free us providing we accepted their Imperialistic Constitution. Wanting our freedom we jumped at the chance of accepting the Constitution we were given, but this constitution was designed in such a way that we would muddle through hopelessly claiming we are free, while according to the Constitution we remained subjected to the Crown and still remain so until this day.

How can we ever be free if we are a subjected people? Although this promised freedom took over 10 years to materialise no attempt was made to prepare us for Government. One had to accept the impossible position which we inherited, a people who for years were deprived of any status in the Government of their country, a people who were uneducated, with three quarters of the population almost illiterate, were told they were now free.

While our Masters who had ran the country for over 400 years took their wealth, which they had accumulated over the centuries and left the country, leaving their Constitution and their stooges to continue the exploitation of the people. At the same time the continuing destabilisation of our Government by the MI5 and the CIA made it impossible for us to govern. One will remember Philip Agee the Head CIA Officer who was in charge of the destabilisation of Michael Manley's Government in Jamaica who came to England in the 1970's and exposed the American Government for what they were doing in that country.

There is no example shown by the two powerful countries who preach democracy, which does not exist within their own country. Neither does the United States of America or the United Kingdom with their two party system, each having the same policies, while at the same time being able to condition the minds of their electorate that when they vote they are voting for a change, when in fact the real Government of the countries are the same Civil Servants who advise each party when they are in power. No wonder our leaders failed to govern, as the Constitution was designed for failure.

Will There Ever Be A World Where We Are Colour Blind?

Racism in the European countries seems to differ from that of the United States and South Africa. England practises the most acute and subtle kind of racism. In other countries victims of racism know where they stand, and how to fight back against the portrayal of one of the most obscene and despicable ideologies any human being can comprehend, man's inhumanity to man.

The United Kingdom lulls its victims into a false regime based strictly on a class conscious society, so riddled with class divisions against their own people, in the form of the shelf system which has been in operation since the Industrial Revolution. The enslaving by the English in the 15th, 16th and 17th and 18th centuries in the Caribbean, the United States, and Australia and in some cases the Latin American Countries is well documented.

We can still see remnants of slavery by the Europeans remaining today, resulting in the mixture of races in all these countries, apart from the areas where we see the outright destruction of the native inhabitants of these countries.

The enslavement of the black man from Africa, which resulted in the fall of the Ghana and Songhi Empire was indicative of white slavery, hence the white slaves of the Caribbean and the black slaves who took their place had the same slave masters. The conditioning of the black man was easy because of their insularity within the islands of the West Indies, to accept their position in life as one of servitude, depending on the white man for his mere existence.

176

To be grateful to his oppressors when small aspects of decency were shown in the realm by overlooking small misdemeanours committed in disobeying their masters, sometimes leading to disquiet and discontent among the victims, brought in its wake the law of divide and conquer, at the same time using the oppressed against the oppressed thereby causing deeper and deeper division sometimes leading to hate and malice by one oppressed to the other oppressed, while the oppressors themselves gloated when they succeeded in destroying the minds and breaking the will of the oppressed, leading to hate and mistrust among themselves, leaving them distorted to the state of destruction.

At the same time their masters in far away countries like the United Kingdom celebrated with glee the conquest of the so-called master-race over people who they later described as sub-human and mere animals. The essence of this division was based on the masters themselves, their infidelity by using the women of the inferior class as sexual objects to carry out their lust and depravity by forced sexual intercourse, creating an in-between nation not knowing where they belonged and who they are.

These backward and limited people from the Caribbean, never in their wildest imagination believed they would enter and stand on the soil in the country they were told flowed with milk and honey, where the streets of London were paved with gold. In their servitude it would be sacrilege to dream of a black man entering heaven, even in disguise. They were conditioned to believe their masters were from a land so precious, so godly and superior that it gave them the right to use and abuse as they saw fit.

The masters themselves never thought that one day the people so inferior would enter their domain, they had done everything possible to stop this happening.

First there was the law of illegitimacy where an illegitimate child could not accede to his father's wealth or any part thereof of his

177

father's property, hence even the illegitimate sons and daughters were not expected to cross the seas. As late as 1971 an act of Parliament tried to enforce these actions when they brought in the Immigration Act in an effort to stop the flow of their sons and daughters, who by then were skeletons in the cupboard in the homes of the landed gentry and aristocrats of Britain, the patrons of the art who were slave masters, and great great grandfathers and mothers.

A clause was brought in by Parliament namely the Patriality Act of 1971, in order that the Immigration Act applied to black people only and not people from Canada, New Zealand, Australia and the United States. We were told to prove our patriality, we had to prove ourr great grandmother and father were citizens of the British Isles, and a marriage certificate had to be presented, that at a time of such union a legal state of marriage had taken place.

Of course this excluded all the hundreds of thousands of black people living in Britain, because at the time of such union the British Parliament knew that no such marriage took place, therefore the patrial from the Caribbean could not prove their patriality, so could be repatriated back to the Caribbean if the occasion ever arose when it was expedient to do so.

The people still in their ignorance, still bearing the inbred inner belief of their inferiority were so patriotic that they volunteered en mass as Soldiers, Airman and Merchant Navy Personal and later on after the War, came in droves, to rebuild the Mother Country, which was destroyed by the English themselves and other Europeans. These people sacrificed all they could to sustain a land which they loved deeply, not realising in that land there was no love, gratefulness or respect, and were disillusioned in their belief spiritually and morally.

This disinvestment was exacerbated when the doors of the Churches were closed in their faces as they discovered they were neither Roman Catholic nor Anglican as they believed, and had entered a country which was void of Christianity and where the full force of racism was brought to bear against them. The pain of such

178

disillusionment and sorrow, after being stripped of all the things they believed in, and the realization that all our hopes both spiritually and morally all forms of human decency and the pride which was deep within, believing we were a part of a great nation, which we were prepared to die for was only an illusion.

This is what makes us what we are today, stripped of our Christianity, of our belief in our dignity and pride, our hopes and aspirations for ourselves and our children, our disillusionment is complete.

To some of us not even death is the answer as we pine to return to the land of our birth, knowing we have to leave our offspring behind in a no man's land. In our deep sorrow we try not to be bitter, not to moan over our misfortune, not to destroy ourselves with hatred, but endeavour to let the light of friendship flow within us in the hope that together, we will build the nation we once believed in, a nation free of racism, free of hate, free of contempt for one to another.

Hoping one day history may be recorded for once in our favour, that we have contributed to a world where we are colour blind, where class no longer exists, a world where equality, justice and love prevail.

This is my hope for the future of mankind and our species, if we are to continue and not disappear like the dinosaur, to be found in the dust of the earth, where our destiny lies in a history of self destruction.

Immigration update

The 1962 Immigration Act had a considerable public impact through the media following demands for control and reduction in immigrants from non-white Commonwealth countries to Britain. Nearly fifty years later it is still a major concern for the media and the white population. Even many non white people who are descendants from the Commonwealth since 1962 are opposed to the increase in immigration, which in recent years, has come mainly from Eastern Europe.

In 1965, the government's White Paper on Immigration from the Commonwealth, noted that "at the moment restrictions apply to members of the white as well as the black Commonwealth. If this comes in practice to prevent the entry of a number of say, Australians and Canadians who would bring nothing but benefit to British life, there should be no hesitation about changing the rules". The rules were changed in the 1971 Immigration Act to allow people with a white parent or grandparent to enter Britain. As this would mainly apply to white immigrants it was seen as a 'racially motivated piece of legislation implemented by the Conservative government.

Immigration and in particular black people entering Britain has been a major issue especially for the right wing media, politicians and racists and fascist groups since the 1960's. The many anti-immigration laws passed since Britain entered the European Union has mainly affected black immigration, as there is free movement of workers within the 27 countries that constitutes the EU. For decades the term 'immigrants' has been synonymous with black people and immigration control in Britain.

Those who argued for an end to immigration claimed that there were already far too many non-white people in the country and that an end to immigration would enable those already in Britain to integration and improve race relations. Other extremists argued for 'repatritation of blacks'. The liberal minded people blamed the problems associated with poor race relations were due to the failure of local authorities, estate agents and building societies to provide housing for the minority population, race discrimination within the workplace by employers and the unions, politicians and the right wing media. Nevertheless governments of all political persuasions implemented and supported racist immigration laws, since the 1962 Immigration Act.

Commonwealth immigration had been encouraged from the 1950s, to fill vacancies in the NHS, public transport and a number of industries that were in the process of either expanding or restructuring. Recruiting offices were set up in the West Indies and employers

180

actively recruited in parts of Pakistan. By the turn of the decade the UK had become a country of net Commonwealth immigration. This became the occasion for racist campaigning in Parliament and amongst sections of the wider public. One dismal highlight of the agitation for an immigration colour bar came in 1958 when young white men attacked black residents in Notting Hill. Notting Hill was an area of London in which there was competition for housing, parts of the district were run down, with large houses being broken up into flats or rooms to let. The British Union of Fascists, under the slogan 'Keep Britain White' sought to mobilise the disaffected white youth of the area against the black population, resulting in the so called 'Notting Hill race riot'. One outcome of the political agitation over 'race' was the passage of the 1962 Commonwealth Immigrants Act which regulated the numbers of immigrants by requiring would-be immigrants to acquire work permits issued by the government.

Many employers in the private and public sectors in towns and cities were desperate to attract immigrants to fill key positions in the local labour market whilst making no provision of extra housing or other services to meet their needs. Many white workers and institutions including trade unions soon found themselves in competition and potential as well as social and economic conflicts with local residents and workers for the scarce and reasonably priced housing and services that were available. Public discussions and sometimes violent confrontations between white people and immigrants took place across Britain especially in urban areas which were increasingly being expressed in racial terms.

'Race' was also international news. There had been major uprisings of black populations in large cities of the USA, resulting in extensive destruction of property, deaths and injuries: Philadelphia (1964), Watts (1965) Newark and Detroit (1967). From television and press reports it seemed as if the USA was in flames. In South Africa demands for emancipation were also growing against a repressive white regime which used a range of methods of violent repression. In 1960 sixty nine black people were killed and around 200 injured (many shot in the back) in Sharpeville by the South African police. In 1965 Ian Smith, the leader of the minority white regime in what was then Rhodesia, declared independence from the UK, amplifying the conflict between black and white populations within Rhodesia and again making racial conflict international headlines. These events in the USA, the UK and southern Africa were taking place against the background of an increasingly brutal war conducted by the USA in Vietnam, this war generated protest movements world-wide and enabled protesters to bring together events in different continents, linking analyses of colonialism with domestic racial and class oppression. All of these events attracted major coverage in the mass media for many years.

The Race Relations Act 1968 made it illegal to refuse housing, employment or public services to people because of their ethnic background. The Race Relations Act 1975 was a major landmark for black people in Britain which offered greater protection in employment and services. However racism continued in almost every area of life in Britain even 26 years after the legislation to outlaw discrimination was passed. The 2000 Race Relations (Amendment) Act was introduced to ensure that all public bodies were fully compliant with the spirit of the 1968 and 1975 Race Relations Acts.

Non-European immigration rose significantly during the period from 1997, not least because of the government's abolition of the primary purpose rule in June 1997. This change made it easier for UK residents to bring foreign spouses into the country.

The former government advisor Andrew Neather stated in a newspaper, that the deliberate policy of ministers from late 2000 until early 2008 was to open up the UK to mass migration. This enabled a large number of black people to work in areas such as caring for the elderly, public bodies, hotel and service industries and to do the jobs which British workers refused to do despite nearly 3 million people being unemployed.

European Union

One of the Four Freedoms of the European Union, of which the United Kingdom is a member, is the right to the free movement of people as codified in the Directive 2004/38/EC and the EEA Regulations (UK). Since the expansion of the EU on 1 May 2004, the UK has accepted immigrants from Central and Eastern Europe and many other countries totalling over 2 million people.

In February 2011, the Leader of the Labour Party, Ed Miliband, stated that he thought that the Labour government's decision to permit the unlimited immigration of eastern European migrants had been a mistake, arguing that they had underestimated the potential number of migrants and that the scale of migration had had a negative impact on wages

In April 2006 changes to the managed migration system were proposed that would create one points-based immigration systemfor the UK in place of all other schemes. Tier 1 in the new system – which replaced the Highly Skilled Migrant Programme – gives points for age, education, earning, previous UK experience but not for work experience. The points-based system was phased in over the course of 2008, replacing previous managed migration schemes such as the work permit system and the Highly Skilled Migrant Programme.

The points-based system is composed of five tiers, described by the UK Border Agency as follows:

- Tier 1 – for highly skilled individuals, who can contribute to growth and productivity;
- Tier 2 – for skilled workers with a job offer, to fill gaps in the United Kingdom workforce;
- Tier 3 – for limited numbers of low-skilled workers needed to fill temporary labour shortages;
- Tier 4 – for students;

- Tier 5 – for temporary workers and young people covered by the Youth Mobility Scheme, who are allowed to work in the United Kingdom for a limited time to satisfy primarily non-economic objectives.

In June 2010, Britain's new Conservative-Liberal Democrat Coalition government brought in a temporary cap on immigration of those entering the UK from outside the EU, with the limit set as 24,100, in order to stop an expected rush of applications before a permanent cap is imposed in April 2011. The cap has caused tension within the coalition, with business secretary Vince Cable and employers arguing that it is harming British businesses.

The onslaught on immigration continues despite the fact that immigrants represent a net economic gain to Britain and not a liability or a drain on the public and welfare services. This evidence was brought about by a report acknowledged by the government in 2014.

The Borders, Citizenship and Immigration Act 2009, designed to simplify immigration law, strengthen borders and extend the time it takes to gain citizenship was reported in the Guardian Newspaper, 20 January 2010 as: "An act ... brought forward to strengthen border controls, by bringing together customs and immigration powers, and to ensure that newcomers to the United Kingdom earn the right to stay." At the same time the Act::

• Allows immigration officers to perform revenue and customs functions that have up to now been exercised by Her Majesty's Revenue and Customs (HMRC). The UK Border Agency will focus on border-related customs matters, while HMRC will retain responsibility for revenue and customs functions inland.

• Creates new powers to allow customs officials and immigration officers to share information.

• Amends the rules on naturalisation. Those who are resident in the UK will need to have a certain residential status for eight years before being eligible, and those seeking to naturalise on the basis of marriage will take five years. These periods can be reduced to six years or three years respectively if the applicant meets the "activity condition" (see below). In order to qualify towards naturalisation, the period of time spent in the UK has to be while resident on a certain type of visa or entitlement, which will be determined by secondary legislation.

• Creates a new category of temporary leave to remain, entitled "probationary citizenship leave". This will form part of the new route to citizenship and will constitute an additional period for which migrants are denied access to services and welfare.

• Introduces the concept of voluntary community service for migrants, whereby undertaking an "activity condition" can reduce the length of the naturalisation process by up to two years. The type of activity that will count as an "activity condition" will be spelt out in secondary legislation.

• Imposes a duty on the secretary of state to safeguard and promote the welfare of children in the UK. The duty does not apply outside the UK.

• Allows fresh claim judicial review applications to be transferred from the High Court to the upper tribunal.

• Rectifies some irregularities in the awarding of British citizenship and remedies a discriminatory practice that allowed citizenship to pass to children born abroad to British fathers before 1961 but not to children born to British mothers.

• Grants automatic British nationality to a child born in the UK where at least one parent is a foreign or commonwealth member of the British armed forces.

• Allows conditions restricting studies to be imposed on those given limited leave to enter or remain in the UK.

185

• Allows for fingerprints to be taken from foreign criminals liable to automatic deportation under the scheme created in the UK Borders Act 2007.

Other recent legislation has ensured that welfare benefits and other support for immigrants will be either withdrawn, subjected to time limitations, reduced or delayed. Both the government and the opposition Parties are responding to the recent growth and electoral success of the(United Kingdom Independence Party (UKIP) which is by far the most anti-immigrant mainstream Party in recent years. UKIP came on top of the poll during the European Elections in May 2014, ahead of the Conservative and Labour Parties. Anti-immigration feels and Parties are gaining public support and parliamentary seats in many of the 27 EU countries. In several countries they are in coalition government with mainstream Parties.

PART 2

Various contributions

Chapter Eight

NELSON MANDELA

World Statesman and Liberator

Nelson Mandela born 18 July 1918

Family and childhood

Nelson Mandela was born on 18 July 1918 in the Transki. He became the foster son of a Thembu Chief and raised in a traditional tribal culture during his childhood as part of the Thembu ruling family in the Transkei where he herded sheep and learnt to plough. His first name
188

was Rolihlahla; the Nelson was added later by a primary school teacher. Nelson's boyhood was peaceful until the death of his father landed him in the care of a powerful relative who was the powerful Thembu Chief. From his Methodist school he went on to study at the missionary Fort Hare College, but was suspended for organising the students. He was involved in organising protests against white colonial rule of the College.

To complete his studies and to avoid a threatened arranged marriage he went to Johannesburg where he met Walter Sisulu – a self-educated fighter against apartheid in South Africa. Sisulu arranged for Mandela to study law. Through his work in the law firm he saw at first hand the suffering of the African people. Being Black under apartheid meant that life for Africans was cruel, unequal, harsh and miserable. Mandela was opposed to apartheid and the associated cruelty and injustice. He committed himself towards the struggle for justice and freedom of the Africans and was prepared for the suffering and sacrifices, which he would encounter in the road towards personal and national liberation.

The South Africa of Mandela's childhood and early life was shaped by centuries of colonial rule which had concentrated all political, military and economic power and control in the hands of a white minority. Access to education, health, employment and freedom was severely controlled and restricted. The wealth of the country was owned overwhelmingly by the white minority. The great mass of the non-white population had been humbled and humiliated into submission by racism, which pervaded the whole of society. For Mandela the options towards liberation were few given that Africans did not have the vote or power to determine their future through the democratic process. Mandela decided to go along the non-violent route as a strategy.

Mandela became the first member of his family to attend a school, where his teacher Miss Mdingane gave him the English name "Nelson".

189

When Mandela was nine, his father died of tuberculosis, and the regent, Jongintaba, became his guardian. Mandela attended a Wesleyan mission school located next to the palace of the regent. Following Thembu custom, he was initiated at age sixteen, and attended Clarkebury Boarding Institute. Designated to inherit his father's position as a privy councillor, in 1937 Mandela moved to Healdtown, the Wesleyan college in Fort Beaufort which most Thembu royalty attended. At nineteen, he took an interest in boxing and running at the school.

After enrolling, Mandela began to study for a Bachelor of Arts at the Fort Hare University, where he met Oliver Tambo. Tambo and Mandela became lifelong friends and colleagues. At the end of Nelson's first year, he became involved in a Students' Representative Council boycott against university policies, and was told to leave Fort Hare and not return unless he accepted election to the SRC. Later in his life, while in prison, Mandela studied for a Bachelor of Laws from the University of London External Programme

Political activities

Shortly after leaving Fort Hare, Mandela relocated to Johannesburg. Upon his arrival, Mandela initially found employment as a guard at a mine. However, the employer quickly terminated Mandela after learning that he was from a well known family. Mandela later started work as an articled clerk at a Johannesburg law firm, Witkin, Sidelsky and Edelman, through connections with his friend and mentor, Walter Sisulu. While working at Witkin, Sidelsky and Edelman, Mandela completed his B.A. degree at the University of South Africa via correspondence, after which he began law studies at the University of Witwatersrand, where he first befriended fellow students and future anti-apartheid political activists Joe Slovo, Harry Schwarz and Ruth First.

In 1944, when he was 26, Mandela joined the African National Congress (ANC) and with Sisulu and Oliver Tambo helped to form its Youth League. Mandela, with his determination to rid the people of a

190

sense of inferiority after years of oppression, was elected its General Secretary. Mandela and the ANC became involved in passive resistance against the pass laws of the apartheid regime, which helped to control the non-white population and keep them in servility. By 1949 the League had persuaded the ANC to adopt a more militant programme of strikes, boycotts and civil disobedience.

After the 1948 election victory of the Afrikaner-dominated National Party, which supported the apartheid policy of racial segregation, Mandela began actively participating in politics. He led prominently in the ANC's 1952 Defiance Campaign and the 1955 Congress of the People, whose adoption of the Freedom Charter provided the fundamental basis of the anti-apartheid cause. During this time, Mandela and fellow lawyer Oliver Tambo operated the law firm of Mandela and Tambo, providing free or low-cost legal counsel to many blacks who lacked attorney representation.

Mahatma Gandhi influenced Mandela's approach, and subsequently the methods of succeeding generations of South African anti-apartheid activists. Mandela later took part in the 29–30 January 2007 conference in New Delhi marking the 100th anniversary of Gandhi's introduction of satyagraha (non-violent resistance) in South Africa.

Initially committed to nonviolent resistance, Mandela and 150 others were arrested on 5 December 1956 and charged with treason. The marathon Treason Trial of 1956–1961 followed, with all defendants receiving acquittals. The ANC leadership decided to bolster their position through alliances with small White, Coloured, and Indian political parties in an attempt to give the appearance of wider appeal than the more militant African political activists.

On 26 June 1955 at Kliptown 3,000 people adopted the Freedom Charter of the ANC. There, Mandela and other members went out of their way to include everyone in their vision: "South Africa belongs to all who live in it, Black and white". But the government did not like the growing support of the ANC and its ability to attract a mass

191

membership. In 1956 Mandela and 155 others were arrested and charged with treason – an alleged Communist-inspired coup. After an investigation taking four and a half years, the Treason Trail failed; nothing was proved. It was during this time Mandela met and married Nomzamo Winnie Madikizela, a social worker. Despite the fact that for most of their married life, Mandela was either forced into hiding or in jail, she herself was subject to frequent restrictions and house arrests by the government.

In 1959, the ANC lost its most militant support when most of the Africanists, with financial support from Ghana and significant political support from the Transvaal-based Basotho, broke away to form the Pan Africanist Congress (PAC) under the direction of Robert Sobukwe and Potlako Leballo.

From then on the government played cat-and-mouse with Mandela – imprisoning him for his politics, outlawing him, forcing him to go underground and into exile. "I found myself restricted and isolated from my fellow men, tailed by officers of the Special Branch wherever I went.... I was made, by the law, a criminal, not because of what I had done, but because of what I stood for."

Exile then trial

The Sharpeville massacre in 1960 was a watershed in South African politics. Groups like the ANC realised that peaceful protests were not enough. In 1961 Umkhonto we Sizwe (Spear of the Nation), the armed wing of the ANC, was created. And Mandela had, once again, to go into exile. He returned to South Africa and, in 1962, was captured and charged with inciting Africans to go on strike. He used his time in court to make political speeches which he knew would be conveyed not merely to his own people, but across the world. And at the famous Rivonia Trial in 1963 he spoke for four hours in his own defence. "The ANC has spent half a century fighting against racism. When it triumphs it will not change that policy... It is a struggle of the African people, inspired by their own suffering and their own experience. It is a struggle for the right to live..."Mandela and seven other activists were sentenced to life imprisonment.

Armed anti-apartheid activities

In 1961 Mandela became leader of the ANC's armed wing. He coordinated sabotage campaigns against military and government targets, making plans for a possible guerrilla war if the sabotage failed to end apartheid. Mandela also raised funds from abroad and arranged for paramilitary training of the group. Fellow ANC member Wolfie Kodesh explains the bombing campaign led by Mandela: "When we knew that we were going to start on 16 December 1961, to blast the symbolic places of apartheid, like pass offices, native magistrates courts, and things like that ... post offices and ... the government offices. But we were to do it in such a way that nobody would be hurt, nobody would get killed." Mandela said of Wolfie: "His knowledge of warfare and his first hand battle experience were extremely helpful to me."

Mandela described the move to armed struggle as a last resort; years of increasing repression and violence from the state convinced him that many years of non-violent protest against apartheid had not and could not achieve any progress. Later, mostly in the 1980s the ANC waged a guerrilla war against the apartheid government in which many civilians became casualties. For example, the Church Street bomb in Pretoria killed 19 people and injured 217. After he had become President, Mandela later admitted that the ANC, in its struggle against apartheid, also violated human rights, criticising those in his own party who attempted to remove statements mentioning this from the reports of the Truth and Reconciliation Commission.

Arrest, trial and imprisonment

On 5 August 1962 Mandela was arrested after living on the run for seventeen months, and was imprisoned in the Johannesburg Fort. Three days later, the charges of leading workers to strike in 1961 and leaving the country illegally were read to him during a court appearance. On 25 October 1962, Mandela was sentenced to five years in prison.

While Mandela was imprisoned, police arrested prominent ANC leaders on 11 July 1963, at Liliesleaf Farm, Rivonia, north of Johannesburg. Mandela was brought in, and at the Rivonia Trial they were charged by the chief prosecutor Dr. Percy Yutar with four charges of the capital crimes of sabotage (which Mandela admitted) and crimes which were equivalent to treason, but easier for the government to prove. They were also charged with plotting a foreign invasion of South Africa, which Mandela denied. The specifics of the charges to which Mandela admitted complicity involved conspiring with the African National Congress and South African Communist Party to the use of explosives to destroy water, electrical, and gas utilities in the Republic of South Africa.

In his statement from the dock at the opening of the defence case in the trial on 20 April 1964 at Pretoria Supreme Court, Mandela laid out the reasoning in the ANC's choice to use violence as a tactic. His statement described how the ANC had used peaceful means to resist apartheid for years until the Sharpeville Massacre. That event coupled with the referendum establishing the Republic of South Africa and the declaration of a state of emergency along with the banning of the ANC made it clear to Mandela and his compatriots that their only choice was to resist through acts of sabotage and that doing otherwise would have been tantamount to unconditional surrender. Mandela went on to explain how they developed the Manifesto of Umkhonto we Sizwe on 16 December 1961 intent on exposing the failure of the National Party's policies after the economy would be threatened by foreigners' unwillingness to risk investing in the country. He closed his statement with these words:

"During my lifetime I have dedicated myself to the struggle of the African people. I have fought against white domination, and I have fought against black domination. I have cherished the ideal of a democratic and free society in which all persons live

together in harmony and with equal opportunities. It is an ideal which I hope to live for and to achieve. But if needs be, it is an ideal for which I am prepared to die."

All those on trial, except Rusty Bernstein were found guilty, but they escaped the gallows and were sentenced to life imprisonment on 12 June 1964

Mandela was imprisoned on Robben Island where he remained for the next eighteen of his twenty-seven years in prison. While in jail, his reputation grew and he became widely known as the most significant black leader in South Africa. On the island, he and others performed hard labour in a lime quarry. Prison conditions were very basic. Prisoners were segregated by race, with black prisoners receiving the fewest rations. Political prisoners were kept separate from ordinary criminals and received fewer privileges. Mandela describes how, as a D-group prisoner (the lowest classification) he was allowed one visitor and one letter every six months. Letters, when they came, were often delayed for long periods and made unreadable by the prison censors.

Whilst in prison Mandela undertook study with the University of London by correspondence through its External Programme and received the degree of Bachelor of Laws. He was subsequently nominated for the position of Chancellor of the University of London in the 1981 election, but lost to Princess Anne.

Mandela's influence nationally and internationally, continued to grow during his time in prison. His vision for a just and democratic South Africa – as expressed in his speeches and writings – became widely circulated around the world. During his imprisonment his release became the focus for the international anti-apartheid movement. Many student organisations, trade unions and radical political groups and Parties around the world did their best to keep alive the vision of Mandela and his comrades in prison through demonstrations, protests outside the South African Embassy in London and providing financial and practical support for the banned ANC.

Free at last

On 2 February 1990, State President F. W. de Klerk reversed the ban on the ANC and other anti-apartheid organisations, and announced that Mandela would shortly be released from prison. Mandela was released from Victor Verster Prison in Paarl on 11 February 1990, age 71 years. The event was broadcast live all over the world.

On the day of his release, Mandela made a speech to the nation. He declared his commitment to peace and reconciliation with the country's white minority, but made it clear that the ANC's armed struggle was not yet over when he said "our resort to the armed struggle in 1960 with the formation of the military wing of the ANC (Umkhonto we Sizwe) was a purely defensive action against the violence of apartheid". Mandela made a dignified return to the political arena. In 1993 he shared the Nobel Peace Prize with President F. W. de Klerk who helped to dismantle apartheid and white rule after centuries of domination. In 1994 his lifelong ambition was achieved when South Africa became a country in which blacks and whites had equal political freedom.

Presidency of South Africa

South Africa's first multi-racial elections in which full enfranchisement was granted were held on 27 April 1994. The ANC won 62% of the votes in the election, and Mandela, as leader of the ANC, was inaugurated on 10 May 1994 as the country's first black President, with the National Party's de Klerk as his first deputy and Thabo Mbeki as the second in the Government of National Unity. As President from May 1994 until June 1999, Mandela presided over the transition from minority rule and apartheid. Mandela became the oldest elected President of South Africa when he took office at the age of 75 in 1994. He decided not to stand for a second term and retired in 1999, to be succeeded by Thabo Mbeki.

A person of peace

At his inauguration as President of the new regime in 1994 he said: "Let there be justice for all. Let there be peace for all. Let there be work, bread and salt for all. The time for the healing of the wounds has come". Through the Truth and Reconciliation Commission, he tried to get those responsible for apartheid's atrocities to admit to their past mistakes. Mandela in a massive demonstration of faith, hope, charity and forgiveness even invited his jailer to his inaugural ceremony as President.

Since retiring from the Presidency of South Africa Mandela has played a major role on the international political stage to foster peace and harmony in Africa and elsewhere. He has always been a great moral and political leader and these characteristics have grown since his release from prison. He is regarded by many as an international hero and a lifelong fighter against racial oppression and for universal human rights. Despite his age and the fact that he is no longer a leader of a country Mandela continues to seek to influence world affairs on health, investment, conflicts and wars. He recently described America as a threat to world peace and condemned the invasion of Iraq by America and Britain.

Criticism of American and British attack on Iraq

Nelson Mandela had strongly opposed the 1999 NATO intervention in Kosovo and called it an attempt by the world's powerful nations to police the entire world. In 2002 and 2003, Mandela criticised the foreign policy of the administration of US president George W. Bush in a number of speeches. Criticising the lack of UN involvement in the decision to begin the War in Iraq, he said, *"It is a tragedy, what is happening, what Bush is doing. Bush is now undermining the United Nations."*

Mandela stated he would support action against Iraq only if it is ordered by the UN. Mandela also insinuated that the United States may have been motivated by racism in not following the UN and its secretary-general Kofi Annan on the issue of the war. "Is it because the secretary-general of the United Nations is now a black man? They never did that when secretary-generals were white". General Colin Powell, the first of two African-Americans appointed by Bush to the position of US Secretary of State, presented to the United Nations Assembly the case for the war in Iraq and overthrow of Saddam Hussein.

Prior to the war in Iraq Mandela telephoned President George Bush to warn him against the invasion of Iraq. The President refused to take his call which was answered by Colin Powell, Secretary of State. Mandela then telephoned Bush senior who had led America during his time as President in the first invasion of Iraq more than a decade ago to dissuade his son from attacking Iraq.

Mandela urged the people of the US to join massive protests against Bush and called on world leaders, especially those with vetoes in the UN Security Council, to oppose him. "What I am condemning is that one power, with a president who has no foresight, who cannot think properly, is now wanting to plunge the world into a holocaust." He attacked the United States for its record on human rights and for dropping atomic bombs on Japan during World War II. "If there is a country that has committed unspeakable atrocities in the world, it is the United States of America. They don't care." Nelson Mandela also harshly condemned British Prime Minister Tony Blair and referred to him as the "foreign minister of the United States".

Unfortunately, Mandela was not successful in persuading the American government against attacking Iraq. Since his retirement from active politics Mandela has supported numerous important causes for peace and for better quality of life for the poor, the sick and the exploited. He has severely criticised the Americans who dominate international economic, financial and political affairs, being the only super-power with its mighty army and control over international financial structures. Mandela stated that "they [the Americans] think they are the only power in the world. They're following a dangerous policy. One country wants to bully the world".

Despite his age Mandela is actively seeking to shape world affairs. Many politicians and leaders can learn a great deal from this giant of the second half of the 20th century.

His speeches and writings have been published in a book called *'The Struggle is My Life'* and his autobiography called *'Long Walk to Freedom'* is also available.

Until July 2008 Mandela and ANC party members were barred from entering the United States - except to visit the United Nations headquarters in Manhattan - without a special waiver from the US Secretary of State, because of their South African apartheid-era designation as terrorists.

Mandela's 90th birthday was marked across the country on 18 July 2008, with the main celebrations held at his home town of Qunu A concert in his honour was also held in Hyde Park, London. In a speech to mark his birthday, Mandela called for the rich people to help poor people across the world. Despite maintaining a low-profile during the 2010 FIFA World Cup in South Africa, Mandela made a rare public appearance during the closing ceremony, where he received a rapturous reception.

In November 2009, the United Nations General Assembly announced that Mandela's birthday, 18 July, is to be known as "Mandela Day" to mark his contribution to world freedom.

Editor's update:

Rest in peace Madiba

NELSON MANDELA 1918 - 2013: Freedom fighter, prisoner, liberator, socialist, president, celebrity, global icon and much more. The world mourns the passing of man who freed his country from apartheid and became an inspiration to billions around the world.

199

On 5 December 2013, Nelson Mandela passed away at his home in Houghton Johannesburg from prolonged respiratory infection. After ten days of mourning in his homeland a state funeral was held on 15 December 2013, in Qunu, in the Eastern Cape Province, a relatively remote village, where he grew up as a child. After his long walk to freedom, Nelson Mandela reaches his final resting place and is buried at his ancestral home.

During his last few years Mandela suffered from relatively poor health, which worsened during the last year of his life. However, it did not prevent him from making important and timely comments about the situation in South Africa and around the world. Many important world leaders including Presidents, Prime Ministers, politicians, celebrities and others made their way to Mandela's home to meet him and to be photographed with him. It was ironic that several of these same world leaders and politicians regarded him as a terrorist whilst he was in prison.

Unfortunately, Mandela was not successful in persuading the American government against attacking Iraq. Since his retirement from active politics Mandela has supported numerous important causes for peace and for a better quality of life for the poor, the sick and the exploited. He has severely criticised the Americans who dominate international economic, financial and political affairs, being the only super-power with its mighty army and control over international financial structures. Mandela stated that "they [the Americans] think they are the only power in the world. They're following a dangerous policy. One country wants to bully the world".

Mandela urged the people of the US to join massive protests against Bush and called on world leaders, especially those with vetoes in the UN Security Council, to oppose him. "What I am condemning is that one power, with a president who has no foresight, who cannot think properly, is now wanting to plunge the world into a holocaust." He attacked the United States for its record on human rights and for dropping atomic bombs on Japan during World War II. "If there is a country that has committed unspeakable atrocities in the world, it is the United States of America. They don't care." Nelson Mandela also harshly condemned British Prime Minister Tony Blair and referred to him as the "foreign minister of the United States".

This is so true considering what is happening in the Middle East and the continuing onslaught by Israel against the almost defenceless people of Gaza who have been under occupation and blockade for many years. The massacre of mainly civilians in Gaza is continuing as I write this update. The Americans have also tactically endorsed the military coup against the first democratically elected President and government in Egypt, and intervened militarily, with Britain and other NATO countries which removed Muammar Gaddafi who ruled Libya for 42 years until his murder by Western backed forces on 20 October, 2011. The Americans and their European and NATO allies are also back in Iraq as a strategic operational military force and also continuing its final operations in Afghanistan. The last military adventure by the Americans and NATO in the Middle East is to destroy the extremist and terrorist group ISIS, which refers to itself as the "Islamic State" and is committed to spread its beliefs across the Middle East and the world. The ironic thing is that ISIS has successfully used the weapons supplied by the Americans and NATO to attack the Syrian government, which has resulted on over 300,000 deaths, mainly civilians in Syria and millions seeking refuge in the region. ISIS in the eyes of America, Britain and NATO which has grown from their support is now "the most dangerous group that threatens America and the world."

Tribute to Mandela

US President Barack Obama said Mr Mandela "was a fountain of wisdom, a pillar of strength and a beacon of hope for all those fighting for a just world order. He achieved more than could be expected of any man".

Pope Francis said Mr Mandela had forged "a new South Africa built on the firm foundations of non-violence, reconciliation and truth".
201

Great men and women have walked this earth but only a few are remembered. It is their actions and words that make a difference and are remembered. Nelson Mandela is no longer with us in body, but his thoughts and spirit will always be with those of us who shared his words , feeling and love for freedom and humanity. I hope his quotes will serve as a reminder of what he stood for. Many of us will not see the likes of Madiba again in our lifetime, so it falls to us to the example that this great person has set. He taught us to make decisions guided not by hate, but by love; to never discount the difference that one person can make; to do what is right not for the few, but for the many; to oppose injustice, poverty, corruption, racism, inequality and to strive for a future that is worthy of his sacrifice.

His speeches and writings have been published in a book called 'The Struggle is My Life' and his autobiography called 'Long Walk to Freedom' is also available.

Nelson Mandela quotes:

"I was called a terrorist yesterday, but when I came out of jail, many people embraced me, including my enemies, and that is what I normally tell other people who say those who are struggling for liberation in their country are terrorists. I tell them that I was also a terrorist yesterday, but, today, I am admired by the very people who said I was one." – Larry King Live, 16 May 2000.

"No one is born hating another person because of the colour of his skin, or his background, or his religion. People must learn to hate, and if they can learn to hate, they can be taught to love, for love comes more naturally to the human heart than its opposite." – Long Walk to Freedom.

"Education is the most powerful weapon which you can use to change the world." - University of the Witwatersrand South Africa, 2003

"I do not deny that I planned sabotage. I did not plan it in a spirit of recklessness nor because I have any love of violence. I planned it as a result of a calm and sober assessment of the political situation that had arisen after many years of tyranny, exploitation and oppression of my people by the whites".

"To deny people their human rights is to challenge their very humanity"

"Where globalization means, as it so often does, that the rich and powerful now have new means to further enrich and empower themselves at the cost of the poorer and weaker, we have a responsibility to protest in the name of universal freedom".

"I am fundamentally an optimist. Whether that comes from nature or nurture, I cannot say. Part of being optimistic is keeping one's head pointed toward the sun, one's feet moving forward. There were many dark moments when my faith in humanity was sorely tested, but I would not and could not give myself up to despair. That way lays defeat and death."

"I have walked that long road to freedom. I have tried not to falter; I have made missteps along the way. But I have discovered the secret that after climbing a great hill, one only finds that there are many more hills to climb. I have taken a moment here to rest, to steal a view of the glorious vista that surrounds me, to look back on the distance I have come. But I can only rest for a moment, for with freedom come responsibilities, and I dare not linger, for my long walk is not ended."

"Overcoming poverty is not a task of charity; it is an act of justice. Like Slavery and Apartheid, poverty is not natural. It is man-made and it can be overcome and eradicated by the actions

of human beings. Sometimes it falls on a generation to be great. YOU can be that great generation. Let your greatness blossom."

"During my lifetime I have dedicated myself to this struggle of the African people. I have fought against white domination, and I have fought against black domination. I have cherished the ideal of a democratic and free society in which all persons live together in harmony and with equal opportunities. It is an ideal which I hope to live for and to achieve. But if needs be, it is an ideal for which I am prepared to die."

"I had no epiphany, no singular revelation, no moment of truth, but a steady accumulation of a thousand slights, a thousand indignities and a thousand unremembered moments produced in me an anger, a rebelliousness, a desire to fight the system that imprisoned my people. There was no particular day on which I said, henceforth I will devote myself to the liberation of my people; instead, I simply found myself doing so, and could not do otherwise."

"Let there be justice for all. Let there be peace for all. Let there be work, bread, water and salt for all. Let each know that for each the body, the mind and the soul have been freed to fulfil themselves."

"What counts in life is not the mere fact that we have lived. It is what difference we have made to the lives of others that will determine the significance of the life we lead."

"For a revolution is not just a question of pulling a trigger; its purpose is to create a fair just society"

Chapter Nine

John Richard Archer - first Black Mayor of a London Borough

Archer's presidential address to the inaugural meeting of the African Progress Union, 1918, taken from *Staying Power – The History of Black People in Britain* – by Peter Fryer, Published by Pluto Press,1984.

John Archer, Mayor of Battersea

John Richard Archer was born on 8 June 1863. He died in July 1932. He was a British race and political activist for many decades. Archer was elected a councillor for Battersea, in London before becoming Mayor. He was born to Richard Archer, from Barbados, and Mary Teresa Burns, from Ireland, in Liverpool. He travelled the world as a seaman, living in the USA and Canada, then settled in Battersea with his wife, Bertha, a black Canadian. He ran a small photographic studio at a time when photography was in its infancy.

Archer became involved in politics and was noted for his radical socialist views. In 1906 he was elected as a Liberal to Battersea Borough Council for Latchmere ward; at the same time, successfully campaigned for a minimum wage of 32 shillings a week for council workers and was re-elected in 1912. In 1913, he was nominated for the position of Mayor. There were negative, and racist , aspects to Archer's campaign to become the Mayor, with allegations that he did not have British nationality. The result was very close and Archer won by 40 votes to 39 among his fellow councillors. On securing victory Archer made a truly memorable speech:

"My election tonight means a new era. You have made history tonight. For the first time in the history of the English nation a man of colour has been elected as mayor of an English borough. "That will go forth to the coloured nations of the world and they will look to Battersea and say Battersea has done many things in the past, but the greatest thing it has done has been to show that it has no racial prejudice and that it recognises a man for the work he has done."

Archer was re-elected to the Council as a Labour representative in 1919. He stood without success for parliament the same year. In 1918 he became President of the African Progress Union, working for black empowerment and equality. In 1919 he was a British delegate to the Pan-African Congress in Paris. Two years later he chaired the Pan-African Congress in London.

In 1922, Archer acted as Labour Party secretary election agent for Shapurji Saklatvala, a Communist activist standing for parliament in North Battersea. He convinced the Labour Party to endorse Saklatvala and he was duly elected one of the first black MPs in Britain. He and Saklatvala continued to work together, winning again in 1924 until the Communist and Labour parties split fully. In 1929, Archer was agent for the official Labour candidate who won in the general election, beating Saklatvala.

Archer served as a governor of Battersea Polytechnic and on several Boards and institutions. Before his death in 1932, he was deputy leader of Battersea council. He died on Thursday 14 July 1932, just a few weeks after his 69th birthday. His funeral was held at the Church of Our Lady of Carmel in Battersea Park Road on Tuesday 19 July, and he was buried in the Council's cemetery at Morden.

Presidential address to the inaugural meeting of the African Progress Union, 1918 – by John Archer

I greatly dislike bringing coals to Newcastle, and in addressing you tonight, as one born in England, I fear that is what I am doing, but I take courage from the fact I will not accept second place with any here for love of my race. I am, and always will be, a race-man. That feeling was born in me when quite a little boy in my natal city, Liverpool. A famous company of American Negroes were playing that soul-string Negro tragedy *Uncle Tom's Cabin*. I saw the play, and from that moment the seeds of resentment were planted within me that have resulted in making me the race-man I am.

Too long, much too long, has the Negro race suffered. 'Mislike me not for my complexion, the shadowed livery of the burnished sun.' Why should he suffer because of that shadowed livery? As the Prince of Morocco pleaded to Portia, so the Negroes of today plead. I raise my voice tonight against that plea having to be made in future. We are living in stirring times. We have seen the need of the greatest war in the annals of history, a war that marks an epoch in the history of our race. Side by side with the British Army, for the first time, our compatriots from Africa, America, and the West Indies have been fighting on the fields of France and Flanders against a foreign foe. A war, we have been repeatedly told, the despotism of German rule. The truth of that statement will be proved by the way they deal in America with Afro-Africans, in France with the Negro subjects, in Belgium with their Congo subjects, and in Great Britain with India, Africa and the West Indies. We shall be told the old, old story. Africa is not ready; the time is not ripe; they are not sufficiently advanced. According to some critics the Negroes will only be ready with the Angel Gabriel sounds his trumpet. I do not know when that great day will come, but I am hoping it is far distant, because we are inaugurating tonight an association, which I trust to be the parent of a large number of similar institutions, whose sole reason for existence will be the progress of our African race.

I have said according to some people the African is not ready. Upon whom, then, can the blame be placed more equitably than the white race? What have they done, what are they doing, to rectify the great wrong inflicted upon our forbears? The children of the white race today owe a great debt still to the children of the darker race. We are hearing a great deal about indemnities on the one hand, reparation on the other that the Peace Conference is going to demand from Germany. I venture to submit to each delegate to the Conference this proposition; 'Keep your minds on the patent fact that Negroes have been associated with you in bringing about the possibility of this great conference of the nations who are so desirous for the world's freedom.'

I suggest by way of instalment they put down a motion for the better treatment of the coloured races under their rule, greater facilities for educational advancement in part payment of the debt they owe to them. It is rather significant to me that India is the only country of the darker race, which will be directly represented. One of the greatest blots upon the escutcheon of the white race is their enslavement of our people in America and the West Indies. The discovery and colonisation of America were primarily for greed and this dominant principle was illustrated in different stages of the growth and development of the country. Spain, which in the sixteenth century was not only a worldwide Power, but one of the greatest of modern times, bore a very important part in the conquest and settlement of the New World. It was mainly her merchantmen that ploughed the Main, her capital and the patronage of her sovereigns that led. The Dutch and the English followed in the rear. Her sons made settlements in North America and the West Indies early in the sixteenth century, but it was one hundred years after, at Jamestown, Virginia, in 1607, that the English made the first permanent settlement within the continental limits of the United States of America.

In the early voyages it was not at all remarkable that Negroes were found as sailors, though slaves. It is well authenticated that among the survivors of the Coronado expedition was Esteven, a Negro, who was guide to Friar Narcoz in 1539 in the search for the seven cities of Cibola. The celebrated anthropologist, in *The Human Species*, strongly intimates that Africa had its share in the peopling and the settlement of some sections of South America. The exception but proves the rule that the Negro came to the New World as a slave. He was stolen from or brought on the West Coast of Africa, to add to the wealth of America by his toil as bondman and labourer. The Portuguese imported large numbers of Negroes, but I am more concerned with what England had to do with this traffic in human beings.

The English gentlemen Sir John Hawkins made three trips to America from the West Coast of Africa between 1563 and 1567, taking with him several hundreds of the natives, whom he sold as slaves. Queen Elizabeth became a partner in this nefarious traffic. So elated was she at its profits that she knighted him, and he most happily selected for his crest a Negro head and bust with arms pinioned. It was a lucrative business, and though at first shocking the sensibilities of Christian nations and rulers, they soon reconciled themselves, not only to the traffic, but introduced the servitude as part of the economic system of their dependence in America. That it became a fixture after its introduction in these Colonies was due to the prerogative of the Home Government rather than to the importunities of the Colonists - especially because it was a source of revenue to the Crown.

209

Hence I say we who were born under British rule and are of the Negro race here still need reparation to be made to us. We are the ones to show resentment, if it should be shown. We, the offspring of those islands, are the ones to bear malice, if it should be borne. How have we shown this resentment? How have we borne this malice? Look in France and Flanders, and we get the answer. When England was in dire need, African, American and West Indian Negroes forget justice, forgot wrongs, forget insults, and hastened to the nation's call. How have they been requited?

We come from an ancient race. We have a history to be proud of. Before Romulus founded Rome, before Homer sang, when Greece was in its infancy, and the world quite young, 'Hoary Meroe' was the chief city of the Negroes along the Nile. Its private and public buildings, its markets and public squares, its colossal walks and stupendous gates, its gorgeous chariots and alert footmen, its inventive genius and ripe scholarship, made it the cradle of civilisation and the mother of art. It was the queenly city of Ethiopia – for it was founded by colonies of Negroes. Through its open gates long and ceaseless caravans laden with gold, silver, ivory, frankincense and palm oil poured the riches of Africa into the capacious lap of the city. The learning of this people, embeded in immortal hieroglyphic, flowed down the Nile and like spray spread over the Delta of that time-honoured stream, on by the beautiful and vulnerable city of Thebes – the city of a hundred gates, another monument, to Negro genius and civilisation, and more ancient than the cities of the Delta. Greece and Rome stood transfixed before the ancient glory of Ethiopia! Homeric mythology borrowed its essence from Negro hieroglyphics. Egypt borrowed her light from the venerable Negroes up the Nile. Greece went to school to the Egyptians, and Rome turned to Greece for law and the science of warfare. England dug down into Rome's centuries to establish a government and maintain it. Thus the flow of civilisation has been from the East, the place of light, to the West; from the Orient to the Occident.

Some writers have striven to prove that the Egyptians and Ethiopians are quite a different people from Negro, but Jeremiah the prophet asks: 'Can the Ethiopian change skin or the leopard his spots?' The Prophet was as thoroughly aware that the Ethiopian was black as the leopard spotted. We have in addition to this testimony the evidence of Herodotus, Homer, Josephus, Eusebius, Strabo, and the others, and I am content to accept their evidence. Here is our ancient past. We have no need to be ashamed of it.

Our modern record we can also proudly speak about, since freedom came to Africa's sons. What have we achieved, in spite of prejudice, in the realms of science, literature & art! The race can proudly point to Daniel A. Payne, eminent as a pioneer educator, first President of a Negro college and Bishop of the African Methodist Episcopal Church; Henry Highland Garnet, the orator became Minister and Consul-General to Liberia; Dr. Alexander Crummel, D.D., scholar and brilliant conversationalist; the great Fredrick Douglas (cheers), who visited this country and became the friend of Cobden, Bright, Brougham, O'Connell, Disraeli, Peel; Paul Laurence Dunbar, the poet, who also visited this city in 1897; Booker T. Washington (cheers), the first Negro to receive the distinction of Master of Arts from Harvard University; Mrs. Fanny Jackson Coppin, the first coloured woman to graduate from a recognised college in the United States of America, who visited the country 1888 to attend a missionary congress, and so eloquently did she plead the cause that the Duke of Somerset arose and commended her in glowing terms for her eloquence, and the cause that she so ably represented; Harry Oswa Tanner, the famous artist whose paintings can be seen in the Paris Salon; Ida B. Wells, whom I met here when she was rousing the people to the highest pitch of indignation against the lynching of Negroes- these are a few of the names of Afro-Americans we are all proud of. I could go on giving evidence of our race's progress, but time will not permit. I shall therefore conclude this portion of my address with three names of eminent men of our race, one for Africa, one for the West Indies and one for England.

211

In 1864 the most important event in the life of a great African took place in Canterbury Cathedral, when Samuel Crowther was consecrated first Bishop of the Niger (cheers). Remembering, as doubtless many did, the touching history of his childhood and early struggles as a slave, the crowded congregation must have been moved to tears as this African humbly knelt in Gods glorious house to receive the seals of the high office of Shepherd of His earthly fold. The West Indies have given us that master of erudition, Edward Wilmot Blyden. As linguistic scholar, Dr. Blyden ranked deservedly high. He possessed a working knowledge of French, German, Italian and Spanish among modern languages, and of Hebrew, Greek and Latin among the classics. It has been said of him: ' The life and work of the late Edward Wilmot Blyden, D.D., have attracted the attention of Europeans and Africans as one of the most conspicuous expressions and manifestations of the belief that a man of unmixed African ancestry possesses the mental capacity, the intellectual and imaginative power, of acquiring and assimilating alike the literary culture of the ancient civilisations of the Anglo-Saxons, the Latins and the Arabs.

He must be regarded as one of the first-fruits of a maturing literary harvest which in the fullness of time will be ingathered, and which will thus reveal to all mankind the view-point the outlooks and the ideals of the Westernised Africans of America and the West Indies; and also of the Westernised Africans of the Continent of Africa who have lived throughout all of their generations in Africa, governed and surrounded mainly by Pagan and Mohammedan religious influences and by African laws and institutions.' Lastly, those of us who were born here can point to Samuel Coleridge Taylor, the great composer. His *Hiawatha* proved him to be in front rank of musical composers, and will forever live; in his early death the race lost a great man, and I a personal friend.

It is now my pleasure and duty to pay tribute, very briefly, as time will not permit, to someone of the great and noble men and women of the white race who have stood firmly for African progress. My hero in American history is John Brown, who gave his life for freedom of the

212

slaves. This is part of John Brown's last speech at his trial: 'This court acknowledges, I suppose, the validity of the Law of God. I see a book kissed here which I suppose to be the Bible, or at least the New Testament. That teaches me that all things whatsoever I would that men should do unto me I should do even so to them. It teaches me further to remember them that are in bonds, as bound with them. I endeavour to act up to that instruction. I say I am yet too young to understand that God is any respecter of persons. I believe that to have interfered, as I have done, as I have always freely admitted I have done, in behalf of this despised poor, was not wrong but right. Now, if it is deemed necessary that I should forfeit my life for the furtherance's of the end of justice, and mingle my blood further with the blood of my children and with the blood of millions in this slave country, where rights are disregarded by wicked, cruel and unjust enactments, I submit; so let it be done.'

England is rich in names of grand, fearless and noble men and women who have stood out boldly in the Negro's cause. The chief merit unquestionably belongs to Granville Sharp. He was encouraged by none of the world's huzzas when he entered upon his work. He stood alone, opposed to the opinion of the ablest lawyers and the most rooted prejudices of the times; and alone he fought out, by his signal exertions, and at his individual expense, the most memorable battle for the constitution of his country and the liberties of British subjects of which modern times afford a record. It was Granville Sharp who secured the judgement from Lord Chief Justice Mansfield in the test case of James Somerset, the slave, whether he could be held as a slave in England. Lord Mansfield declared that the claim of slavery can never be supported; that the power claimed never was in use in England; therefore the man James Somerset must be discharged – and so firmly established the glorious axiom that as soon as any slave sets his foot on English ground that moment he becomes free. He lighted the torch, which kindled other minds, and it was handed on until the illumination became complete.

Another honoured name for Negro rights is Bishop Colenso, who gave the major portion of his life to the uplifting of his cause, assisted by his daughter in Africa, and we are honoured in having members of his family here tonight. Little did I think when a boy, struggling with Colenso's Arithmetic, I should live to become the friend and associate of his sons. To the memory of the late M.P., Frank Colenso, I pay my tribute. He was imbued with his father's love for the Negro, and fought for him to the day of his death. He was my guide and helped me through many thorny paths and I cherished the fact that he numbered me among his friends. We also have with us tonight Mr. and Mrs. Fisher Unwin, and again I can speak from personal experiences that their hearts are in sympathy with our cause. There are many, many others that I could mention, but I must conclude with a few words about the objects of our African Progress Union. But they are not forgotten, and the thanks of this African Progress Union will be accorded them.

Now about the objects of the African Progress Union. The objects are to promote the general welfare of Africans and Afro-peoples, through such agencies as may be deemed best; to establish in London, England, a place as 'home from home' where the numbers of the associations may meet for social recreation and intellectual improvement, where movements may be promoted for the common welfare, and where members may receive and entertain their friends, under the regulations of the board of management; to spread by means of papers to be read and addresses to be given from time to time, and by means of a magazine or other publications, a knowledge of the history and achievements of Africans and Afro-peoples past and present; and to promote the general advancement of African peoples.

A very necessary thing. The people in this country are sadly ignorant with reference to the darker races, and our object is to show to them that we have given up the idea of becoming hewers of wood and drawers of water, that we claim our rightful place within this Empire (cheers.) That if we are good enough to be brought to fight the wars of the country we are good enough to receive the benefits of the country. (Renewed cheers.) One of the objects of this association is to demand –

not ask, demand; it will be 'demand' all the time that I am your President. I am not asking for anything, I am out demanding, because I have been speaking all through this election, and we have been telling people that what we want to do is to give advancement for the poorer people, that children of the poor shall have an opportunity of going from the school to the college; and we demand the same right for Africa. (Cheer.) The last is 'To create and maintain a public sentiment in favour of brotherhood in its broadest sense'. Now I do like that. I do not know who it was that suggested this, but I do like 'brotherhood in its broadest sense'. In America they had a brotherhood, and they used to say that God had made of one blood all of nations of the earth to dwell. They preached it all right, but preaching it and practising it was a different thing. (Laughter.) There happened to be a man who fell in love; he was a coloured man, and he fell in love with a white girl, and she fell in love with him. He said: 'Well, what do you think your brother will say?' He had already heard the brother preach a sermon on 'God hath made of one blood all nations', and she said: 'Certainly not.' (Laughter.) Said the coloured man: 'I heard you in the pulpit last Sunday, "God hath made of one blood all nations on the earth to dwell".' 'Yes,' he said, 'and I will do so next Sunday; I do not object to you being my brother in Christ, but I object to your being my brother-in-law.' (Laughter.) Well, that is not the sort of brotherhood we want here; we want a brotherhood that will extend itself right out to the nations of the world, and when that is extended they will find that the darker peoples, because of what they have suffered and because of their future, that fleecy locks and black complexions cannot forfeit a nation's claims; skin may differ, but affection dwells in black and white the same. (Cheers)

Chapter Ten

Marc Wadsworth - The Windrush Pioneers

Jamaicans leaving the Windrush in 1948

Speaking at the 50th Anniversary celebrations organised by Jim Thakoordin, in 1998, Chair of Luton Committee for Racial Harmony

"It's a pleasure to be back in Luton. This is only the second Windrush event I've attended. The other was an exhibition at the museum in London, and tonight I'm going to a West Indies ex-servicemen do.

Folklorist Louise Bennett observed wryly, 'What joyful news Miss Mattie, I feel like my heart gonna burst. Jamaica people colonising England in reverse.' Five hundred and ten migrants from the Caribbean, including 18 stowaways, arrived with a fanfare at Tilbury Docks in Essex on June 22, 1948, a former World War II troop ship dubbed the "Black People's Mayflower". Immigrants dominated the news on that same midsummer morning. The Windrush event ranked second on the Pathe News headlines to the arrival in Britain from Hollywood of Ingrid Bergman, the Swedish actress.

Pathe News boomed out to cinemagoers, 'The Empire Windrush brings to Britain 500 Jamaicans. Many are ex-servicemen who know England. They served this country well. In Jamaica they couldn't find work. Discouraged but full of hope they sailed to Britain, citizens of the British Empire coming to the mother country with good intent.' My father, Simeon George, Rowe was one of them. He first came to Britain in 1943 as a teenaged RAF recruit.

After the war, he returned to the grinding poverty of the Jones Town West Kingston ghetto from which he had come. But, like his comrades, he paid his fare to return to the motherland on the troop deck of the Empire Windrush to escape Jamaica's crippling unemployment. Simeon is listed in the passenger's log as a 'barber' aged 24. Everyone had to give their trade.

All of the mainly Black passengers, who embarked at Trinidad, Jamaica, Bermuda, and Mexico, had responded to job advertisements in their local newspapers and favourable reports of work in Britain. Interestingly, 10 passengers are recorded as having gone to work for the BBC, where I started my broadcasting career. Jamaica's Daily Gleaner newspaper reported on May 13 1948, 'Among those preparing for the long voyage in search of employment are mechanics, welders, machinists, cooks, and many of whom style themselves simply as musicians.'

217

Arrival of the Empire Windrush and the British media

British press response to the arrival of the Empire Windrush a month later was welcoming, even if racism in wider society was soon to confront them. The sensationalist scare stories whipped up by unscrupulous politicians about hordes of Black immigrants threatening to 'swamp' this country were to come afterwards. Daily Mirror bosses sent a light aeroplane to greet the newcomers and the next day the paper trumpeted on its front page, 'Britain's day of rejoicing', over the now familiar photograph of the Empire Windrush.

But an Evening Standard headline indicated that racists, opposed to the black passengers settling in Britain, might cause trouble: 'Double guard on men of Jamaica. They are kept waiting aboard homeland ship.'

A Daily Graphic reporter painted a colourful picture. 'Dusky, eager young faces beneath panamas and pith helmets and sporting the gayest neck ties, mingled with late afternoon shoppers at Clapham South. These 240 tropical and zoot-suited Jamaicans were officially 'the friendless and jobless' immigrants from the liner Empire Windrush'.

The majority of newcomers found work within a month, mostly in factories. Those without places to stay were accommodated in the Clapham Deep Shelter, a part of the Northern Line tube that had been used as an air raid shelter during the war. The location of this shelter and use by its occupants of the nearby Labour Exchange in Coldharbour Lane, Brixton, next to where the The Voice newspaper is based today, gave rise to this part of London becoming the unofficial capital of Black London.

Questions in Parliament

Prime Minister Clement Attlee said, 'It would be a great mistake to regard these people as undesirables and unemployables. The majority of them are honest workers who can make a genuine contribution to our labour difficulties.' In the light of these positive words, the scandal of the bad accommodation given to the Empire Windrush homeless by the government was raised by Labour minister Tom Driberg and Brixton MP Marcus Lipton. As a result of a public row, which embarrassed the radical Attlee administration, better housing was found above ground. Five books by black authors, all of them journalists, have been published, one of them to coincide with the four-part BBC 2 Windrush programme.

Black soldiers in Roman invasion of Britain

Journalists keen to promote good race relations can learn a valuable lesson from the work of our colleagues who reported on the arrival on the Empire Windrush half a century ago. There are also important lessons to be learned from the Windrush. Black people didn't first arrive in Britain fifty years ago. We came here as soldiers in the Roman army before the English arrived. Emperor Severus, an African, was Supreme Commander of the Roman legions. But the Windrush symbolises the pioneer spirit, courage and determination of a colonised people prepared to take risks to start a new life for themselves.

Our parents fought for this country against the Nazis during the war. With their muscles and sweat, they made Britain great. And today, in the World Cup, Black youth are again the backbone of our national pride competing at France '98. I've been privileged to be working recently on a housing estate, which has suffered a bad press, Stonebridge, in Brent, finding and developing the amazing creative talent there with a community journalism course and writing competition.

The winner of the competition, by the way, was a female Somalian student, Fozia Ismail, whose words ring in my ears. If I may quote, 'There are too many who undervalue the importance of education and thus undervalue themselves. This isn't helped by the media's fascination with the gang culture in our area and the all-too-exaggerated images of Jamaican 'yardies' all over the place running riot...'

219

Black youth members of the Anti-Racist Alliance have staged several successful entertainment events. I am going with them to an international summer camp in Italy next week. They have confounded our critics by demonstrating considerable talent.

Black pride, Black politics and Black struggles

I have been a journalist, trade unionist and activist in Black politics for almost two decades. Alongside Jim Thakoordin, I helped to establish the Labour Party Black Section in 1983, which gave us the four black MPs four years later and played a role in founding the Black-led Anti-Racist Alliance in 1991. Increasingly, I am reminded of Malcolm X's comment about the news media, 'It has the power to make the guilty innocent and the innocent guilty'. No community understands this more than one made up of people of African-Caribbean and Asian descent - what I call the black community. Black, for me by the way, is a political term that unites all people of colour in their struggle against racism.

Right-wingers like Lord Tebbit insult us by saying we are not British enough. They want us to abandon our culture, religion, history and major contribution to civilisation as a condition of acceptance by this society. Gandhi poked fun at the Tebbit's view of this world when, on a visit to London, he was asked by a journalist what he thought of British civilisation. The Mahatma replied: 'It would be a good idea.' Professor Bhikhu Parekh, in the forward to the milestone Fourth National Survey of Ethnic Minorities in Britain, states, '...the demand for integration can be taken too far. Every society is articulated at several levels, and immigrants may choose to integrate into some of these and not others. They might fully participate in the economy, the conduct of public affairs, etc., but prefer to marry among themselves or adhere to their own traditional cultural beliefs and practices'. Bhikhu, professor of political theory at Hull University, goes on to say that if some black people choose to 'break out of their communities', obstacles should not be placed in their way., 'But if others decide differently, their choices should be respected. Identification of the wider community does not require the destruction of narrower identifications.'

The racists conveniently forget how Black people got here in the first place. That most reactionary of journalists, Paul Johnson, writing in the Daily Mail recently, described the slave trade which carried many of our ancestors to the Caribbean, Americas and subsequently to Britain, as the 'greatest act of human depravity in history, worse than the holocaust, worst than the Gulag.' Of course, Johnson went on to attempt to lessen the evil of white people involved by focusing on the role played by the Africans who sold their own people into bondage. Cities like London, Liverpool and Bristol were built up from the profits of slavery which paid for the industrial revolution in this country. Some would say it put the 'great' in Britain by making the country the world's major power at the time.

Author Ronald Segal says that, even though Britain was the first Western nation to withdraw from the slave trade, 'racism survived, resurgently accompanying the European scramble for Africa and informing the imperial vision.' Segal goes on to state that today 'individual blacks are acceptable for their success, while Blacks in general are still seen as different and threatening'.

The Black contribution to Britain's wealth did not stop the abolition of slavery. During the war, black servicemen and women fought against fascism; thousands of people, like my father who came as part of what was described as the 'first batch' of RAF recruits. He was sent to Filey camp in North Yorkshire with only sheep as company. Racists feared that if these virile young Black men were allowed any nearer to human life they would pose a danger to chaste English womanhood. After Filey camp, the West Indian RAF recruits were dispatched to the 'deep shelter' under Clapham Common, in south London. It is interesting to note that thing have not changed much in 50 years since the Windrush arrived because reports of the horrendous racism faced by Black servicemen and women are just as bad today.

221

Isn't it ironic that the army is currently using the face of one of their few black captains in a poster campaign titled 'Your Country Needs You'?

Black people in the building of Britain

As we survey Britain in 1998 - two years before the next millennium - and compare it with ten years ago, we can see that, in this nation of shopkeepers, the window display has changed. There are more Black faces. The music business is a good example. With a one billion pound annual turnover, it is Britain's fifth largest industry. But how many Black producers, managers, agents, promoters, or record company executives are there? So often the music business is a case of Black talent and white profit. Black people are grossly under-represented in many institutions. There may be a handful of lower court judges (all 96 High Court Judges are white), a handful of Queen's counsel, and no more than a dozen MPs and Peers who are black.

At government level, we can boast no more than a Junior Minister who is my friend the Brent South MP, Paul Boateng. By contrast, in sport, where talent rather than someone's subjective judgement holds sway, Black footballers dominate the Premier League. There are several Black Olympic gold medal winners.

But look inside Great Britain PLC. Look closer and it is still business as usual for the majority of Black folk, even a year after the election of a reforming Labour government. Broadcaster and chair of race think tank, the Runnymede Trust, Trevor Phillips remarked that if you went to the BBC or ITV early in the morning, you would think that these companies were run by Black people. But no, they are the cleaners, security, drivers, and kitchen staff. Broadcast journalists like Trevor and myself, though more common, are still an exception to the rule.

Blacks are still being denied equal access

Despite the 1976 Race Relations Act, which the government boasts is the toughest of its kind in Europe, black people are more than twice as

222

likely to be unemployed. While white unemployment is running at 8%, for African-Caribbeans it is 24% and Pakistanis and Bangladeshis it is 27%. When Black people do have a job, they are likely to be first in, last out. Ethnic minority men and women on average earn a quarter less than their similarly employed white counterparts. Despite the fact that Black people make up 5.5% of the population, our representation in the upper levels of the civil service, judiciary and corporate sector is less than 1%. There is not a single Black Permanent Secretary in the Civil Service. Only one Black person has risen beyond the rank of police superintendent.

Black people are disproportionately in prison and mental institutions although the levels of criminality and mental illness in our community do not justify this. Successive race relation laws - the last one passed by a Labour government in 1976 to soften the blow of racist immigration legislation they had brought in earlier - have pretty much eliminated the overt 'colour-bar' in our society. The one which openly allowed landlords to advertise 'No Blacks, No Irish, No Dogs'.

The 'colour bar' has been replaced by the 'glass-ceiling' of institutional racism, which is ever present. There is a more murderous form of discrimination in existence in the form of racist attacks that have increased by a staggering 25% over the last year, according to police statistics.

Racial harassment and attacks

The Police Studies Institute's Fourth National Service of Ethnic Minorities in Britain [that was] published last year suggests that as many as 250,000 Caribbeans and Asians experience racial harassment every year, including insults and abuse at the hands of strangers, neighbours, workmates or even the police. Stephen Lawrence, an 18 year old Black student, was murdered on the night of April 22, 1993, by a mob of racist thugs while he stood with a friend at a bus stop in Eltham, minding his own business.

223

I was telephoned by a family friend of the Lawrences the following day at the Anti-Racist Alliance office and from then onwards we spent every available hour with Stephen's parents, helping in whatever way possible. This senseless killing became the national cause celebre that symbolised all racist murders, perhaps because Stephen Lawrence was a clean-cut, A-Level student from a Christian family.

The boy next door, who wanted to be an architect, and just happened to be Black. His brutal murder was taken up, at the ARA's invitation, by Nelson Mandela, when he visited London. Yet, revealingly, no British government minister or member of the Royal family saw it fit to express any similar public concern. Rolan Adams, a 15-year-old black youth, was murdered by racist in 1991, at Thamesmead near to Eltham. So were Rohit Duggal and Orville Blair in the same area, leading the ARA to call this part of southeast London the 'racist murders capital of Britain'.

Yet the earlier racist murders were ignored by the media and politicians. It is no coincidence that the fascist British National Party had based their headquarters at nearby Welling. They mounted an aggressive 'rights for whites' campaign from their 'Nazi bunker'.

Persistent peaceful campaigning by the ARA and others led to the eventual closure of the headquarters. Meanwhile, Middle England, in the form of the previously hostile Daily Mail, joined the labour and anti-racist movement in championing the 'Justice for Stephen Lawrence' campaign. After the lamentable failure of the police murder investigation - starkly exposed at the current public enquiry - and the Lawrence family's own aborted private prosecution, the Daily Mail took the unprecedented step of naming Stephen's killers on its front page.

As well as agreeing to the family's demand for a judicial inquiry into the murder and the issues it raised, Home Secretary Jack Straw also announced his intention to bring into law all the legislation proposed by the ARA in our Racial Harassment Bill. A huge victory, some people might say, but one not credited to us by the news media or politicians who have instead dwelt on past political differences in the ARA to write us off. What they fail to say is that those differences are about an essential political principle: the right of the oppressed to lead their own struggle.

As a result of the weakness of the anti-fascist movement, it has been easier for prominent Black people to be victimised and our communities ignored. Local governments funding to Black groups has been slashed, forcing leading organisations to close and their vital work to be abandoned. Against this backdrop, there is the international scandal of Britain's record on the deaths of Black people in custody - something the ARA has raised with the Committee on the Elimination of Racial Discrimination at the United Nations. According to the pressure group Inquest, between 1969 and 1991 there were 69 'identified' Black deaths in custody. Of those, 37 were in police custody. Since 1991 there have been a further 43 identified Black deaths in custody of which 14 were in police custody.

Unlawful killing verdicts were returned by inquest juries recently in four cases of police custody deaths and yet no action was taken against the officers involved, who were not even suspended from duty during the investigation of their behaviour. This leads me to conclude that in Britain the police have a licence to kill black people in custody. The ARA is currently involved in the production of a pan-European educational anti-racist CD-ROM project being co-ordinated by the Danielle Mitterand Foundation in Paris. The French version of this important multi-media tool for educators was launched in Belgium, in the presence of a government minister and other dignitaries, on the anniversary of the end of the Second World War last year. We will be launching a British version in similar style later on this year.

We need to take advantage of the very latest new technologies - harness the huge talent that black people have in the field of electronics. Look how computer literate our children are. The way they dismantle computers, amplifiers, sound systems, and rebuild them. We're not just

225

dancers, musicians, sportsmen and women. We have the genius of inventors - traffic lights, light bulb, heart transplants.

Racism in the workplace

One humiliating example of racism that we put on CD-ROM involved two black waitresses, Freda Burton and Sonia Rhule. They were subjected to a torrent of racist and sexist abuse by 'comedian' Bernard Manning at a Derby Round Table dinner at the city's Pennine Hotel on 1st December 1994. Freda and Sonia at first lost their industrial tribunal case against the management of the hotel at which they had been working, but eventually they won substantial financial compensation on appeal.

The case set the important precedent that an employer has a duty to protect staff from racial discrimination. Local authorities are normally the largest employers of labour in our cities and towns. Just as with the transport and health services and, in this area, the motor industry, black labour keeps town halls working. Yet racism stalks us on a daily basis in the workplace.

Hackney council was recently damned in an official report, which found that black staff faced serious discrimination from managers. The pattern is not restricted to London. It is widespread throughout the country. Commission for Racial Equality (CRE) Chair Sir Herman Ousley put his finger on the problem when he told a management publication that 'human talent and energy lies trapped behind structures that discriminate or operate passively against a tradition of disadvantage'. He proposed the creation of 'league tables for employers, highlighting both those that have done well and those that have done badly. The worst performers could expect legal action to be taken against them by the CRE.'

Greenwich, the millennium borough, could go a long way toward redressing the balance through contracts compliance, the enforcement of equal opportunities on public-service providers backed up by ethnic record keeping and monitoring. That means proportional Black contracts and jobs where all the millennium projects are concerned.

When Atlanta hosted the Olympics, that is just what happened, so we can do it here too. Black politicians and their supporters must fight for contracts compliance to be brought in by the Labour government. This, more than most measures, will prove that Prime Minister Tony Blair is as serious as his counterpart President Bill Clinton in America about delivering for the black voters who put him into power.

As Bhikhu Parekh points out, 'Contrary to general belief, judiciously deployed positive discrimination is not incompatible with, but necessary to uphold the liberal principle of equal opportunity.' But we should not all hold our breath because, as Bhiku puts it, 'The fact that New Labour is all white is significant ... Could they not have done for ethnic minorities what they have done for women?'

If New Labour's slogan is 'Education, Education, Education' to this we must add: 'Organise, Organise, Organise'. Only this way will we be able to build on the historical gains of the Windrush generation and take our rightful place in society.

Thank you for listening."

Editor's insert:

Black people petitioning for a National Windrush Day in Britain

Petition Background (Preamble):

There has been a Black presence in Britain since Roman times. Seventeenth Century London was home to more than 10,000 Black residents. However it was the 492 Caribbean men and women and those that followed from other parts of the Commonwealth such as Africa,

227

India and Pakistan that played such a significant role in creating modern Britain. However, it has to be recognised that the seeds of modern migration started with 10,000 Caribbean service men and women who volunteered during World War II.

One of the key contributions of the Windrush Generation is making Britain more open and reflective based on the shared acknowledgment of social injustice and the values of hard work, tolerance and respect. The long history and campaigns for racial equality from the 1950s to the 1970s was the British equivalent of the American civil rights movement. Race relations and subsequent human rights legislation on gender, disability, age, religion and belief, and sexual orientation have made Britain more humane and socially aware.

This was reinforced by cultural dialogue on musical taste, food, life style and fashion, and the relationships by which Black, White, Asian and other communities created the multicultural nature, ethos and lifestyle which are now an accepted part of mainstream thinking and society.

This generation of people born between 1910-1930 will have passed away which means that the next Windrush celebrations in 2018 will be an empty and hollow affair. We will regret this as a nation for not taking individual and collective responsibility in systematically documenting their history as part of a legacy for the young people of all races and nationality regarding our contribution to Britain and beyond.

For Patrick Vernon, Writer and Campaigner, "It's time to commemorate and celebrate the contributions to Britain of black, Asian and other minority communities.

In 2008 after making my documentary *A Charmed Life* about the life of the Ex Serviceman Eddie Martin Noble I suggested that we should choose the day when the Empire Windrush docked at Tilbury in 1948 on the 22 June as a public holiday.

This is arguably the most powerful and iconic symbol of migration and the rise of modern day multicultural Britain to date. The Windrush is not simply about the 492 Caribbean men and women that arrived in Britain on that ship but everyone from the Empire and the Commonwealth who were British subjects and saw Britain as the mother country.

With the success of the Olympic Games in 2012 and with the latest census which highlights the current and future demographics of this country I believe it is time to commemorate and celebrate the contributions to Britain particularly over the last 65 years of Black, Asian and other minority communities. It would also remind us that Britain has been and will always be a nation of migration and a home for political refugees and asylum seekers.

Danny Boyle and Paulette Randle were aware of this history thus ensuring that the Windrush along with the creation of the NHS was part of the national narrative in the Opening Ceremony of the 2012 Olympics in London. There is now a growing demand from faith leaders, equality campaigners, politicians and high profile personalities who think that we should have public recognition of multicultural Britain using the Windrush as a powerful symbol around an annual programme of events or a public holiday.

Sadly the constant drip, drip references to the failure of multiculturalism and the loss of 'Britishness' as an inclusive concept creates much uncertainty and lack of confidence for young people and the most recent migrants to Britain, apart from the super-rich, who now feel under constant attack and scapegoated. A Windrush Day is important if we want a tolerant, respectful society especially if want to tackle all forms of political extremism and terrorism. Also the day could also be considered as an opportunity to celebrate our diversity and our shared history of struggle and achievement.

Such a day would prevent political parties from using the race card and immigration card to appease certain white voters and now a growing established Black and Asian middle class. Windrush Day would be

229

different from celebrating Commonwealth Day which not many people are aware of. It would be similar but not the same as Holocaust Day which takes place on the January 27 every year to commemorate the victims and families of Jewish and other people affected by the Holocaust but also modern genocide and extermination of ethnic groups globally.

This adds to the importance of teaching about the Windrush as part of the national curriculum for a generation of young people who can learn the history, survival techniques and strategies which can help them to influence the world they live in today. Windrush Day would further add value to events such as Black History Month /African History Month, Notting Hill Carnival, Diwali and Eid which have now been embraced by central and local government, education with inclusion in the national curriculum, museums and the arts.

The Windrush Generation is now disappearing as many of these pioneers have passed away, suffering from long term health conditions or languishing in residential or nursing homes. A number have immigrated back to their countries of birth.

Many of those born between 1910-1940 may not be around at the next Windrush celebrations in 2018.The question we need to ask ourselves is why wait either every five or 10 years to celebrate this achievement.

We will regret it as a country if we fail to take individual and collective responsibility for systematically documenting their history and contribution to Britain and beyond, as a legacy for young people of all ethnicities and nationalities."

Please write to your Member of Parliament if you wish to support the Campaign for a National Windrush Day.

Chapter Eleven

Jim Thakoordin - Race Relations in Britain

Paper delivered to Race Equality Advisers, Local Government Officers and University Staff, at Dalhousie University, Halifax, Canada in 1994.

Mrs Jayaben Desai strike leader
At Grunwick, 1976

Introduction

231

This paper is about race relations in Britain and to a lesser extent Europe. It briefly examines both the historical and contemporary aspects of race relations; including the social, economic, political and cultural experience of Black people. Black people in the context of this document refer to descendants of Africans, Asian and other non-white visible minorities. This paper identifies some of the difficulties facing Black people and the various attempts by Governments, institutions, employers and local authorities to address the racial discrimination and disadvantage through legislation; positive action and measures; policy and strategy initiatives and racism/anti-racism awareness training.

In order to understand racism and race relations in contemporary Britain one should have some knowledge of when and how Black people settled in Britain. It is important to understand the historical, economical and power relations, which have characterised the perceptions and feelings of white people towards Black people. Historically Blacks have been seen as being inherently inferior, morally, mentally, culturally and spiritually. They were regarded as being uncivilised, sub-human savages who were lazy, dirty and undesirable. Some of these stereotyped assumptions still exist today amongst substantial numbers of Europeans.

The presence of Blacks in Britain has always caused considerable concern. The stereotyping of Blacks has changed very little during the centuries and so has the perceived remedies. Restriction of Black immigrants; repatriation; discrimination; prejudice and marginalisation are still pervasive in Britain in the 1990's despite extensive legal, organisational and policy changes even in the public sector.

Historical Aspects

According to Peter Fryer, "Staying Power – The History of Black People in Britain", Pluto Press, 1984, there were Africans in Britain before the English came here. Some were soldiers in the Roman Imperial Army, which invaded and occupied the southern part of

232

England for three and half centuries. Africans remained in Britain for some 400 or 500 years after the Romans had left. Amongst the Black population were soldiers, slaves and servants.

During imperialism, colonialism, and slavery Blacks were brought to Britain in sizeable numbers. By the 16th century Blacks had settled in many areas of the United Kingdom especially around the large ports and urban areas such as Liverpool, Bristol, London, Manchester, Cardiff and Glasgow. The Black population in Britain constantly increased during the 16th, 17th and 18th centuries with the continuation of the slave trade until its gradual abolition in Britain, which started with the Mansfield Judgement in 1772. Slavery was not formally abolished until 1834 in the colonies although historians have argued that it continued in some shape or form for many years after formal abolition.

Blacks were brought to Britain between 1500 and 1600 mainly for the purpose of being servants to wealthy families; used as status symbols by the rich; as prostitutes or sexual conveniences for the rich; and as court entertainers. Many Blacks ran away from their owners and masters and lived independent lives as sailors, entertainers or labourers. In the 1570s Queen Elizabeth was shown with a group of Black musicians and dancers entertaining her courtiers and herself. However entertaining the Queen may have found the Black entertainers, she was nevertheless opposed to their presence in her country, arguing that there were enough people in England without blackamoors.

On 11th July 1596, when the population of England was only 3,000,000 Queen Elizabeth sent an open letter to the Lord Mayor of London, and the Mayors and Sheriffs in other towns in the following terms:

> *"Her Majesty understanding that several blackamoors have lately been brought into this realm, of which kind of people there are already too many here..... Her Majesty's pleasure therefore is that those kind of people should be expelled from*

233

the land...."

In 1601 the Queen issued a proclamation in which she declared herself:

> *"Highly discontented to understand the great number of negars and Blackamoors which (as she is informed) are crept into this realm.... Who are fostered and relieved here to the great annoyance of her own people that want the relief, which those people consume, as also for that the most of them are infidels, having no understanding of Christ or His Gospel" (Peter Fryer "Staying Power – The History of Black People in Britain").*

From 1621 onwards the trade in Black people as slaves was quite common in the large cities of Britain. In 1770 there were 8,000 Black slaves in London alone, forming some 3% of the capital's population of about 650,000. However, despite various attempts to rid the realm of Blacks they continue to increase in many towns and cities. The gradual reduction of the slave trade in Britain resulted in many freed Blacks trying to find work to support themselves. It was extremely difficult for many of them who drifted into prostitution, vagrancy, unemployment and destination.

When the government's attention was drawn to the plight of the freed slaves its response was to repatriate them. It offered free passage and £12 per head for every Black who agreed to be deported to Freetown in Sierra Leone in Africa. 411 Blacks and 60 white prostitutes were bundled off to Freetown in 1786. A hundred years later the number of Blacks in Britain reduced drastically because of fewer newcomers, inter-marriage and those returning to their country of origin.

However, with the growth of colonialism; imperialism; growth in world trade; and the economic and political domination of many African, Asian and Caribbean countries, Black people began to arrive in Britain in sizeable numbers as students and seamen in the late 19th Century.

Slavery and the Industrial Revolution

Slavery, which was linked with colonialism and imperialism, generated the wealth, which was instrumental in the creation of the industrial revolution in Britain. According to Ramsay Muir, "A History of Liverpool" published by Williams and Northgate, 1907.

> *"The slave trade was the pride of Liverpool, for it flooded the town*
> *with wealth which invigorated every industry, provided the capital*
> *for docks, enriched and employed the mills of Lancashire, and*
> *afforded the means for opening out new and ever new lines of trade.*
> *Beyond a doubt it was the slave trade which raised Liverpool from*
> *A struggling port to be one of the richest and most prosperous trading*
> *centres in the world."*

The same could be said for all the major towns and cities and the industries which grew from the highly profitable slave trade and colonialism. The cruelty of slavery both in Britain and her colonies which lasted for around 400 years; the exploitation, suffering and oppression of tens of millions of the Blacks for centuries; and the exploitation of the natural resources of the countries under colonialism, coupled with economic subordination to the British economy cannot be ignored by either the Black or White people in Europe and North America.

Blacks in Britain 1914 – 1945

The outbreak of the First World War in 1914 brought about dramatic changes for Blacks in Britain. Opportunities were created for many workers including women and Blacks. Black labourers were recruited to work in munitions and chemical factories recruited to the merchant

235

navy and replaced white men who joined the army and navy. Many Blacks in Britain and in the colonies joined the war on behalf of the allies and fought in Europe and elsewhere. By the end of the war there were some 20,000 Black people in Britain. During the war regiments made up almost entirely of Black soldiers fought in Europe and Africa. Many were commended for their bravery. Racism was rife in the army and even on the battlefield. Blacks were often referred to by the white soldiers as 'monkeys' and 'apes'. Shortly before the end of the War in 1918 about 2,000 wounded soldiers including some 50 Blacks were brought back to military hospital in Belmont Road, Liverpool. The Black soldiers were subjected to regular racial taunts and abuse. On one occasion some 400 to 500 white soldiers went into battle with 50 Black soldiers. The Blacks were blamed for the rioting but a War Office enquiry found otherwise, ("The Belmont Hospital Affair", African Telegraph. 1/8 December, 1918).

After the war Blacks found themselves once again at the rough end of life in Britain. White workers demanded jobs occupied by Blacks. Many White workers refused to work with Black workers. Black workers were being sacked to make way for White workers in the sugar refineries in Liverpool and in the docks in Cardiff. There were riots in Liverpool, Cardiff and elsewhere in Britain as Blacks were attacked on site. Racial violence was very common. Blacks organised to defend and protect themselves against constant racism. Blacks were often turned out of their accommodation for having no jobs and no money. Even hostels accommodating Black men were targets for the racists. (Peter Fryer, "Staying Power – The History of Black People in Britain" Pluto Press, 1994, pages 289 –321).

Blacks were not only attacked and ridiculed by self confessed fascists and racists but were also ridiculed and stereotyped by those who claimed to be radicals, liberals, socialists, trade unionists and feminists. The post-war depression of the 1920's and 1930's made the conditions for Blacks much worse than the rest of the population. Many blacks lived in terrible poverty and some turned towards the trade unions and radical political parties for support and involvement. A

236

number were elected as Councillors, Mayors and Members of Parliament.

Black soldiers fought for the allies

During the Second World War there was a substantial increase in the number of Black people in Britain, which included some 35,000 Black American soldiers. Between 1939 and 1945 many regiments consisting mainly of Black soldiers fought in Europe once again, on the side of the allies. Racial tensions, harassment and attacks inside and outside the army and other services were commonplace. Many White Americans brought their prejudice and racism with them to Britain. Several questions were raised in the House of Commons and debates took place in the Cabinet about situation faced by the Black soldiers in Britain. Many institutions and organisations were apprehensive about the way they should treat or respond to Black soldiers.

Sikh and Muslim soldiers along with millions of Others fought for the allies against the fascists. Over 2 million Asians and African soldiers died in the war around the world.

237

For example, the wife of a vicar in Weston-Super-Mare during a talk to local women suggested a six-point code of behaviour, which included the following advice:

- White women must have no relationship with coloured men;
- On no account must coloured troops be invited to the homes of white women;
- If she is walking on the pavement and a coloured soldier is coming towards her, she should cross to the other pavement.

Quoted in the Sunday Pictorial, 6 September 1942.

The major General responsible for Administration in Southern Command issued to District Commanders and Regional Commissioners a set of "Notes on Relations with Coloured Troops." According to the author, wherever they lived, however, they possessed certain fundamental characteristics, which had to be borne in mind when dealing with them in a British context:

> "While there are many coloured men of high mentality and cultural distinction, the generality are of a simple mental outlook.
> They work hard when they have no money and when they have money prefer to do nothing until it is gone. In short they have not the white man's ability to think and act to a plan. The spiritual outlook is well know and their nature. They respond to sympathetic treatment. They are natural psychologists in that they can size up a white man's character and can take advantage of a weakness. Too much freedom, too wide association with white men, tend to make them lose their heads and have on occasions led to civil strife. This occurred after the last war due to too free treatment and associations which they had experienced in France."

Appendix to Sir James Grigg, Secretary of State for War memorandum for the Cabinet 3 October 1942, WP (42) in CAB 66/29.

238

After the war Black people in Britain continued to suffer from racial discrimination and racism. A number of soldiers stayed on in Britain after the war and a number of Black people began to arrive in Britain in search of work. The first wave of economic immigrants from British colonies started with the landing of the SS Windrush at Tilbury Dock on 22 June 1948. The 1948 Nationality Act had granted United Kingdom citizenship to citizens of Britain's colonies and former colonies. The British passport gave them the right to come live and work in Britain.

Race Relations during the 1950's & 1960's

Between 1948 and 1958 Black immigration from Africa, the Caribbean and the Asian sub-continent grew steadily. In 1948 less than 1,000 Black people arrived in Britain to seek employment. By 1954 some 24,000 Black immigrants arrived from the Caribbean. 26,000 arrived in 1956, 22,000 in 1957 and 16,000 in 1958. By the end of 1958 there were some 125,000 Caribbeans/West Indians and around 55,000 from the Asian sub-continent.

Many Blacks in the Caribbean, India and Pakistan were recruited by London Transport and the Department of Health with full support of the British Government to fill the jobs which many white workers were reluctant to do. These jobs were in transport, the health service and in manufacturing. They were characterised by low pay and unsociable hours.

Post-war Britain needed labour to sustain the growth and development and it was not surprising that immigrants from the colonies and ex-colonies filled this gap. The cycle had turned a full circle from being unwelcome to Britain and subject to repatriation nearly two hundred years previously to being recruited to work in Britain. However, despite the presence of less than 200,000 Blacks in Britain there were enormous debates regarding the uncontrolled flow of Black people to Britain; and Blacks being responsible for crime and prostitution; slum housing; unemployment; disease and poor environment. Many private employers, and even public sector employers apart from the Health Service and London Transport employed Blacks only when white labour was not available. Blacks were employed in the lower paid and low status jobs. Many industries such as banking, insurance retail, administrative, clerical supervisory, management, construction, mining, hotel and catering, gas, water, electricity, telecommunication and local government jobs were generally unavailable to Blacks. Employers, landlords and providers of services were free to discriminate against Blacks on the basis of skin colour or ethnic origin.

The Notting Hill Riots

Racial discrimination, harassment and marginalisation of Blacks continued almost unchecked for centuries in Britain. In 1958 there were riots in London (Notting Hill) and in Nottingham some 200 miles away from London. By the end of 1958 and the beginning of 1959 open conflicts involving Black and white people were common in London and in many large towns and cities in Britain. This led to calls from politicians of all persuasions for an end to immigration. Racial tension and conflicts escalated in 1960 and 1961. People openly talked about the colour problem. Blacks were seen as the problem. Instead of addressing white racism politicians and institutions as well as the media pandered to racism. The Conservative Government against opposition from the Labour Opposition, introduced the Commonwealth Immigration Act 1962, which became operative on 1 July.

This measure restricted Black immigration to those who had been issued with employment vouchers and dependants of Black people already settled in Britain. At the time of the 1962 Act, which grossly restricted the flow of Blacks in Britain, the Black population totalled only around 200,000 out of a population of over 50,000,000 people.

By 1962 the following arguments were dominant in discussions relating to race, racism and race relations:

- Britain had a colour problem because too many Blacks were here;
- Black people were the source of the problem;
- Good race relations was dependent on the size of the black population;
- Race relations would improve with severe restrictions on newcomers;
- Black people should integrate and assimilate into British culture and lifestyles;
- There were insufficient jobs, housing and health care for the indigenous people let alone foreigners;
- Blacks were lazy, dirty, and were exploiting the welfare state;
- Blacks were not welcome as neighbours, their presence would lower the standard of the neighbourhood;
- Blacks were bad neighbours. They were living in overcrowded houses, and they were noisy, uneducated and much less desirable as neighbours than British people;
- Blacks were taking jobs, houses and health care from British people;
- All Blacks were immigrants/non British even though they had settled in parts of Britain for centuries;
- Blacks were a liability to Britain;
- They were prepared to work for less money and accept a lower standard of living;
- British culture, standards, values and way of life were being swamped by Black people; and
- Britain was a small over-crowded island, and had to have a strict immigration policy.

The 1964 General Election, which resulted in a Labour Government after 13 years of rule by Conservative Governments, was a bitterly fought contest. Race was a major topic of discussion. A conservative candidate Peter Griffiths fought on an openly racist platform: demanding the ending of immigration and the repatriation of "the coloureds." His slogan was: "if you want a nigger for a neighbour

241

vote Labour." Peter Griffiths defeated a senior Labour minister and won the Smethwick seat in Parliament.

The 1960's especially from 1965 onwards were a period of growing politicisation and Black awareness particularly in America, Britain, France, Africa and the Caribbean. Black radicals either formed separate civil rights organisations or attached themselves to radical socialist, or liberal political and liberation movements. Both confidence and militancy increased amongst Black people and their organisations. Many liberal people, including feminists, students and politicians, supported the demands for an end to discrimination and racial violence against Black people. Demands for equal access, rights and justice for Black people were widely debated alongside the arguments by the right wing and racist politicians and people who were arguing for further immigration and repatriation of Black people.

Labour's Record on Race

The Labour Government elected in 1964 having initially opposed to the Immigration Act 1962, boldly implemented the 1962 Act having accepted that it was necessary for good race relations. However, having decided that strict immigration control was a necessary prerequisite to good race relations and racial integration, it decided to impose further control of Black immigration to Britain by restricting the number of employment vouchers available to potential Black immigrants from 30,000 to 8,500 annually through the 1965 White Paper "Immigration from the Commonwealth. The White Paper was commonly regarded by anti-racists as further concessions to racists. Institutional racism became respectable to some extent. Extremism was increasingly being regarded as 'common-sense.' Of course, the racists would never be satisfied. At first they were opposed to Black immigration, then they shifted towards restricting the number of entrants, followed by the call for an end to immigration, and finally, repatriation. The numbers game meant little to the racists whose strategy was clearly designed to intimidate the Black population and to reverse the flow of Black immigration.

In 1968 the Labour Government introduced yet another piece of nakedly discriminatory legislation. The Commonwealth Immigration Act 1968 was steam-rollered through Parliament in a record time of only three days of emergency debate. The sole purpose of this legislation was to restrict the entry into Britain of East African Asians who were mainly living in Kenya and were holders of British passports. The British government broke a pledge by previous governments to honour rights of British citizens to enter Britain. This right of entry was removed from East African Asians who were holders of British passports. It did not restrict the right of white British passport holders living abroad for generations to enter Britain.

Amongst the most vocal, respectable, and powerful voices supporting the anti-immigration lobby was the Right Honourable Enoch Powell, Conservative Member of Parliament for Wolverhampton Southwest. On 9 February 1968 he stated:

> *"There is a sense of hopelessness and helplessness which comes over persons who are trapped or imprisoned, when all their efforts to attract attention and assistance brings no response. This is the kind of feeling which you in Walsall and we in Wolverhampton are experiencing in the case of continued flow of immigration into our towns... Recently those of us who live in the Midlands and in other areas directly affected have been startled to learn that a provision in the Kenya Independence Act and similar British legislation has the unexpected effect that some 200,000 Indians in Kenya alone have become literally indistinguishable from the people of the United Kingdom, so that they have an absolute right of entry to this Country." (Smithies B and Fiddick P. Enoch Powell on Immigration, London Sphere Books Ltd. 1966).*

The speech had the effect of panicking the Labour government into passing the 1968 Immigration Act.

This legislation together with the 1962 Immigration Act, and the 1965 White Paper, legitimised the notion that Black people were the source of racial tension and conflict, and that they were responsible for what was seen as the "race problem."

The sole purpose of these Acts was to restrict Black immigration and to allow entry to white immigration. The 1968 Act Immigration Act also included the setting-up of a Body to foster good race and community relations through a national and local framework, which established local Community Relations Councils. Many white people including substantial numbers of trade union members were pleased about the further restrictions imposed on Black immigration, but angry at what they saw as appeasement of Black people, by seeking to ban discriminatory advertisements.

Before the 1968 Race Relations Act discriminatory advertisements which included "No Coloured" or, "Europeans Only" were quite common. Whilst the Act stopped such advertisements being openly displayed, it had very little effect in stopping discrimination in practice.

The various official and research documents continued to highlight the severe inequality experienced by Black people in almost every sphere of British society. Racial discrimination was widely practised by institutions, organisations and individuals in jobs, housing, services and access to opportunities. The PEP (Political & Economic Planning) Reports of 1967 and 1974 explained in detail the extent and implications of the systemic discrimination against Black people which pervaded and transcended every aspect of life in Britain.

During the 1960's the revival and growth of the fascist and racist organisations were met with organised resistance by Blacks, especially those who were proclaiming and projecting Black liberation through "Black Power" and "Black is Beautiful." Throughout the history of the Black presence in Britain there were indigenous people who were supportive of their struggles for equal treatment. Such radicals joined with Blacks in marches, demonstrations and at meetings expressing solidarity in fighting racism.

244

Race Relations in the 1970's

The Immigration Act of 1971 which was introduced by a Conservative government, and came into force in 1973, changed the status of most Commonwealth immigrants to that of aliens. The Act divides people into 'patrials' and 'non-patrials.' Patrials are British passport holders who were born, or whose parents or at least one grandparent were born in the U.K. The Act opens the door to immigration wider than at any time since restriction began, because it grants unlimited rights of entry to millions of Commonwealth whites settled in Canada, America, Australia, New Zealand and Southern Africa. This Act is blatantly racist and has been accepted as such by many politicians and writers on the subject of race, immigration and nationality. The Labour opposition in Parliament bitterly criticised the 1971 Act but as before retained it during their return to power between 1974 and 1979.

During the 1970's racial discrimination, harassment and violence continued. By the end of the 1970's almost half of the Black population living in Britain were born here. Britain was rapidly becoming a multi-cultural, multi-racial society. There were some two million Black people in Britain. The Trade Union & Labour Relations Act 1974; the Employment Protection Act 1975, and the Employment Protection (Consolidation) Act 1978, passed by a Labour government provided some protection for Black workers in employment. However the most important piece of legislation was the Race Relations Act 1976 (RR Act) which replaced the Race Relations Acts of 1965 and 1968, and passed by a Labour government covers discrimination in employment and training, education, housing, and the provisions of goods and services. The 1965 Act created the criminal offence of incitement to racial hatred, which made it an offence to use speech, written word or illustration in public which were either abusive, threatening or insulting, or were likely to stir up racial hatred. The 1976 RR Act transferred this offence to the Public Order Act 1936 and it is now contained in the Public Order Act 1986. The overwhelming majority of people prosecuted under the 1965 Act were Black people.

Few white people were prosecuted under the Public Order Act 1936 or the Race Relations Act 1965.

Race Relations Act 1976

The 1976 RR Act with certain exceptions outlaws both direct and indirect discrimination on grounds of colour, race nationality and ethnic or national origin. It excludes; however, discrimination based on religion, politics or culture. The RR Act established the Commission for Racial Equality (CRE) whose stated goals include working towards the elimination of discrimination; providing advice and assistance to institutions, employers and the public in promoting equality of opportunity and good relations between the races; keeping under review the working of the Act; drawing up and submit proposals for amending the Act to the Secretary of State.

The CRE has the power to:

- Investigate organisations that it thinks may be practising racial discrimination, and to warn people and institutions to stop discriminatory practices and if they fail to comply, to issue non-discrimination notices where investigations disclose unlawful acts of discrimination;
- Request compliance with the Act and instruct those who have been issued with notices to keep the CRE informed for up to five years of progress relating to changes aimed at ending any discriminatory practices;
- Power to apply to a court of law for an order requiring compliance by the offender; and
- Power to issue Codes of Practice (good practice guide) which are not legally binding but could be taken into consideration when addressing cases of racial discrimination.

The CRE reviewed the Act in 1986 and again in 1992. The recommendations made in 1986 and 1992 are yet to be addressed by the

Secretary of State. Amongst the recommendations made in 1986 were the following:

- Improving the definition of discrimination;
- Reducing the number of exemptions from the provisions of the Act;
- Providing for specialist tribunals to hear all discrimination cases;
- Redefining the CRE's formal investigations powers;
- Providing for the CRE's formal investigations powers;
- Providing for the CRE to have access to an independent tribunal of fact across the range of its law enforcement activities;
- Improving the remedies for dealing with proven discrimination; and
- Improving a number of the mechanisms for bringing about change.

Changes recommended in the 1992 review of the Act included the following:

- Employers should have a statutory obligation to carry out monitoring;
- Employers should develop equality targets;
- All public authorities should ensure that all their contractors are equal opportunities employers;
- The CRE should be able to act like an inspectorate to examine major areas for racial equality;
- A special division of industrial tribunals should be developed, to handle discrimination cases;
- Legal aid should be extended to cover racial discrimination cases; and
- Compensation levels should be raised for victims of discrimination.

Cases related to racial discrimination at work are normally dealt with at industrial tribunals and the maximum compensation is around £11,000. Most cases for racial discrimination when proven are settled for awards of between a few hundred pounds to the maximum. The average compensation is about £1,000. A private Member's Bill is currently going through Parliament to remove the maximum award in line with recent changes in cases of sex discrimination.

The Act itself is seen as being weak and to a large extent ineffective. There are certain exemptions from the Act. For example government activities are outside the remedial provisions of the Act. The Act could easily be altered by Ministers of the Crown through Orders in Council; or in pursuance of any instrument made under any enactment by a Minister of the Crown; or in order to comply with any condition or requirement imposed by any Minister of the Crown.

Section 41(2) extends to these government circulars and to ministerial pronouncements, where they concern matters of nationality and residence. The government is therefore free to discriminate by decree, and without having proper debates in Parliament relating to changes of the Act.

The RR Act (section 71) states that "it shall be the duty of every local authority to make appropriate arrangements with the view to securing that their various functions are carried out with due regard to the need:

- To eliminate unlawful racial discrimination; and
- To promote equality of opportunity, and good race relations, between persons of different racial groups.

Section 11 of the 1966 Local Government Act also provides local authorities with additional funding to address specific needs of Black people. Most of the additional funding has been used for education and training in schools.

The scheme of the Race Relations Act 1976 closely mirrors that of the Sex Discrimination Act 1975. The first three types of discrimination are direct discrimination, indirect discrimination and victimisation.

Race Relations in the 1980's and 1990's

In May 1979 a Conservative government was elected and the following general elections in 1983, 1987 and 1992 resulted in victories for the Conservatives. Whilst the question of race was never a major issue during general election campaigns it was always a card which certain conservative politicians would play. For example even the Prime Minister Mrs Thatcher stated on television her concerns and the concerns of "the British people" that "Britain was perceived as being swamped by people of a different culture."

During this period the focus on race moved substantially from immigration and ethnocentric racism to Eurocentric racism with major concerns on refugees, asylum seekers and illegal Black immigration. Faced with social and economic destabilisation; high unemployment; increased levels of crime and violence; and less resources allocated to social and welfare needs the European countries particularly those which constitute the European Community (EC) were anxious not to encourage refugees, asylum seekers and illegal immigrants to Europe. The EC countries collectively introduced measures to achieve this and as a result the percentage of asylum-seekers granted asylum in Europe decreased from about 65% to around 10%. Individual EC members such as Britain, France and others introduced additional arrangements to reduce if not to stop more Black people entering their country under whatever status.

Racism within a Western European Context

Two new phenomena have raised their heads since 1980 in Western and Eastern Europe and in other parts of the world. The first one is the "new racism" which emerged with the decline of the Soviet Union; the decline and substitution of socialist ideals and the attempts to divide the

249

world on racial borders. The second phenomenon is the revival of monetarism linked with an increasingly right wing ideology and practices, had gradually transformed into a tide of xenophobia and the revival of neo-fascist, nationalist and populist political parties.

The re-enforcement of capitalist ideals and the restructuring of the capitalist economies resulted in mass unemployment; attack on living standards and the rights of workers; reductions in the public sector and public expenditure; rising poverty and homelessness; increasing criminal behaviour; urban unrest; and destabilisation of various institutions, cultures and values. For the racists the continuing situation for over a decade of high unemployment (some 12 million in the EC and around 3 million in the UK); the fear of unemployment; decline in inner city areas; and threats to living standards have provided opportunities to revive the irrational and destructive racist ideology.

This ideology and its growth amongst the young people in Europe may of whom are unemployed and disappointed with their lives, the racist/fascist ideology provided a framework for them to become involved and to self achieve esteem and recognition. This "new racism" constitutes a serious threat not only to Blacks and good race relations in Europe but also a serious threat to liberal and democratic forms of politics and institutions. This links up with the concept that sees racism as being composed of a triad of "isms": "classism" which for example, reflects the hierarchisation of society along class lines; "sexism" which is based on the establishment and defence of supremacy in respect of gender, and "racism" which constitutes the social demarcation of power, and the abuse/misuse of that power to deny people their civil, economic, social, political rights and liberties."

For some people the "new racism" reflects the decline of industrialisation and the class conflict, whilst others see it as a combination of the end of colonialism, and the emerging of situations where groups of people, especially in poor inner city areas are increasingly becoming a new underclass. The white people generally blame the Blacks for the decline in living conditions; poorer welfare services and the weakening of certain socio/economic safeguards. The destabilisation and dis-integration of nation states, particularly in Eastern Europe, and conflicts based on ethnic and religious differences results in reshaping not only geographical boundaries, but also race relations in the whole of Europe.

The "new racism" could also be linked with the globalisation of the world's economy; the emergence of powerful economies like the Japanese and South Korea; the marginalisation of certain groups of skilled workers due to rapid technological changes; serious decline in certain traditional industries and occupations; and the decline of power, influence and control resulting from the global re-structuring of the global capitalism.

Over 20 million Black people in Europe

There are some 20 million Black people in Western Europe (the majority were born in Europe) and they all faced the common enemy of racism which manifests itself in racial harassment and attacks; disproportionately high levels of unemployment and poor housing; marginalisation; less power and resources; high poverty levels; stereotyping; prejudice and discrimination; and fear of the future. In Britain alone 31 Black people have been murdered by racists as defined by the police. Since the 1980's racial attacks and violence have become increasingly common throughout Europe. In German, France, Belgium, Britain and in other European countries racial attacks and murders motivated by racial hatred are on the increase. Black communities are becoming increasingly worried, afraid and isolated. In many cases of racial violence and murders the Black community often expressed their disappointment at the failures of the law to identify and prosecute the criminals. Confidence in the law in preventing and dealing with racial violence by Black people is minimal. Attempts to make racial harassment and attacks a criminal offence in Britain has so far failed to secure Parliamentary support, even though the CRE is and has been advocating this policy for many years.

251

Black People in Britain and the impact on Race Relations

Demographic Factors

The 1991 Census of Population of Great Britain was the first to contain a specific question of the ethnic origin of respondents. Whilst the Census figures are by far the most up-to-date statistics available on demographic details they are not wholly accurate. In fact it is estimated that they could very well under-represent the Black population by up to 5% because of failures to include all the residents for a variety of reasons.

However, according to the Census there were some 58.9 million people in Great Britain, of whom 94.5% were white, and 2.7 million or, 5.5% were non white (Black).

Of the Black population, 1.5% were of Indian origin, 0.9% Pakistanis; 0.9% Caribbeans/West Indians; 0.4% Africans; 0.3% Bangladeshi, 0.3% Chinese; 0.3% Black-other and 0.9% (one in every six non-white person) were listed as other. The "other" non-white population is likely to represent a substantial number of people from mixed (Black and White) parentage. The Labour Force surveys of 1985 and 1986 reported that some 10% or, 255,000 non-white people in Britain were of mixed race. Almost one in every hundred marriages in Britain is a mixed marriage involving a white and a Black person.

Over a quarter (25.6%) of Black population was living in inner London; 16.9% in outer London; 14.6% in the West Midlands and 8.2% in West Yorkshire. Over 50% of the Black population was living in London and South East of England. The Black population is very concentrated and in many local urban areas it can represent up to 55% of the local population. The majority of the Black population, particularly the Muslim population is growing at a much higher rate that the rest of the total British population due to less family planning and larger families. In many schools in the large urban areas the overwhelming majority of the school population in Black, mainly Asians. The Black population is a relative young population and there were some 1.6 million, representing 4.7% of the total population of working age.

Employment/Unemployment Characteristics

For Black men in employment 53% were in manual occupations compared with around 52% for white workers. The proportion of Black workers in non-manual work was broadly similar to that of white workers (47%). However, there were considerable variations between Black workers from different ethnic and age groups. According to the Labour Force Surveys 1989 and 1991 unemployment for Black men was 12.7% compared to 6.9% for white men. The situation for women was 11% and 6.8% respectively. Unemployment for men from Pakistan and Bangladesh was 21.4%, compared to African/Caribbean at 15.1% and 9.9% for Indians. For young Blacks
between 16 and 24 years the unemployment rate was 22% compared to 12% for white people within the same age group.

As far as qualifications are concerned the situation is almost similar for Black and white people in the 16 to 24 age group; 6% of Black and white people have higher qualifications; 73% of white people have other qualifications and 65% of Black people have similar qualifications; and 21% of white people have no qualifications compared to 30% of Black people in the 16-24 age range. The situation is not a great deal dissimilar for the 25-44-age range. These statistics are broadly reflected in various reports produced by the CRE and the Policy Studies Institute (PSI) in 1992 and 1993. The figures quoted are mainly official figures representing those who have registered as unemployed. These figures reflect only around 7- to 80 per cent of the actual numbers unemployed. A very high proportion of Asians is in self-employment in the retail and catering trade with high levels of under-employment.

Black people are grossly over-represented in shift working (25% compared to 15% for white workers); low paid and low status jobs despite their qualifications; and are paid much less for doing

253

similar work to white workers because of poor promotion prospects and lower status work. Black applicants have to apply for up to five times the number of jobs before they are offered a post. Racial discrimination, harassment and marginalisation of Black workers in employment are on the increase, and this trend is reflected in various official reports.

Racial Harassment and Racial Attacks

Racial harassment and racial attacks are well under-represented in official statistics because of the fear of further attacks. In July 1993, the Minister of State for the Home Office reported to a Home Affairs Select Committee on Racial violence that there might be between 130,000 and 140,000 racially motivated attacks reported each year, and that the "true figure" could be as high as 330,000. In 1992 ten people died as a result of what are believed to have been racially motivated murders. Between 1981 and 1993 it was estimated that up to 55 people might have lost their lives through racially motivated violence in Britain. Many Black and Jewish families are living in constant fear of racially motivated attacks and invariably the police appear to be unable to prosecute even a fraction of the aggressors, even when they are known to the police. The fascists are also targeting Jews for their attacks.

Fortunately, very few Jews live in the decaying/deprived parts of the inner city areas. The police will not proceed with prosecutions unless there are independent witnesses who are prepared to attend court and give evidence against the aggressors. Racial attacks are more likely to take place in working class areas with poor housing stock often owned by local authorities. These areas are also likely to have high crime rates; high unemployment; poor environment and less opportunities available locally. Blacks are frequently seen as being responsible for most of the problems in the deprived inner city areas even when they are the worst victims, and suffer more than the white residents from multiple deprivation of poor employment opportunities; housing; education; health and welfare services.

Racist and Fascist Groups

The increase in racial violence must be seen against the growth of racist and fascist groups in Britain and indeed Europe. The British National Party (BNP) is a fast growing political movement in Britain. Fascist parties are growing in every Western European country. The Neo-nazi parties in Germany are growing in confidence and support, and so is the BNP in Britain. On 13th September 1993, the BNP won its first ever Council election in one of the most deprived areas of London with around one third Black population. The BNP lost the seat to Labour, which also won control of the Council on 5th May 1994. The BNP did not create the racism in the area; instead racism gave rise to the BNP. The local Liberal Democrats Party, which controlled the Tower Hamlets Council since 1986, had a long history of marginalising the local Black population (mainly Bangladeshis other Asians. The Labour Party, which controlled the Council for decades prior to 1986, did very little to support or win the confidence of the local Black community. This neglect by the Labour Party is typical of the urban inner city areas invariably controlled by the Labour Party. The Liberal Democrats and the Conservatives are no better in supporting the Black people in areas where they exercise political control. Labour is the most popular Party for Black people with up to 70% or more of the voters supporting Labour at local and general elections.

The overwhelming number of local and national Black politicians in Britain has been elected as Labour Party candidates. There are currently five Black Labour Members of Parliament (four men and one woman, including two Asians and three African/Caribbean).

Local Authorities and Anti-Racism Strategies

Local authorities have been in the forefront of anti-racism strategies through their equal opportunities policies and practices in recruitment, training and development, promotion, positive action and access to services. More than half of the 514 local authorities in Britain –

255

ranging from budgets of £10 million to over £1,000 and workforces form 300 to nearly 50,000 have introduced some sort of equal opportunity policy which includes an element of anti-racism strategy (see appendix 3) for a summary of a comprehensive anti-racism/equal opportunity local authority policy. Local government is one of the largest employers in Britain with some 2.7 million workers representing around 12% of the total workforce. Anti-racism/equal opportunity arrangements took off with the Greater London Council and the Inner London education Authority in around 1981 (both abolished by the government in 1985). Many authorities are still trying to move from simple policy statements to more strategic policies.

Some reflection on Race relations Arrangements in Canada and Great Britain

Britain is relatively small in size in comparison to Canada. The population of Britain is over twice that of Canada (59 million compared to 26 million). In 1962, Canada brought the immigration policy which gave preference to white immigrants to an end, whilst in the same year Britain introduced the 1962 Immigration Act which restricted the number of Blacks coming to Britain from the British colonies and the Commonwealth. Canada had what could be described as a "tri-partisan" approach to immigration policy much earlier than Britain. Up to now the Labour Party is seen as being more sympathetic to immigration that the Conservative Party.

Canada created a Department of Immigration which deals with the administrative functions related to immigration, whereas immigration, nationality, asylum and citizenship issues are dealt with by the Home Office with a Cabinet Minister at its Head. The 1972 Review of Immigration Policy which consisted of a special joint all party committee, and which reported to the Canadian Parliament in 1975, was a much fairer policy than the 1971 Immigration Act passed by the British Parliament which is often referred to as "one of the most racially biased pieces of legislation in practice in Britain." This Act was designed primarily to restrict Black immigration and to keep open

256

the door for white immigrants. It would appear that Canada was strongly influenced in its immigration policy by foreign policy considerations (by wanting to appear non-racist) as well as labour market and economic needs.

Conclusion

Race and race relations are major concerns in Britain for both Black and white people. The "new racism" is destabilising community relations and creating greater divisions, fear and conflicts between white and Black people. Despite the various British, EC and international laws to protect all citizens irrespective of colour or race, Black people in Britain are disproportionately disadvantaged in almost every aspect of life. Racism is pervasive and systematic in almost every area of economic, political, social and cultural activity in Britain. Covert discrimination is widely practised by institutions, individuals and organisations despite the Race relations Act 1976, Sex Discrimination Act 1975 and 1986. The current legislation and framework are insufficient/inadequate to substantially eliminate racial discrimination and disadvantage.

The extent of racism in Britain appears to fluctuate with economic growth; levels of unemployment; the relative state of the economy in relation to the rest of the world; living standards and the level of commitment by political parties to good race relations.

The next six years leading up to 21st century will be crucial for what is now and irreversibly a multi-cultural/multi-racial Britain. The Black population is here to stay. They are an integral part of British life and society. Deterioration in race relations will damage everyone irrespective of colour or race. Good race relations are in everyone's interests.

Thank you for listening to me.
Editor's note:

Update on the latest statistics on ethnic

257

make-up of the population in the UK

According to the 2011 Census, the ethnic composition of the United

Kingdom was as set out in the table below.

The non- white population is likely to increase to 20% by 2050.

Ethnic group	2011 population	2011%
White: Total	**55,010,359**	**87.1**
Gypsy/Traveller/ Irish Traveller: Total	**63,193**	**0.1**
Asian or Asian British: Indian	1,412,958	2.3
Asian or Asian British: Pakistani	1,174,983	1.9
Asian or Asian British: Bangladeshi	451,529	0.7
Asian or Asian British: Chinese	433,150	0.7
Asian or Asian British: Other Asian	861,815	1.4
Asian or Asian British: Total	**4,373,339**	**6.9**

Black or Black British: Total	1,904,684	3.0
Mixed Multiple: Total	1,250,229	2.0
Other Ethnic Group: Total	580,374	0.9
Total	63,182,178	100

The non-white population in the UK now stands at around 13% of the total population representing over 10 million people. The non-white population is rising at a much faster rate than the white population and it is likely to double in size within the next 20 years. This will have considerable impact on a whole range of social, cultural, economic and political issues for both the white and black population.

Chapter Twelve

Zita Holbourne - The Freedom to Express Who we Are

Lee Jasper, Zita Holbourne, Marcia Rigg and Jim Thakoordin at the TUC Black Workers Conference 2012

Article first appeared in Defending Multiculturalism: A Guide for the Movement, Edited by Hassan Mahamdallie, and published by Bookmarks Publications, 2011

"The struggles Enrico Stennett was engaged in sixty years ago, is still continuing by the present generation and no doubt by future generations until equality for all is achieved."

Multiculturalism is many things to many people but one thing it most definitely is not is a government policy. Multiculturalism is about respecting, celebrating, sharing and honouring our many traditions, cultures, languages, religions, non religion, histories and lifestyles.

Multiculturalism is sometimes seen as a celebration of diversity, but it's much more than that.

It's about having the freedom to express who we are without fear of repercussions if we do, and about celebrating who we are. It cannot be defined with one phrase and it can't be limited to a definition decided by a politician. Multiculturalism is more powerful than the government of the day – it's about who we are, where we come from and where we are going and no politician can take that away.

It's what makes us a strong, vibrant and enriched society. It's about self-definition and self-determination and it helps us to have the confidence to share and embrace our traditions and uniqueness. Multiculturalism is ever-changing and ever-evolving as we embrace traditions that are ancient, handed down to us through generations while adopting, adapting and experiencing new ones so the two fuse together to create an eclectic explosion of religion, culture, music, food, language and lifestyle.

Why should we defend it?

So why should we defend multiculturalism? If you take away multiculturalism, which you could never do anyway, you take away the very essence of what makes us who we are and what makes the UK the country it is. You take away our strength and our unity. In order to take away multiculturalism you would have to erase history – centuries of enslavement, invasion and migration.

David Cameron is trying to link multiculturalism to extremism. This is dangerous and irresponsible. In effect it is racist and Mr Cameron as leader of the government has a responsibility to promote harmony between different races and religions and a duty of care towards all citizens not just a chosen few that he feels he can relate to. The aspects of multiculturalism he does not like are not the aspects embraced by the upper class Oxbridge educated millionaire circles he moves in but the aspects embraced by working class black and Asian people. His attack on multiculturalism is a direct attack on certain

261

faiths, specifically Islam, and on race equality. David Cameron wants to strip us of our right to celebrate and embrace who we are as individuals, as communities and as UK citizens, but only some of us – he's not suggesting his Eton-educated chums branch out and make new friends or that Sloane Rangers come down to the East End and hang out with the locals in the Boleyn pub. His comments were directed at specific sections of the population and he has expressed negative and wrong perceptions about those sections.

This is not the first time that he has attacked multiculturalism. In a debate hosted by the Equality and Human Rights Commission in 2008, Cameron defined "state multiculturalism" as the idea that we should respect different cultures within Britain to the point of allowing them and encouraging them to live separate lives, apart from each other and apart from the mainstream. So in effect stating in 2011 that "state multiculturalism" has not worked he is saying that we should disrespect different cultures, not allow them to live separate lives and that we should all live together. Cameron therefore seems to be advocating for communes for clones and for people to discriminate against each other. It would seem that the attack on multiculturalism is likely to rear its head again and this is why it is important that we counter the negative and dangerous comments about it that do nothing to promote equality and are more likely to provide ammunition for the far right to use towards black and Asian people.

As a second generation black woman of mixed race heritage there are many aspects to my culture, and while it is impossible for me to stop embracing my multiculturalism, if it were possible I would refuse. It was a long and painful journey for me to understand and deal with the racism I faced growing up, to not just accept but grow to like and be proud of the person I was, to shake off several layers of negative assumptions and prejudice towards me because of how I looked, my black heritage, my mixed heritage, the cultural traditions I embraced. Promotion of multiculturalism is one of the ways I was able to do this because through multiculturalism came an acceptance of different cultures and our right to be. While once I had kept quiet about those traditions in the company of those I didn't know well, even trying to conform sometimes to a fake "norm", I became not only emboldened but delighted in both owning my cultural traditions in public and sharing them. My multiculturalism is where I draw my strength and confidence from. Muhammad Ali said, "I am American. I am the part you won't recognise. But get used to me. Black, confident, cocky, my name, not yours, my religion, not yours, my goals, my own, get used to me."

Embracing my culture and traditions manifests in all aspects of my life. As a poet, as a visual artist, as a trade union representative and a community activist it plays a key part. My life path has been influenced not just by my own culture but the cultures I have experienced throughout my life both in the UK and other countries. I am fortunate to have friends and family in many different parts of the world and travelling to a range of countries and continents has afforded me the opportunity to observe, learn from and identify with many different cultures, religions and traditions which have in turn enriched my life experience. Within my family there are English, Welsh, Irish, Trinidadian, Venezuelan, St Lucian, Barbadian, American, Canadian, Colombian, Spanish, French, Sri Lankan, Native American, Italian and Gibraltarian members observing five different religions or none at all.

In the UK I have friends and colleagues who are from many different religions and ethnicities and these, along with the family members, mean my life experience is more interesting and exciting as a result of us all sharing the cultural traditions we embrace. It is because of multiculturalism that we are enriched and stronger as a society. It's for these reasons and many more that it is essential for us to defend multiculturalism.

The key role of the trade union movement

As a trade union representative I am very committed to combating discrimination and achieving equality. In fact it was my interest in equality and justice that led me to become a trade union representative.

263

I believe there is a strong link between equality and multiculturalism because both are positive forces in challenging discrimination.

The trade union movement has a key role to play in defence of multiculturalism. Trade unions, just like employers and service providers, have a legal and moral duty to promote good relations between people of different races, colours, ethnicities, religions and cultures.

Equality is supposed to be at the heart of everything a trade union does and tackling discrimination while promoting and practicing equality is an integral part of every campaign and policy it has. Embracing multiculturalism is a positive way of promoting equality.

While multiculturalism is being attacked by the far right and linked to race and religion in a negative way, defending it needs to be embedded in anti-racist and anti-fascist activities and campaigns by unions and activists and within equality policies and initiatives.

Because there are different understandings of what multiculturalism means, including the bizarre definition of "state multiculturalism" Mr Cameron talks about , it's important that dialogue takes place in the first instance within the union movement at all levels about what multiculturalism both represents to the trade union movement and means to different people, because you can't have a collective defence of something that is not understood by those who are defending it, and without that dialogue there is potential for division caused through misunderstanding. If unions include multiculturalism in their equality and anti-racist/anti-fascist work this gives an opportunity to discuss, define and defend. Alongside this an awareness of and understanding of different religions is important, particularly Islam given the rise of Islamaphobia and Cameron's linking of multiculturalism with extremism.

The TUC and all trade unions have equality policies and multiculturalism can be included in those policies and anti-racist/anti-fascist policies. There are charters for equality and a charter in defence of multiculturalism could be drawn up at TUC level that could be signed up to by trade union leaders giving a commitment at top level to its defence. This top level commitment should not be instead of anything else but in addition to gaining the same kind of commitment from individual trade unions and from equality structures within them. Unions could write model motions in defence of multiculturalism to aid the debate but also so that it becomes part of union policy. Workshops and discussion forums could be facilitated and organised. It is important that these involve anti racist organisations, faith groups, black community organisations and those on the receiving end of prejudice and discrimination linked to attacks on multiculturalism.

My trade union, the Public and Commercial Services union (PCS), has already started the process of forming policy and awareness. My union provided some awareness sessions on main religions a few years ago. In April 2011 PCS submitted an emergency motion to the TUC Black Workers Conference titled "Condemn David Cameron's attack on multiculturalism", which I moved and the Communication Workers Union seconded, as follows:

• Conference notes that David Cameron's speech at the Munich Security Meeting (5 February 2011) claimed multiculturalism had failed the UK and referred to extremist/terrorist incidents to justify the false claim.

• Conference is concerned by Cameron's speech on the same day EDL extremists besieged Luton to vent fascist/anti-Islamic poison. Yet he chose not to condemn EDL extremism.

• Conference agrees that Cameron should focus on sorting out the economic mess caused by financial institutions; investing in Britain's future, not stoking disharmony across Europe by denouncing multiculturalism. Conference condemns Cameron for playing the hate-mongering "trump" immigration card.

• Conference agrees the TUC Race Committee

- should seek the signatures of all affiliated members, general secretaries and others, to challenge the attack on multiculturalism

265

- encourage all affiliates to actively affiliate to, support and promote the "One Society, Many Cultures" campaign to showcase the positive contributions that Black people and multiculturalism continue to make to Britain

- demand an explanation from Mr Cameron as to why he chose to conflate multiculturalism with extremism and

- ask David Cameron to outline how he will tackle extremist elements within groups like the EDL and BNP.

The motion was carried unanimously which means that it is now union policy to carry out the instructions in the motion.

Key things trade unions can do to kick start the process

• Union equality committees to put defence of multiculturalism and combating islamophobia on their agendas and initiate discussion.

• Draw up model motions defending multiculturalism .

• Enter discussions with anti-racist/anti-fascist organisations about how we can work together.

• Call on the TUC to draw up a charter in defence of multiculturalism.

• Invite speakers to union meetings to talk about why the defence is important and relevant to trade unions.

• Publish articles in union journals about multiculturalism.

• Publish articles in union journals about different religions including Islam and/or provide fact sheets about key religions including Islam.

• Dispel any myths about Islam through dialogue and publications, eg fact sheets.

• Campaign against any attacks on Islam or other religions.

• Enter discussions with employers.

• Hold celebratory events to promote multiculturalism.

• Hold celebratory events on key religious dates.

• Hold awareness sessions on different religions including Islam.

• Invite religious leaders or observers which could include union reps and members to give talks on what their religion means to them.

• Ensure that their policies and practices take into account religious observance and practices, ie time off for religious observance/holidays, provision of faith observance rooms, arranging meetings and events to take into account key religious dates.

We must ensure that the defence of multiculturalism is debated and agreed wider than within union structures and among union members and taken to our workplaces and the communities we live in. Trade unions could look at the sectors they represent in and agree a process of discussing attacks on multiculturalism with employers and gaining commitment from them to include multiculturalism in their policies and initiatives.

Con-Dem cuts will reduce the amount spent on equality initiatives and cultural events such as Black History Month meaning that there is less scope for promotion of multiculturalism. The knock-on impact of public sector cuts on the voluntary sector who provide unique services to our multicultural communities will mean that funding is cut to important initiatives that promote equality and diversity and celebrate multiculturalism. As the cuts will hit the poorest and most vulnerable the hardest, many of whom are used as scapegoats by the far right and right wing press, defending those communities goes hand in hand with defending multiculturalism.

Perhaps, therefore, in the same way as public sector organisations have a duty to assess the equality impacts of any cuts they are proposing, we should call on Mr Cameron to carry out an equality impact assessment on his plan to scrap multiculturalism? Will it have a disproportionate impact on race grounds – it most certainly will have an

267

overwhelming negative and disproportionate impact – and as such Mr Cameron will need to reconsider his proposal or put forward his mitigation.

I believe that in the same way we tackle the discrimination of cuts towards black people, women, disabled people, LGBT people, pensioners and children we must tackle the impact of cuts on celebrating and promoting multiculturalism.

It is important that the positive messages about multiculturalism are brought to our schools, colleges and universities and multiculturalism continues to be celebrated in our schools while being debated, defended and promoted within the student movement. The National Union of Students and education sector unions have a key role to play here.

One way to bring the message to our wider communities about why we are defending multiculturalism is to celebrate it. Unions regularly combine debate with art and culture in order to bring messages of unity, hope and equality to wider audiences; unions could hold multiculturalism seminars, concerts and socials and use these to not only defend multiculturalism but also raise funds for causes they support and campaigns they are running. Trade unions have a responsibility to challenge the government when they get things wrong and trade union leaders could write to the government setting out the arguments for defending multiculturalism. They can challenge any negative responses by the press to Cameron's comments and dispel any myths or lies.

Multiculturalism is here to stay

Multiculturalism is here to stay; the task ahead is about defending our right to embrace multiculturalism in an open way, to have dialogue about it and to celebrate it without fearing repercussions for doing so from the far right, racists and the current government. People should be free to embrace their own cultures without living in fear, we should be able to respect the differences between us while celebrating how those differences bring us together and unite us in such a way that we can be open about who we are.

We are not clones, we are not the same and that should be celebrated. Multiculturalism is not just important to us as individuals or ethnic and religious groups but as a response to racism and discrimination. Our right to recognise and enjoy multiculturalism is a human
right and any threat to multiculturalism is a threat to our freedom. "To be free is not merely to cast off one's chains, but to live in a way that respects and enhances the freedom of others" – Nelson Mandela.

MULTICULTURALISM

POEM WRITTEN BY ZITA HOLBOURNE, COPYRIGHT FEBRUARY 2011

I embrace my Multiculturalism
As I do my Afrocentrism
As I do my Feminism
And even my *Englishism*

I have African and European roots but I'm a Londoner
I'm both Caribbean and an Eastender
My Sunday dinners include both roast potatoes and *rice n peas*
I can slip between 'BBC English', 'Cockney' and 'Patois' *with ease*
I was raised in the church but respect all religion
Some of my friends are atheist but doesn't cause division
I relax with Jazz, dance to Hip Hop
Chill with Lovers, but I love BeBop!

You can't define me with a single entity
That's because I have a multiple identity
I'm not just ***multicultural***

I'm also *multiracial*

I'm proud of my history and my roots
I dress, speak and communicate as it suits
You can't define me with *just one word*
To limit my multiculture *would be absurd!*

The complexities of my multiple identities
Manifest in my eccentricities
They're wrapped up in my DNA, my blood, invasion, freedom
In Empire, enslavement, in race, belief, religion
In class and gender, language and dialect
Skills and talent, knowledge and intellect
Add to this the food I eat, the music I adore
The traditions I embrace and the passions I live for

If *I* am *multicultured* as *I* alone stand
I'm afraid *Mr Prime Minister,* I don't **understand**
How you expect a whole population *collectively*
To be single cultured and have just one *identity*
And how you can believe multiculturalism's dead
When I'm a living legacy of it's success

It's *deep rooted*, sometimes understated
Always there but never overrated
It's in the way we ♪sing♪ and the way we talk
The way we dance and the way we walk

Multiculturalism cannot fail to succeed
It's not in the gift of a politician to proceed
With it's termination

IT'S NOT YOUR CREATION!
It's in our blood and in our bones
You can't create multicultural free zones

It's on our airwaves and in our streets

270

In our attire and rhythm and beats
It's in street food and haute cuisine
It's even in her Majesty the Queen
It's in the theatre and in literature
In places of worship and holy scripture

It's CELEBRATION!
It's JUBILATION!
It's *pomp and glory*
And it's **OUR STORY!**

You can't erase what makes us who we are!
It's not something you can permit or bar!
And you can't take away what brings us *together*

RECOGNISE *Mr Prime Minister*
MULTICULTURALISM'S here forever!

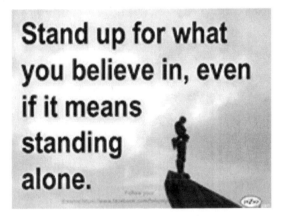

Chapter Thirteen

Jim Thakoordin –
Black Self-organisation within Trade Unions

Jim Thakoordin with Francis O'Grady
General Secretary of the TUC 2014

Black trade unionists starting organising together as a response to the pervasive racism in British society during the 13 years of Conservative rule from 1951 to 1964. Throughout the 1960s, race and immigration featured negatively on a daily basis in the media, particularly the right-wing tabloid press. The Labour Party, nurtured by the trade-union movement, seemed less overtly racist; yet beneath the surface lurked institutional racism in trade union branches and constituency parties. So African Caribbean and Asian workers organised themselves to fight for their rights. This is the context within which the Black Trade Unionist Solidarity Movement (BTUSM) came about and grew rapidly.

Black workers in Britain have for centuries faced racism, joining forces with sympathetic white radicals to highlight and oppose it at work, in politics and in society at large. During the 1964 General Election that toppled the Tory government, race became a major issue. The Tories had introduced the 1962 Immigration Act, which denied people from former British colonies the right to enter the UK to work. The Labour Party appeared to be somewhat critical of the legislation and promised to re-examine it when they returned to power. So, in many respects Black workers trusted Labour and were far more likely to join trade unions than White workers. However, despite the rising numbers of Black members of the Labour movement, they were not represented at decision-making level within the unions or the Labour Party.

Black workers began to raise questions about equality and representation at the workplace, election to positions within the structures and access to office in local and central government. In the unions there were White members who were reluctant to treat Black members as equals or represent their interests. Some were quite vocal in seeing Black workers as unwanted foreigners competing for jobs and services. The National Front was among various racist political groups active within the unions and even the Conservative Party. As a result, during the 1970s Black workers waged numerous struggles against being treated less favourably than their White counterparts. Where the unions were either reluctant to support them or opposed their actions, Black workers joined together to take on the employers themselves.

In 1965 and 1968 the Labour government passed legislation aimed at reducing racism in employment. When in 1970 the Tories returned to power they passed the 1971 Immigration Act, further restricting the flow of Black workers to Britain. Re-elected in 1974, Labour passed the 1976 Race Relations Act outlawing racism in the workplace. The unions took some note and began to organise courses on anti-racism. By 1979, a handful of Black trade-union full-time officials included Bernie Grant, in the National Union of Public Employees (NUPE), Bill Morris, in the Transport and General Workers

Union (TGWU), and myself, in the General Municipal and Boiler Makers Union (GMB).

The 1970s and early 1980s were characterised by Black struggles within trade unions and in communities with sizeable Black populations like Birmingham, Brent, Bristol, Tottenham, Southall, Brixton, Burnley, Liverpool and elsewhere.

Black people were beginning to organise in small groups at work, especially in town halls, where the National Association of Local Government Officers (NALGO) - forerunner of Unison - was a strong union. The Labour Party, mindful of the huge importance of Black votes to its electoral fortunes, issued discussion papers on race in October 1977, followed by a major conference, and promised changes to improve race relations in its 1979 election manifesto. Having defeated Labour that year, after the notorious comments of prime minister-to-be Margaret Thatcher about migrants "swamping" Britain, the Tories continued to attack the unions and give little consideration to the plight of Black workers.

By 1979 Black workers were organising in local government under the banner of Black NALGO, to the annoyance of the trade-union movement. At this time I met with Bernie Grant - my countryman from Guyana, where we had a solid tradition of union organisation - and he fully backed Black workers grouping independently within unions.

We organised a meeting at the Greater London Council (GLC) that year, with the support of activists from Camden Black Workers Group, made up mainly of NALGO activists and other interested trade unionists who wanted to find out more about Black self-organisation. Among the most active Black workers in London local government were Azim Hajee, Judy Bashir, Gulam Mayet, Chris Khamis, John Ohen and John Fernandez. Continuing to build Black networks within the unions, in 1980 we organised a Black Workers' Conference in Bradford attended by more than 150 NALGO members. We lobbied the Trades Union Congress and supportive unions such as the National Union of Miners, Fire Brigades Union and NUPE. On 22 November

274

1981, at the GLC, we launched The Declaration on racism within the Labour movement and society at large. The meeting, where more than 30 unions were represented, agreed that Black workers needed to work within the unions rather than split off to organise separately.

We pledged to:

- Organise a London-based conference of Black trade unionists to discuss a programme of action
- Make links with other Black workers' organisations, with a view to launching a national Black Trade Unionists Solidarity Movement (BTUSM)
- Work to improve Black participation at all levels of the union and labour movement
- Work for changes within the trade union and labour movement to restore Black people's confidence.

An Annual General Meeting was called in 1982, with more than 75 delegates. Unfortunately, it was disrupted by a group of people arguing about the definition of "Black", after a Turkish woman insisted on her right to attend even though she did not see herself as Black. Very little was therefore achieved and it was agreed to convene a further BTUSM meeting in 1983.

In December 1982 John Fernandez, a respected race awareness lecturer, exposed the vicious racism among cadets at the police training college at Hendon, north London. He was dismissed from his post soon afterwards and the case became a cause célèbre. BTUSM fully supported John Fernandez and his union, the National Association of Teachers in Further and Higher Education (NATFHE); however, a group calling itself the Racism Awareness Programme Unit (RAPU) took a different view. By early 1983 the TUC Race Advisory Committee was established. The GLC Ethnic Minorities Unit was also focusing on anti-racism issues. On 29 May 1983, BTUSM convened a meeting to agree a constitution.

Five months later, on Sunday 2 October 1983, at the party conference in Brighton, the fledgeling Labour Party Black Section tabled its first resolutions demanding official recognition. A fringe meeting was arranged with GLC councillor Frances Morell (who later became the leader of the Inner London Education Authority), Russell Profitt, Marc Wadsworth, Diane Abbott, Bernie Grant and me.

On Monday, during the debate on why Labour lost the 1983 General Election, I made a speech attacking the Labour Party and the unions for not empowering Black people. The following day, I was quoted in the national newspapers. Other Black delegates later joined the debate and raised issues of Black representation. Paul Boateng, Russell Profitt and Keith Vaz (who was active in the Labour Party Race Action Group with his mother and sister Valerie Vaz, elected to Parliament in 2010) also played a part.

At a meeting in June 1984, BTUSM adopted its new constitution. That year, there were frequent disagreements within BTUSM, which was funded by the GLC and had full-time workers. By the end of 1984 most BTUSM activists had transferred support to the Labour Party Black Section. BTUSM was dissolved in 1985. I was elected Convenor of the Black Section, with Russell Profitt as Chair, Marc Wadsworth as Vice-Chair and Billy Poh as Secretary.

Jim Thakoordin, Linda Bellos MBE, Narendra Makanji And Marc Wadsworth at a meeting in London in 2014. They have all been involved in the Black struggles since the 1970's.

Chapter Fourteen

Jim Thakoordin –
When Black History Month started and Why

**Jim Thakoordin: speech delivered to Lambeth UNISON
Black Workers Group, in October 2007**

Greetings colleagues

Thank you for inviting me to this important event. I want to start off by
saying a few things about Black History Month before I go on to talk of
Black History and what we have contributed to civilisation over the
centuries.

277

When Black History Month Started

Black History Month (BHM) started in America in February 1926. It started as "Negro History Week" by African and white American scholars as a serious platform to address the widespread ignorance, and deliberate distortion of Black history, civilisation, culture and contributions to the development of humankind in all areas of activity over thousands of years.

BHM started in Britain as part of the process of Black self-organisation following the Civil Rights activities during the 1960's and 1970's. It started off with Black Studies and issues relating to Black Liberation and self organisation in trade unions, the Labour Party and the response to racism during the 1970's 1980's and culminated in a number of local authorities in partnership with Black community organisations formally organising activities associated with Black culture, art, politics, music, history and racism. The first major BHM activity I attended was organised by Ealing Council in 1989 and addressed by Mrs Mugabe, Neil Kinnock, Leader of the Labour Party, Bernie Grant and others.

Why Black History Month

To plan our journey ahead we need to know where we have come from and how we got where we are. History is important for all of us Black and white. Unfortunately, the history of Black and Asian people until the 20th Century was denied, distorted and denigrated by Europeans in Europe, North America, Australia and in other countries where the descendents of white Europeans ruled.

Black and Asian people, especially Africans were dehumanised, stereotyped, labelled and described as uncivilised, inferior and unequal to white people. White colonialists, merchants, slavers, imperialists, capitalists, plantation owners, traders, churches, monarchs and scholars had convinced themselves and brainwashed their fellow white citizens that Black and Asian people had never created any civilisation of any kind.

This belief was essential in order to justify slavery, colonialism, imperialism and the right of Europeans to conquer and exploit countries inhabited by Black and Brown people. Racism was given respectability and accepted by white states, the nobility, churches, institutions and the powerful. The legacy of centuries of racism still distorts our history and contributes substantially to the world in which we all live and work.

It is no coincidence that Africa has been the poorest continent soon after Europeans arrived in the 15th century, and is likely to remain so for a long time. It is no coincidence that the white population of the world which represents less that 25 % of the world population has by far the majority of the wealth and control almost all the key economic, political, military and scientific decisions which affects the majority Black and Asian population.

BHM provides all of us with an opportunity to critically and objectively reflect and evaluate not only our history, but also our present and where we want to be in the future. Our world has become a small village given the advances in transport and the media. Look around your workplace, your community and your cities and you will see a variety of races, cultures, religions, lifestyles and skin colours. Our world is multi-racial and multi-cultural. We all need to come to terms with our history, our environment and the society in which we live.

BHM is a timely reminder that we are one race – the human race. We need to celebrate of differences as well as the things we have in common such as human rights, freedom, justice, liberty, equality, democracy. We need to use build on activities and awareness created during BHM to ensure that we respect each other and that we commit ourselves, our union, our government and our nation to work towards real and positive freedom, justice, equality and access to health, education, economic and social justice in our modern world.

We must never forget the reasons which enabled inequality, exploitation, degradation, inhumanity and injustice endured by Black

279

and Asian people, especially Africans and the poor around the world through slavery, colonialism, imperialism, nationalism, chauvinism or uncontrolled capitalism to influence our relationship.

Who is supposed to celebrate Black History Month

We should all celebrate BHM. BHM should be positively and proactively celebrated by all races, ethnic groups, religion, ages, and institutions. It is not only for Africans or people of African descent. We must find ways of learning about the history of all racial groups including the indigenous community, so we can work towards greater understanding of each other and build trust and respect for each other throughout the year. BHM should be a major catalyst to bring us physically and emotionally towards each other.

Why Black History Month is important for all of us, whether we are trade unionist, or not

My interest in Black History, trade unions and radical politics led me to discover that far from being uncivilised, or failed to contribute towards the development of our world in all areas of human activities, we were in fact the first race on this planet. Black people in Africa, Asia and North America were the first people to be civilised and have given the rest of the world the ideas, tools and resources from which our modern was built. Our history and glorious past have been distorted and hidden from us for too long.

Here is some brief information I want to share with you today. There is not enough time for me to go into the massive contributions to every aspect of our world today, that were made possible by natives from Asia, North America and Central America as well as the Middle East, so I will concentrate mainly in Africa.

African History, Civilisation, and Inventions

African culture, art, and creativity were recognised and much valued by ancient Egypt, Greece, Rome, and other empires. It as not until the

Europeans conquered, colonised, and enslaved much of Africa between the fifteenth and nineteenth centuries that Africa was labelled the "Dark Continent." Stereotypes of Africans as uncivilised, barbaric, and biologically inferior were nurtured in European literature, myths, culture, and values simply to justify the inhuman and barbaric treatment of Negroes.

Prior to the European involvement, much of Africa was as developed as Europe, with agriculture, arts, language, learning, crafts, trading, mining, and other areas of activity which were at least as complex as sophisticated as elsewhere in the world. Before the colonisation and enslavement of Africa by the Europeans, the Africans were approximately on the same levels of economic, human, and cultural development as most of Europe. Colonisation and slavery were significant turning points for African development.

Four centuries of the capture, slaughter, and enslavement of millions of Africa's most able people – the young, the strong, and the economically active – robbed Africa of its opportunity to develop its independent, economic, social, and political structures and infrastructures such as roads, transport, communication, and education. Various sources have estimated that up to fifty million Africans perished due to enslavement and persecution by the deliberate actions of Europeans. The history of Africa over the last four centuries was largely written by the European conquerors in such a way that it denies Africans and others the opportunity to reflect on the rich history and civilisation.

Before European intervention

The ancient emperors of Ethiopia, Sudan, Mali, Songhay, Egypt, and other areas of Africa were highly developed, civilised, and scientific.

The Ghanaian Kingdom, founded in about 300 AD, expanded west from the Niger basin to the Atlantic coast and north to the Sahara Desert. It included present day Mali, Mauritania, and Senegal until it

281

was conquered in 1076 AD. The Royal Palace was "adorned with sculptures, paintings, and glass windows," wrote the historian El Idrise in 1152. The King of Ghana, Kanissa'ai, who ruled at the end of the seventeenth century, had over one thousand horses, which neither "slept except upon carpet, nor were they tied except by silken rope around their necks and feet" (from The World of Africa, by W. E. B. Dubois).

The city of Ghana consisted of two townships that were six miles apart. One of the townships was inhabited mainly by Muslims and the other, by pagans. There were twelve mosques in the Muslim township and one in the pagan township. The city of Ghana was "one of the most populous cities in the world. The people wore clothes made out of wool, cotton, silk, and velvet. Trading in wood, textiles, copper, jewels, silver, gold, armour, and weapons was carried out extensively in the empire" (from Histoire des Berberes, by Idn Kaldoun, 1925).

Over the last few decades, Africans and, indeed, Black people around the world who were victims of imperialism and colonialism, are beginning to discover their history and civilisation which the colonists either denied or stole from them. Africans around the world are becoming increasingly aware of their history and are able to refute the characterisation of Negroes as "savages", barbarians, or as people who have contributed very little towards civilisation. The European and American economies starting with the industrial revolution, which originated in Britain, was largely financed by wealth accumulated through slavery, colonisation, and the exploitation of Africa, Asia, and South America. It is important, not only for Africans but for everyone, to recognise and to understand the history of Africa and the immense contributions that Africans have made towards the world, civilisation, and economic development over the centuries.

Ancient Ghanaians, Egyptians, Ethiopians, and other Africans valued education and learning highly. Great universities and places of learning were constructed, where students studied medicine, science, philosophy, literature, agriculture, politics, and architecture.

Imhotep of Ancient Egypt was the true father of medicine. He was born in about 2300 BC. Rome, Greece, and other civilisations gained much of their knowledge of medicine, language, and architecture form Africans like Imhotep. He was worshipped in Rome as the Negro Prince of Peace. He was the Prime Minister to King Zoser, as well as the foremost architect of his time. The saying, "Eat, drink, and be merry, for tomorrow we die" has been attributed to him. Hippocrates, who is generally heralded as the Father of Medicine was born 2000 years after Imhotep (from Ancient Egypt: the Light of the World, by Gerald Massey, 1907).

The universities of ancient Africa were more advanced than the European universities. Even in remoter parts of Africa, including Timbuktu, Gao, Jenner, and Samkoze, there were universities that brought together thousands of scholars to study law, literature, grammar, geography, science, and humanities long before such centres of learning had been established in England, France, or Germany.

Books on reading, writing, and mathematics, with substantial input from Negroes, were published and housed in both public and private libraries in Egypt long before such advancements reached Europe. According to Herodotus, "The records on the monuments and in the tombs have attested to the pictorial wonders which have rendered Greece and Italy illustrious were derived from the efforts and achievements of African Mothers" (from The Mothers, by Robert Briffault).

Queen Makeda of Sheba, who ruled Ethiopia in 960 BC and who was attracted to the "dark olive –coloured" King Solomon, gave the King the richest gift ever recorded, consisting of "120 talents of gold, and of spices very great store and precious stones." Solomon, in turn, "prepared an apartment built of crystal from the floor to the ceiling for her ... and had a throne set up for Makeda beside his. It was covered with silken carpets, adorned with fringes of gold and silver, and studded with diamonds and pearls. From this she listened while he delivered judgement."

283

Makeda possessed all the qualities of a great ruler. She has been mentioned in two great books, the Bible and the Koran. Her fame extended even into distant parts of savage Europe. The Romans spoke of her as the "Black Minerva" and the "Ethiopian Diana" (from Makesa, Reine de Saba by Le Roux Hugues, 1914).

King Akhnaton and Queen Nefertite, who ruled ancient Egypt in 1254 BC, were both Black Africans. "Living centuries before King David, Akhnaton wrote psalms as beautiful as those of the Judean Monarch thirteen hundred years before Christ. Akhnaton preached and lived a gospel of perfect love, brotherhood, and truth. Two thousand years before Mahomet, he taught the doctrine of One God. Three thousand years before Darwin, he sensed the unity that reigns through all living things" (from Worlds of Great Men of Colour, by J. A. Rogers).

Tiro, The Inventor of Shorthand

Negroes were not only great inventors, academics, and scientists in Africa; their influence followed their presence in Europe. Tiro was born on the estate of the Roman Knight, Marcus Tullius Cicero in 103 BC and, in 63 BC, became Cicero's personal servant and secretary. Cicero recognised Tiro's potential and financed his education. Tiro followed Cicero during to several of his country estates, where Cicero repeatedly sent him to transact private business. Eventually, Tiro developed a system of shorthand that enabled him to take dictations from Cicero. After Cicero's death, Tiro opened a school in Rome where he taught shorthand. In the ninety-nine years of his life, he published several documents, including a collection of his letters, which have survived.

The Invention of Mathematics

Mathematics was invented in Egypt. The word mathematics, come from the Greek, "Mathesis", which means science. Mathematics "passed from Egypt to Greece and Thales of Miletus is believed to have carried it thither at his return from his travels" (from The Ancient History, by Charles Rollins).

As many other Europeans have done throughout the centuries, many Greeks tried deny Africans, Indians, Chinese, and other non-white civilisations or to claim for themselves inventions and discoveries associated with Black people. Air J. G. Wilkinson wrote in his book, The Ancient Egyptians, in 1854, "I have also known that Herodotus and others ascribe the origin of geometry to the Egyptians, but the period when it commenced is uncertain. Anticledes pretends that Meoris was the first to lay down that elements of that science, which he says was perfected by Pythagoras; but the latter observation is merely the result of the vanity of the Greeks, which claimed for their countrymen (as in the case of Thales, and other instances) the credit of enlightening a people on the very subject which they had visited Egypt for the purpose of studying."

The Egyptians and other non-white civilisations invented and discovered numerous areas of science, agriculture, medicine, engineering, and mechanical instruments, which other countries have improved and which are essential to our daily lives. Included among these are dentistry, iron smelting and converting it into tools and machinery, weaving, and even the first alphabet.

Conclusion

- Black people have taken part in the struggles to establish trade unions, democracy and political parties in Britain since the 17th century.
- Africa, Asia and South America had great civilisations long before Europe became civilised
- Black people lived and worked in Britain for hundreds of years. At least since the Roman invasion of Britain.
- Millions of Blacks and Asians fought against Germany in the First and Second World Wars.
- Black and Asian people contributed enormously to the civilisation of mankind in every area of activity, including science, language, education,

285

mathematics, medicine, art, music, culture, architecture, transport and material things for centuries, which we all use on a daily basis.

- Blacks and Asians were great inventors, pioneers, philosophers, and adventurers for centuries.
- African culture, art, and creativity were recognised and much valued by ancient Egypt, Greece, Rome, and other empires. It as not until the Europeans conquered, colonised, and enslaved much of Africa between the fifteenth and nineteenth centuries that Africa was labelled the "Dark Continent."
- Stereotypes of Africans as uncivilised, barbaric, and biologically inferior were nurtured in European literature, myths, culture, and values simply to justify the inhuman and barbaric treatment of Negroes.
- Prior to the European involvement, much of Africa was as developed as Europe, with agriculture, arts, language, learning, crafts, trading, mining, and other areas of activity which were at least as complex as sophisticated as elsewhere in the world.
- Before the colonisation and enslavement of Africa by the Europeans, the Africans were approximately on the same levels of economic, human, and cultural development as most of Europe. Colonisation and slavery were significant turning points for African development.
- Four centuries of the capture, slaughter, and enslavement of millions of Africa's most able people – the young, the strong, and the economically active – robbed Africa of its opportunity to develop its independent, economic, social, and political structures and infrastructures such as roads, transport, communication, and education.
- Various sources have estimated that up to fifty million Africans perished due to enslavement and persecution by the deliberate actions of Europeans.
- The history of Africa over the last four centuries was largely written by the European conquerors in such a way that it denies Africans and others the opportunity to reflect on the rich history and civilisation.

Let me introduce you to some examples of recent African inventions:

The following pages contain just a few examples of inventions and improvements on inventions designed by people of African origins in the nineteenth century. The extracts are taken from Black Innovators,

286

by Dr. Irene Diggs (Institute of Positive Education, 7524 South Cottage Grove Avenue, Chicago Illinois, 60619).
- The extracts are taken from Black Innovators, by Dr. Irene Diggs (Institute of Positive Education, 7524 South Cottage Grove Avenue, Chicago Illinois, 60619).

Invention	Inventor	Date	Patent Number
Cotton Planter	Blair, Henry	31 August 1836	Unknown
Folding Bed	Bailey, L. C.	18 July 1899	629, 286
Ladder Scaffold Support	Bailes, William	5 August 1879	218, 154
Rotary Engine	Beard, A. J.	5 July 1892	478, 271
Car-Coupler	Beard, A. J.	23 November 1897	594, 059
Letter Box	Becket, G. E.	4 October 1892	483, 525
Railway Signal	Blackburn, A. B.	10 January 1888	376, 362
Spring Seat for Chairs	Blackburn, A. B.	3 April 1888	380, 420
Street Sprinkling Apparaus	Binga, M. W.	22 July 1879	217, 283
Ironing Board	Boone, Sarah	26 April 1892	473, 653
Lawn Mower	Burr, J. A.	9 May 1899	624, 749
Switching Device for Railways	Burr, W. F.	31 October 1899	636, 197
Rapid-Fire Gun	Burkins, Eugene	Unknown	649, 433
Parcel Carrier for Bicycles	Certain, J. M.	26 December 1899	639, 708
Street Car Fender	Cherry, M. A.	1 January 1895	531, 908
Ice-Cream Mold	Cralle, A. L.	2 February 1897	576, 395
Steam Feed Water Trap	Creamer, H.	17 March 1885	313, 854
Steam Trap	Creamer, H.	8 March 1887	358, 964
Automatic Stop Plug for Gas Oil Pipes	Cosgrove, W.	17 March 1885	313, 993

287

entilator	F.Darkins, J. T.	19 February 1895	534, 322
Photographic Print Wash	Dorticus, C. J.	23 April 1895	537, 968
Chamber Commode	Elkins, T.	9 January, 1872	122, 518
Refrigerating Apparatus	Elkins, T.	4 November, 1879	221, 222
Convertible Settees	Evan, J. H.	5 October 1897	591, 095
Valve	Ferrell, F. J.	27 May 1890	428, 671
Furniture Castor	Fisher, D. A.	14 March 1876	174, 794
Guitar	Flemming, R. F., Jr	3 March 1886	338, 727
Motor	Gregory, J.	26 April 1887	361, 937
Registers	Hilyer, A. F.	14 October 1890	438, 159
Portable Weighing Scales	Hunter, J. H.	3 November, 1896	570, 553
Heating Apparatus	Jackson, B. F.	1 March 1898	599, 985
Gas Burner	Jackson, B. F.	4 April 1899	622, 482
Automatic Locking Switch	Jackson, W. H.	23 August 1898	609, 436
Grass Receivers for Lawn Mowers	Johnson, D.	10 June 1890	429, 629
Bicycle Frame	Johnson, I. R.	10 October 1899	634, 823
Swinging Chairs	Johnson, P.	15 November 1881	249, 530
Eye Protector	Johnson, P.	2 November 1880	234, 039
Velocipede	Johnson, W.	20 June 1899	627, 335
Paint Vehicle	Johnson, W. A.	4 December 1888	393, 763
Egg Beater	Johnson, W.	5 February 1884	292 821
Spring Gun	Lewis, E. R.	3 May 1887	362 096
Bridle-Bit	Little, E.	9 March 1882	254, 666
Pencil Sharpener	Love, J. L.	23 November 1897	594, 114
Fire Extinguisher	Marshall, T. J.	26 May 1872	125, 063
Nailing Machine	Matzeliger, J. E.	25 February 1896	421, 954

288

Lubricator for Steam Engines	McCoy, E.	2 July 1872	129, 843
Ironing Table	McCoy, E.	12 May 1874	150, 876
Lawn Sprinkler	McCoy, E.	26 September 1899	631, 549
Elevator	Miles, A.	11 October 1887	371, 207
Cotton Chopper	Murray, G. W.	5 June 1894	520, 888
Fertiliser Distributor	Murray, G. W.	5 June 1894	520, 889
Air Ship	Pickering, J. F.	20 February 1900	643, 975
Device for Sharpening Edged Tools	Purdy, W.	27 October 1896	570, 337
Fountain Pen	Purvis, W. B.	7 January 1890	419, 065
Paper Bag Machine	Purvis, W. B.	28 January 1890	420, 099
Electric Railway Switch	Purvis, W. B.	17 August 1897	588, 176
Safety Gate for Bridges	Reynolds, H. H.	7 October 1890	437, 937
Life Saving Guards for Locomotives	Robinson, J. H.	14 March 1899	621, 143
Clothes Dryer	Sampson, G.T	7 June 1892	476 416
Curtain Rod	Scottron, S. R.	30 August 1892	481, 720
Potato Digger	Smith, P. D.	21 January 1891	445, 206
Oil Stove	Standard, J.	29 October 1889	412, 689
Refrigerator	Standard, J.	14 July 1891	455, 891
Metal Bending Machine	Stewart & Johnson	27 December 1887	375, 512
Propeller for Vessels	Toliver, George	28 April, 1891	451, 086
Corn Husking Machine	Washingotn, Wade	14 August 1883	283, 173
Fire Escape Ladder	Winters, J. R.	7 May 1878	203 517
Telephone Transmitter	Woods, G. T.	2 December 1884	308, 817

289

Electro Mechanical Brake	Woods, G. T.	16 August 1887	368, 265
Telephone System and Apparatus	Woods, G. T.	11 October 1887	371, 655
Railway Telegraphy	Woods, G. T.	15 November 1887	373, 383
Overhead Conducting system for Electric Railway	Woods, G. T.	29 May 1888	383, 844

History is important for all of us, as it informs us of where we have come from, where we are at and where we are going. I am proud to be Black, I am proud to be a trade unionist and I am grateful to you for allowing me to share my thoughts on Black History with you.

Thank you for listening sisters and brothers.

Additional information 2014

Inventors and Discoverers

Apart from the rich history of inventers, philosophers, scientists, artists, engineers, architects, astronomers, doctors and academics, who existed in Africa and in other continents of the world thousands of years before Western civilisations, African American inventors have been in the forefront of discoveries for more than three centuries, and this played a substantial role in promoting the industrial revolution in Europe and North America. .

Africans, Asians, Chinese and other non-white civilisations have invented and discovered a wide range of gadgets, machinery, medical cures, and life saving techniques, theories, structures and practices that have had a huge impact on modern life. Much of this progress has been either, stolen or falsely claimed to have been created by Europeans and

290

have been incorporated in subsequent inventions and discoveries which affect our daily lives today across the world.

Of course the Europeans who have largely been involved in colonising, enslaving, controlling and recording the history of the continents and countries they have dominated have painted a very sad and inaccurate picture of the history, civilisations, richness in wealth, knowledge and experience of these people and their civilisations that spanned thousands of years. Only in relatively recent years have we had access to so much of our history and civilisations over the last 7,000 years. Far from being uncivilised savages with inferior mental and intellectual capacities, our ancestors were well ahead of Europe in every field of creation and discoveries. Our ancestors have populated every continent in the world and advanced agriculture, engineering, learning and teaching, medicine, astronomy, trading and finance, architecture, military tactics and structures designed to resolve disputes and social issues.

The history and contributions of black people towards human civilisations and advancements have been marginalised by Western nations especially in North America and Europe. Africans have journeyed across the entire face of our planet and have become Emperors and rulers in every corner of the world, including Africa, Asia, China, Japan, North and South America, the Caribbean, Middle East and in parts of Europe.

Ever during the centuries of colonialism, enslavement and control by the Europeans black, Asian and indigenous non-white natives have made enormous contributions to human kind in every aspects of our lives right up to today, and will continue to do so in even greater number and in a wider range of inventions, discoveries and creations in the future.

Some Black American inventors, assisted sources and links:
www.black-inventor.com/
www.blackinventor.com
www.african-americaninventors.org
http://blackinventions.org/
http://www.africanaonline.com/2010/09/virgie-ammons-the-damper/
http://inventors.about.com/od/bstartinventors/a/Bessie_Blount.htm
http://blogs.oregonstate.edu/jessicahaynes/2009/04/15/marie-van-brittan-brown-inventor/)
http://inventors.about.com/od/bstartinventors/a/Patricia_Bath.htm
http://inventors.about.com/library/inventors/blboone.htm
http://www.csupomona.edu/~plin/inventors/goode.html
http://inventors.about.com/library/inventors/bljoyner.htm
http://www.greatfemaleinventors.com/pages/marjoriejoyner.html
http://web.mit.edu/invent/iow/cjwalker.html

Chapter Fifteen

Marc Wadsworth - Speech on Race relations in Britain

Speech delivered by Writer and Journalist Marc Wadsworth, of the Anti-Racist Alliance, at a public meeting, held by Luton Committee for Racial Harmony, on Saturday, 22 November 1997

Police stop and search in London

My thanks go to Jim and Doreen Thakoordin, Cecil Harrison and everybody who organised this event. I would also like to pay tribute to all of you, including your MP Kelvin Hopkins, who founded Luton Racial Harmony Committee and successfully fended off the threat from the National Front fascists in the County of Bedfordshire more than a decade ago. I have personally known Jim since he and a few others started the Black Trade Unionist Solidarity Movement in 1979 and in 1983 formed the Black Section within the Labour Party. Myself and others were inspired and motivated into becoming part of the Black struggle during the 1970's and 1980's because of people like Jim who were in the forefront of raising Black issues within the trades union and labour movement.

Colleagues, if you read the tabloid press yesterday you will have noticed how two remarkable parliamentary by-election results in Winchester and Beckenham were knocked off the front pages by a scandal about a boxer. Frank Bruno – a very British Black hero, disgraced in a court battle with his wife about alleged domestic violence. Not so long ago it was the turn of O J Simpson – an all-American hero. Two sports stars. Models of integration. Icons for White people. Sometime role models for Black youth. Built up then brought down by the very system that made them great. Each case, with all its tragedy, demonstrates how fragile is Black success in a White world.

I have been a journalist, trade unionist and activist in Black politics for almost two decades. I helped to establish the Labour Party Black Section in 1983, along with Jim Thakoordin and others, and played a role in founding the Black-led Anti-Racist Alliance eight years later. Increasingly I am reminded of Malcolm X's comment about the news media: "It has the power to make the guilty innocent and the innocent guilty." No community understands this more than the one made up of people of African-Caribbean and Asian descent – what I call the Black community. Black, for me by the way, is a political term which unites all people of colour in their struggle against racism.

Right-wingers like Lord Tebbit insult us by saying we are not British enough. They want us to abandon our culture, religion, history and major contribution to civilisation as a condition of acceptance by this society. Gandhi poked fun at the Tebbits of this world when, on a

294

visit to London, he was asked by a journalist what he thought of British civilisation. The Mahatma replied: "It would be a good idea."

Professor Bhikhu Parekh, in the foreword to the milestone Fourth National Survey of Ethnic Minorities in Britain, states: "...the demand for integration can be taken too far. Every society is articulated at several levels, and immigrants may choose to integrate into some of these and not others. They might fully participate in the economy, the conduct of public affairs, etc., but prefer to marry among themselves or adhere to their own traditional cultural beliefs and practices."

Bhikhu, professor of political theory at Hull University, goes on to say that if some Black people choose to "break out of their communities" obstacles should not be placed in their way. "But if others decide differently, their choices should be respected. Identification with the wider community does not require the destruction of narrower identifications." The racists conveniently forget how Black people got here in the first place. That most reactionary of journalists Paul Johnson, writing in the Daily Mail recently, described the slave trade which carried many of our ancestors to the Caribbean, Americas and subsequently to Britain, as "the greatest act of human depravity in history, worse than the Holocaust, worse than the Gulag". Of course, Johnson went on to attempt to lessen the evil of the White people involved by focusing on the role played by the Africans who sold their own people into bondage.

Cities like London, Liverpool and Bristol were built up from the profits of slavery which paid for the industrial revolution in this country – some would say, it put the "great" in Britain by making the country the world's major power at that time. Author Ronald Segal says that, even though Britain was the first Western nation to withdraw from the slave trade "racism survived, resurgently accompanying the European scramble for Africa and informing the imperial vision". Segal goes on to state that today "individual Blacks are acceptable for their success, while Blacks in general are still seen as different and threatening".

The Black contribution to Britain's wealth did not stop with the abolition of slavery. During the war, Black service men and women fought against fascism; thousands of people like my father who came to Britain as a member of the RAF in 1943. Part of what was described as the "first batch", he was sent to Filey's camp in north Yorkshire with only sheep as company. Racists feared that if these virile young Black men were allowed any nearer to human life they would pose a danger to chaste English womanhood. After Filey's camp, the West Indian RAF recruits were dispatched to the "deep shelter" under Clapham Common, in south London. To their credit, Socialist MPs like Brixton's Marcus Lipton and the government minister Tom Driberg protested at this racist treatment and some of the men were moved to accommodation above ground.

That, in brief, is how Brixton became the capital of Black Britain. The first street to be settled was Somerleyton Road, opposite where The Voice newspaper is based today. My father left the RAF in 1946, disillusioned with Britain, and returned to Jamaica. But unemployment and the grinding poverty of the west Kingston ghetto where he lived forced him back to the so-called motherland, aboard the SS Empire Windrush, in 1948 along with almost 600 other Black former servicemen. It is interesting to note that things have not changed much in 50 years since then because reports of the horrendous racism faced by Black servicemen and women are just as bad today. Isn't it ironic that the Army is currently using the face of one of their few Black captains in a poster campaign titled Your Country Needs You?

Millennium

As we survey Britain in 1997 – three years before the next millennium – and compare it with 10 years ago we can see that, in this nation of shop-keepers, the window display has changed.

There are more Black faces. The music business is a good example. With a £1bn annual turnover, it is Britain's fifth largest industry. There are an abundance of Black artists. But how many

Black producers, managers, agents, promoters or record companies or record company executives are there? So often the music business is a case of Black talent and White profit. Black people are grossly under-represented in many institutions. There may be a handful of lower court judges (all 96 High Court Judges are White), Queens Counsel, more than a dozen MPs and Peers who are Black. At government level, we can boast no more than a junior health minister.

By contrast, in sport where talent rather than someone's subjective judgement holds sway, Black footballers dominate the Premier League. There are Black Olympic gold medal winners. But look inside Great Britain PLC. Look closer and it is still business as usual for the majority of Black folk, even six months after the election of a reforming Labour government.

Broadcaster and chair of race think tank the Runnymede Trust, Trevor Phillips remarked that if you went to the BBC or ITV early in the morning you would think these companies were run by Black people. But, no they are the cleaners, security, drivers and kitchen staff. Broadcast journalists like Trevor and myself - though more common – are still an exception to the rule. Despite the 1976 Race Relations Act, which the government boasts is the toughest law of its kind in Europe, Black people are more than twice as likely to be unemployed. While White unemployment is running at eight per cent, for African-Caribbeans it is 24 per cent and Pakistanis and Bangladeshis 27 per cent. When Black people do have a job they are likely to be the last in and first out. Ethnic minority men and women on average earn a quarter less than their similarly employed White counterparts.

Despite the fact that Black people make up 5.5 per cent of the population, their representation in the upper levels of the civil service, judiciary and corporate sector is less than one per cent. There is not a single Black Permanent Secretary in the Civil Service. Only one Black person has risen beyond the rank of police superintendent. The 1991 census found that a third of Pakistani and a half Bangladeshi households are overcrowded compared to less than two per cent of

297

White homes. Black people are disproportionately in prison and mental institutions though the levels of criminality and mental illness in our community do not justify this.

Successive race relations laws – the last one passed by a Labour government in 1976 to soften the blow of racist immigration legislation they had brought in earlier – have pretty much eliminated the overt "colour-bar" in our society. The one which allowed landlords to openly advertise: "No Blacks, No Irish, No dogs".

Indians, mainly those from East Africa, have by and large been an economic and educational success. They have done disproportionately well in retail sectors, for instance as the owners of newsagents. One might say they have become the new English shop-keeper. But this Asian success story is an exception and owes much to enterprise and hard work and little to government policy. The "colour bar" has been replaced by the "glass-ceiling" of institutional racism which is ever present. And there is a more murderous form of discrimination in existence in the form of racist attacks which have increased by a staggering 25 per cent over the last year, according to police statistics. The Policy Studies Institute's Fourth National Survey of Ethnic Minorities in Britain published this year suggested that as many as 250,000 Caribbeans and Asians experience racial harassment every year – including insults and abuse at the hands of strangers, neighbours, workmates or even the police.

Stephen Lawrence, an 18-year-old Black student, was murdered on the night of April 22 1993, by a mob of racist thugs while he stood with a friend at a bus stop in Eltham, minding his own business. I was telephoned by a family friend of the Lawrences the following day at the Anti-Racist Alliance office and from then onwards we spent every available hour with Stephen's parents helping in whatever way possible. This senseless killing became the national cause celebre which symbolised all racist murders, perhaps because Stephen Lawrence was a clean-cut, A Level student from a Christian family. The boy next door, who wanted to be an architect, and just happened to be Black. His

298

brutal murder was taken up, at the ARA's invitation, by Nelson Mandela, when he visited London. Yet, revealingly, no British government minister or member of the Royal Family saw fit to express any similar public concern. Rolan Adams, a 15-year-old Black youth, was murdered by racists in 1991, at Thamesmead near to Eltham. And so were Rohit Duggal and Orville Blair in the same area, leading the ARA to call this part of south east London the "racist murders capital of Britain".

Yet the earlier racist murders were ignored by the media and politicians. It is no co-incidence that the fascist British National Party had based their headquarters at nearby Welling, and mounted an aggressive "rights for Whites" campaign from their "nazi bunker". Persistent peaceful campaigning by the ARA and others led to the eventual closure of the headquarters. Meanwhile, middle England, in the form of the previously hostile Daily Mail, joined the labour and anti-racist movement in championing the Justice for Stephen Lawrence campaign. After the lamentable failure of the police murder investigation and Lawrence family's own aborted private prosecution, the Daily Mail took the unprecedented step of naming Stephen's killers on its front page. The new Labour Home Secretary Jack Straw granted the family's demand for a judicial inquiry into the murder and the issues it raised. Jack Straw also announced his intention to bring into law all the legislation proposed by the ARA in our Racial Harassment Bill.

A huge victory, some people might say, but one not credited to us by the news media or politicians who have instead dwelt on political differences in the ARA to write us off. What they fail to say is that those differences are about an essential political principle; the right of the oppressed to lead their own struggle. Self-proclaimed anti-racists like Ken Livingstone MP, an arch political opportunist who until his defeat by the membership co-chaired the ARA, have proved themselves no more than old fashioned White supremacists who would rather see an organisation destroyed than concede to Black leadership.

The weakening of the ARA, with Livingstone and his allies forming a breakaway group, has been calamitous for the whole anti-racist movement. As a result, it has been easier for prominent Black people to be victimised and our communities ignored. Local government funding to Black groups has been slashed, forcing leading organisations to close and their vital work to be abandoned. Against this backdrop, however, there is the international scandal of Britain's record on the deaths of Black people in custody – something the ARA has raised with the Committee on the Elimination of Racial Discrimination at the United Nations (ARA official report, February, 1996).

According to the pressure group Inquest, between 1969 and 1991 there were 69 "identified" Black deaths in custody. Of those, 37 were in police custody. Since 1991 there have been a further 43 identified Black deaths in custody of which 14 were in police custody. (The use of the word "identified" denotes the fact that up until 1997 the Home Office only monitored the age and gender of those who died. Following huge public pressure, the ethnic origin of victims is now recorded.) Unlawful killing verdicts were returned by inquest juries recently in four cases of police custody deaths and yet no action was taken against the officers involved who were not even suspended from duty during the investigation of their behaviour. This leads me to conclude that in Britain the police have a licence to kill Black people in their custody.

ARA Film

The Black star of BBC's hit soap Casualty, Patrick Robinson, played the lead role in an ARA promotional film Wonderful World which highlighted racial violence. The film captured the imagination of the editor of the Daily Mirror who telephoned me for a copy and then featured it on two pages of his newspaper. Since then, our advertising agency Maher Bird Associates has won a top national award with a newspaper ad on the same subject and they have run a radio advertisement on London News Direct, in memory of Rolan Adams, titled Waiting for a Bus. This has been followed up with a poster campaign at major billboard sites in London.

Youth ARA has gone from strength to strength organising their own ambitious events like the Black People in the Media conference in October. This attracted a big audience of mainly students to hear keynote speakers including Samir Shah, the head of the BBC's political unit, Sarwar Ahmed, editor in chief of the Ethnic Media Group, the editor of Pride magazine Marcia Degia, Edward Boateng, a senior executive from the American television cable news station CNN and myself. Youth ARA have also staged conferences on employment and business and have launched an ARA internet site donated free of charge by a company called Blacknet UK.

We were not able to stage the popular youth anti-racist festival ARAfest this year, not least because it would have clashed with the Respect event the Trades Union Congress now hold, with the help of sponsors like British Airways and Ford motor company – big names from which a Black organisation like the ARA could not hope to get support. But then they do say that emulation is the sincerest form of flattery.

Weakened in the workplace by the anti-trade unionism of the Thatcher years and therefore struggling to find a new role for itself, the TUC have capitalised on the fact that Black culture has transformed youth culture.
This is something that has been lost on Prime Minister Tony Blair but not new Conservative Party leader William Hague who attended both the Notting Hill Carnival and the Music of Black Origin Awards.

Shahid Miah and other members of Youth ARA are involved, with Tony O'Hara, of Harrow ARA, and me, in the pan-European educational anti-racist CD-Rom project being co-ordinated by the Danielle Mitterrand Foundation in Paris. The French version of this important multi-media tool for educators was launched in Belgium, in the presence of a government minister and other dignitaries, on the anniversary of the end of the Second World War this year.

301

We will be launching the British version in similar style early in 1998. Among the case studies put forward for the CD-Rom was the Melanie Purkiss affair. Melanie, a Black 16-year-old international sprinter from Hampshire, uncovered a racist practice British Airways were operating. Check-out staff at Gatwick Airport in 1995 wrongly told her she could not fly to Bordeaux, in France, on a one-way ticket because French immigration officials would not let her into the country despite the fact that she is a British and European Union citizen. She was only allowed to fly after agreeing to sign a "form of indemnity" which would have left her liable to pay a £2,000 fine if the French authorities refused her entry. The same year, a Black British probation officer, Tony Kelly, accused BA of racism after his passport was photocopied without his consent by check-out staff. In both cases, the airline was forced to apologise and end the discriminatory practice.

Airlines, like BA, have been criticised for picking on Black passengers because of the draconian Carriers Liability Act 1994 which can result in them having to face big fines if one of their ticket-holders is deported. A more humiliating example of racism that we put on the CD-Rom involved two Black waitresses, Freda Burton and Sonia Rhule. They were subjected to a torrent of racist and sexist abuse by "comedian" Bernard Manning at a Derby Round Table dinner at the city's Pennine Hotel on 1st December 1994. Freda and Sonia at first lost their industrial tribunal case against the management of the hotel at which they had been working but eventually they won substantial financial compensation on appeal.

The case set the important precedent that an employer has a duty to protect staff from racial discrimination. Local authorities are normally the largest employers of labour in our cities and towns. And, just as with the transport and health services and, in this area, the motor industry, Black labour keeps town halls working. Yet racism stalks us on a daily basis in the workplace.

An Asian former employee of Lambeth Council Don D'Souza was last month awarded more than £358,000 in damages after an eight year race discrimination legal battle against the local authority. Don was deprived of a town hall job he enjoyed doing as a result of a campaign of victimisation by his bosses.

This month Hackney Council was damned in an official report which found that Black staff faced serious discrimination from senior managers. The pattern is not restricted to London. It is widespread throughout the country.

Commission for Racial Equality (CRE) Chair Herman Ouseley put his finger on the problem when he told a management publication that "human talent and energy lies trapped behind structures that discriminate or operate passively against a tradition of disadvantage". He proposed the creation of "league tables for employers, highlighting both those that have done well and those that have done badly. The worst performers could expect legal action to be taken against them by the CRE". Greenwich, the Millennium London Borough, could go a long way towards redressing the balance through contracts compliance – the enforcement of equal opportunities on public-service providers backed up by mandatory ethnic record-keeping and monitoring.

That means proportional Black contracts and jobs where all the millennium projects are concerned. When Atlanta hosted the Olympics that is just what happened, so we can do it here too. Black politicians and their supporters must fight for contracts compliance to be brought in by the Labour government. This, more than most measures, would prove that Prime Minister Tony Blair is as serious as his counterpart President Bill Clinton in America about delivering for the Black voters who put him into power.

As Bhikhu Parekh points out: "Contrary to general belief, judiciously deployed positive discrimination is not incompatible with, but necessary to uphold the liberal principle of equal opportunity." But we should not hold our breath because, as Bhikhu puts it: "The fact that New Labour is all-White is significant...Could they not have done for ethnic minorities what they have done for women?" Political commentator Martin Jacques, writing in The Observer notes: "Blair, at

303

44, is the product of a very White world: Fettes, Oxford, the Bar, the Labour Party and his constituency, Sedgefield. So, less excusably is Labour. The young besuited men of Millbank are almost exclusively White.

Every one of the 54 special ministerial advisors appointed by Labour is White. Labour is not part of multi-cultural Britain." Examine the effective culling of Black Labour councillors around Britain and this becomes even more apparent.

For instance, in my own London Borough of Lambeth, south London, just two Black councillors remain when we had almost a dozen before New Labour. In the recent party selection meetings for council candidates, two Black women who are former Mayors of the borough were deselected in seats whose voters are a majority Black and will now be represented by White men. Some say there should be a law against this sort of affront to democracy.

Race Law

The problem with the 1976 Race Relations Act is that it exempts much government activity from its provisions. It is much less powerful than Northern Ireland's Fair Employment Act which deals with religious discrimination, something which British Muslims, in their campaign against Islamaphobia, point out is needed here too. Individual beacons of courage like the mothers and fathers who fight for justice after a racist murder inspire us. As does the bravery of children like Daniel De Gale, aged 10, who is critically ill with leukaemia at Great Ormond Street Hospital. If Daniel were White he would stand a one in four chance of surviving. Being Black he has only a one in 120,000 chance. It is because of these appalling odds that no Black leukaemia sufferer has had a successful bone marrow transplant in this country. But stars, like footballers John Fashanu and Ian Wright, have joined Daniel's family in their quest to find suitable Black donors.

This campaign, set up by Daniel's mother Bev, is an excellent example of us doing something for ourselves rather than carping on the sidelines. Either Black people organise ourselves or we will get ignored.

Student Success

In education, the stereotyping of Black male pupils and their disproportionate exclusion and expulsion rates are a continuing source of concern. But there are significant success stories. Twelve per cent of British university students are Black and in higher education generally there are many examples of our students out-performing their White counterparts.

As a contribution to this, world champion boxer Lennox Lewis has set a shining example for his fellow wealthy Black sports men and women by making an annual £1m donation to an inner city college named after him. Contrast Lennox's generosity with the meanness of the Cabinet minister responsible for overseas aid Clare Short when faced with the crisis brought about by the Montserrat volcano. She accused the stricken islanders of wanting financial "golden elephants" from Britain. What a cheek! Like the population of Montserrat, Black people want parity not charity.

Clare, who represents a Birmingham parliamentary constituency with the largest number of Black voters in the country, should be made to apologise for this insult whenever she meets Black people. It is a pity the Black MPs were not more vocal in their criticism of their Labour colleague.

But then perhaps this sorry story is an object lesson that movements create leaders, not the other way round, and movements, like the Black Section campaign which won the Black MPs their positions, must keep making their representatives accountable. National Black movements, like the Black Section and Labour Party Black Socialist Society to which it gave birth are close to extinction because the people they propelled into office compliantly went along with rather than defended them against the attacks of the powers-that-be. This means we must go back to basics, concern ourselves less with

305

the Black-faces-in-high-places approach of the middle class, and build from the bottom up again.

From a community level, Black people need to develop groups in workplaces, places of worship, on housing estates, among the youth and women, around specific grassroots issues like racial violence, police brutality, jobs, education and an economic fair deal. As part of the process, we might draw support from anti-racist White people in alliances or coalitions. But we must learn from the mistakes of the past and establish structures which enable us to maintain control of our organisations. This way we will be able to painstakingly relaunch a national Black voice capable of articulating a Black agenda for the next millennium.

The year 2000 will usher in a new dawn for Black people in Europe – across the 27 European Union states and beyond. Because we are part of a global diaspora we are instinctively internationalist What is more, we have made this country and the European continent our home and very much know we are here to stay. I am reminded of a sentence in the maiden speech of Shapurji Saklatvala, the Indian elected the MP for Battersea North in 1922, about whom I have written a book which is being published in 1998. He urged the House of Commons to "burst out of these time-worn prejudices and boldly take a new place".

(Comrade Sak, A Political Biography, Marc Wadsworth, Peepal Tree Books, Leeds.) Black people demand and expect respect, dignity and justice. With your support I know those goals will be achieved.

Thank you comrades. I wish Jim and Doreen Thakoordin and the Luton Committee for Racial Harmony every success.

Editor's Update: No fewer than 127 black and ethnic minority people have died in police custody in the past 20 years. Since the murder of Stephen Lawrence in April, 1993. No police officer has been convicted of any of these deaths.

PART THREE

Famous people involved in the struggles for racial justice, equality and human rights

Chapter Sixteen

MAHATMA GANDHI

Struggles against British Colonialism

Mahatma Gandhi 2 October **1869 – 30 January 1948**

The name of Mohandas Karamchand Gandhi is synonymous with India's struggle for independence from British rule. He was a man who captured the imagination of millions of people in his own country and around the world, with his principle of non-Cupertino and non-violence, or satyagraha, an idea which later inspired the Civil Rights Movement in America, Europe and around the world. Gandhi was a ceaseless crusader for peace, justice, rights, freedom and harmony around the world. He was also deeply committed to equality for women. During his life he wrote over 10 million words, which averages some 500 words every day for 50 years. Many world leaders including Kwame Nkrumah, Dr Martin Luther King Jr., Nelson Mandela and others acknowledged Gandhi's contribution to their leadership qualities.

Childhood

Gandhi was born on 2 October 1869 into an average family in a small town near Bombay, in the province of Gujarat, India. When Gandhi was born he was the sixth child and the youngest child of the family. At Gandhi's birth his father was 48 years old and his mother was in her early twenties. His father was an educated man and worked as a civil servant. He died when Gandhi was still at school. His mother was illiterate but exercised enormous power within the family. Gandhi's childhood was not exceptional in any way; he was shy and quite timid. His achievements at school were regarded as slightly below average. At the age of thirteen, whilst still at school he was married to Kasturba. He left school and started at a college but dropped out after a few months. He was then advised by a family member to go to England and to study law.

Education and Life in England

Gandhi arrived in London after promising his mother that he would not eat meat, get involved with women or drink alcohol. To enable Gandhi to study in England his family had to make a lot of sacrifices. His brother sold some of the family land and his wife sold most of her jewellery and other members of the family made contributions. The local community was unhappy about this journey and decreed that anyone who crossed the seas, or anyone who assisted someone in the crossing of the seas, would be an outcast. Gandhi pleaded with them but to no avail. Nevertheless he left India in September 1888 at the age of 18.

After arriving in London Gandhi had to overcome his shyness, get used to a new lifestyle and culture. He was a hard working student and completed not only the law course but also the London Matriculation examination. He returned to India as a Barrister in Bombay but was unable to establish a successful practice, so he decided to accept an offer to assist a senior lawyer in South Africa for a year and left India in May 1893, age 23.

Experience in South Africa

Within days of arriving in South Africa Gandhi experienced race discrimination. He was on a train journey from Durban to Johannesburg when he was told that, despite having a first class ticket, he had to travel in the coach reserved for non-whites, as only white people were allowed to travel first class. Gandhi was angry with this, as his experience of travelling in London was grossly different. He refused to change carriage and was ejected from the train late at night, on a small station up in the mountains, during the middle of winter. He spent the night on the cold station. The next morning he took the first train and arrived in Johannesburg a much-awakened person to apartheid and racial discrimination based on skin colour. During the long night at the railway station Gandhi reviewed his career and what he wanted from life. He decided that fighting racism and oppression was more important than a high career or making money.

On another journey by coach, he was beaten up by a passenger when he refused to crouch by the driver's feet. In Johannesburg, he was refused a hotel room because he was Indian. From that day, he vowed that he would oppose racial prejudice and discrimination. He decided following his experience so far in South Africa to convene a meeting of local Indians to find out about their situation under such apartheid conditions. He spent the next year fighting the South African authorities on legal grounds against racial discrimination and representing victims of racism in the courts.

At the end of the year, having successfully completed his assignment in South Africa, he was contemplating returning to India, but he discovered that a Bill aimed at preventing Indians from voting was being planned by the government. He therefore decided to stay and to oppose the Bill. He campaigned full-time against the Bill, which was passed a month later. Gandhi then decided to stay as long as it took to fight apartheid. He brought his family to South Africa where he continued his work as a lawyer for 21 years, fighting racism through the courts. Although Gandhi won a number of court cases and secured concessions for the Indians, the government counteracted his success by passing even more draconian legislation against the Indians and Africans.

Gandhi spent a lot of time educating and supporting the Indian community. He believed that Indians in South Africa should maintain their self-respect and keep high standards if they were to prove that they were equal to whites. He worked to overcome differences of religion, caste and wealth amongst Indians through the Natal Indian Congress. Gandhi was determined to fight against unjust laws legally and morally. After his experience with the law he decided to fight apartheid and racism through the moral route.

The Moral Crusade for Freedom

Gandhi felt that it was justified to break unjust laws and developed a "truth force". For Gandhi, the ends never justified the means – all action had to be non-violent. He then turned to journalism to advocate his cause and in 1903 having lived in South Africa for 10 years; he started a weekly newspaper called 'Indian Opinion', in which he outlined the conditions of Indians and Africans in South Africa under apartheid. Journalism had a profound effect on Gandhi. He met many leaders and influential people through his campaigns and crusades. He decided to start living a far more simple life and to live on a farm where

311

he could grow his own food, use basic machinery and experiment with fasting. He also decided to practice celibacy. Gandhi used his newspaper to educate his followers to the concept of non-violence as a means of resisting oppression and creating change. By 1914 Gandhi's philosophy began to attract world attention as he had achieved some success through his philosophy of Satyagraha. The nationalist leaders of India who were opposed to British occupation of their country were aware of Gandhi's reputation and persuaded him to return to India to work with them.

Starving Indian family, British Raj, 1877.

British grain taxation policies, coupled with drought, caused an estimated 12-29 million Indians to starve to death from 1876-1902. The British administration, headed by the viceroy Lord Lytton(who dismissed calls to feed famine victims as "humanitarian hysterics"), not only did nothing to stop the disaster but actually pushed an act of parliament in 1877 that forbade famine relief, for fear it would cut into the record profits being made. They did allow desperate refugees from the countryside to earn their food at work camps in Madras and Calcutta, where their rations were less then that of prisoners at Buchenwald. British troops massacred starving mobs who tried to storm the trains and ships that were exporting their grain to Britain. The Madras Chamber of Commerce suggested the police set up flogging posts to prevent people from stealing the grain.

Back to India

He left South Africa in 1915, age 45 and returned to India. At this time, he was still a great admirer of the British and their influence in India through his experience in England and the contrast he experienced in South Africa, but within 2 years his views had changed. Gandhi felt that in a number of ways the British presence was good for India and even campaigned to recruit soldiers for the British Army during the First World War 1914-18. However, after the war in 1919 the British forces ordered a massacre in Punjab in which 319 Indian men and women were killed and 1200 seriously injured. This shattered his belief in the British Empire. Also on a visit to Champaran at the foot of the Himalayas, he met peasants who worked the land in terrible conditions for English landlords. When he disobeyed a police order for him not to enter the district, he was arrested. He was shocked, but learnt a lesson about what British rule meant, saying, "In Champaran I declared that the British could not order me about in my own country". Gandhi soon emerged as a powerful leader of the national movement for freedom, earning the name "mahatma", meaning "great soul".

Gandhi's influence on the Indian National Congress party was to make it into a mass popular movement. Travelling the country in his simple dress, and living a plain lifestyle, he won the trust of the peasants. Winston Churchill, who believed fully in the rightness of the British Empire, branded Gandhi a "half-naked fakir". He was, perhaps, unable to understand how a man with Gandhi's appearance could be a challenge to British rule. Unlike some nationalist leaders Gandhi was not interested in raising an army against British rule or forcing the rulers out, as he thought that the British were able to rule India because in many ways the Indians needed them. They had been conditioned to British rule especially the Maharajas who were able to maintain their rule and wealth under the British protection. Gandhi wanted the Indians

313

to learn to manage their own affairs effectively without relying on, or co-operating with the foreign rulers. This, he thought, would demonstrate the helplessness of the British and they would leave India voluntarily.

The Philosophy of Satyagraha in India

In 1920, a year after the tragedy of the Jallinawala Bagh Massacre, Gandhi launched his campaign of civil disobedience. He called for a mass boycott of all government institutions, including the law courts, schools and payment of taxes. He said that the only way to drive the British rulers out of India was total non-co-operation. Along with thousands of other Indians, Gandhi was arrested and imprisoned for "political crimes" against the British Government. "Rivers of bloodshed by the government cannot frighten me", said Gandhi in defiance. Typically, Gandhi would not be defeated, even when he was in jail. Whilst serving his 6-year prison sentence, he wrote, "By nature I like solitude. Silence pleases me. And I am able to indulge in studies which I prize, but which I was bound to neglect outside". Gandhi was again the inspiration for the freedom struggle in 1929, when he led the campaign against the salt tax. This tax made it impossible for Indians to make their own salt, and so they had to depend on imported salt from Britain. Gandhi realised that salt was representative of the entire colonial system of enforced dependence. He organised open defiance of the salt tax law. He and his supporters marched over 240 miles to the sea, where they collected water and boiled it for salt.

Gandhi encouraged Indians to grow their own food, weave their own clothes, and run their own schools, colleges, hospitals, courts, railways and law enforcement agencies. He emphasized the need for unity amongst people from different cultures, religions and social status and to present a united front against British rule. He warned his people against violence against each other or against British rule and re-enforced his philosophy on non-violence through the newspapers under his influence. One of Gandhi's most significant successes came in 1930 when he challenged the British Government that he would defy the Salt

Tax if it were not withdrawn within ten days. The Government ignored this threat and Gandhi carried out the defiance by marching 241 miles to the sea on foot over 24 days with his followers in full view of the world media.

Mass Following

The long march by Gandhi attracted worldwide attention and support for non-violence. The event ignited the imagination of millions of Indians who had never witnessed anyone who had challenged the British rule in such a way and to have such an impact without resorting to violence. As a consequence many Indians began to defy the British inspired laws and the Government accepted that they were losing control over India and decided to hold talks with leaders about the possibility of granting them independence.

Ending of British Rule

For the next 16 years the British government used all sorts of techniques to delay independence. Gandhi was seen by most people as the undisputed leader of the movement for independence and was invited with others to meetings with the Viceroy in India and to attend Conferences in London with the British Government. During this period Gandhi and others increased the pressure on the British administration in India, which in turn took a series of actions to subdue the population. Gandhi and many of his followers were frequently harassed, persecuted and imprisoned. Despite these measures the pressure on British rule became more serious. Gandhi's influence grew even when he was in prison. He was not afraid of being in prison and used the time to reflect and to plan new activities. He spent a total of 7 years in prison during his lifetime.

Eventually, in 1942, with India's desire for freedom still bring frustrated by the British administration, Gandhi launched the Quit India Movement. In his famous 'Do or Die' speech, he said"I want freedom immediately, this very night, before dawn, if it can be had…. Congress must win freedom or be wiped out in the effort…..we shall either free India or die in the attempt". Gandhi and all the other Congress leaders were immediately imprisoned, but the movement had been rooted in the hearts of the people, from where new leaders and activists sprang to replace those who had been imprisoned.

Finally, on August 15 1947, 31 years after Gandhi joined the struggle for independence, India was granted independence. One of the most disappointing outcomes for Gandhi was the division of India and the creation of two separate states, one for Indians and the other, Pakistan, for Muslims. Gandhi was opposed to the division of India but people within the Congress Party, which formed the interim government in India and supported the division, outnumbered him by a large majority. His philosophy of non-violence was not adhered to by the Hindus and Moslems factions, which fought each other, and resulted in the death of several hundred thousand people.

While others celebrated India and Pakistan's freedom in August, Gandhi was in Punjab trying to end communal rioting. On 30 January 1948, Gandhi himself became a victim of the violence surrounding the partition of India. He was shot 3 times at point black range by a Hindu, Nathuram Ghose, who blamed Gandhi for allowing India to be divided. The world was left mourning a great man who had brought freedom to his people, and inspired struggles against injustice around the world. Gandhi's last words after being shot were, "Oh God".

Gandhi was a man of God and a man of peace he respected all religions and all cultures. He was genuinely committed to resolving issues through talking and negotiations. Many world leaders claim to believe in peace, yet they prepare their country for wars. If war led to harmony then the problems of the 20th century would have been solved by the First World War in 1914-1918. There would have been no need for a Second World War some 20 years later and dozens of major conflicts around the world since in which tens of millions have been killed around the world. The world still needs the spirit and philosophy of Gandhi. His views and contribution to human kind will live forever.

The Quit India Speech made in 1942 by Mahatma Gandhi

The Quit India **speech** is a speech made by Mahatma Gandhi on 8th August, 1942, on the eve of the Quit India movement. He called for determined, but **passive resistance** that signified the certitude that Gandhi foresaw for the movement is best described by his call to Do or Die. His speech was issued at the Gowalia Tank Maidan in Bombay, since re-named August Kranti Maidan (August Revolution Ground). However, almost the entire Congress leadership, and not merely at the national level, was put into confinement less than twenty-four hours after Gandhi's speech, and the greater number of the Congress leaders were to spend the rest of the war in jail.

Before you discuss the resolution, let me place before you one or two things, I want you to understand two things very clearly and to consider them from the same point of view from which I am placing them before you. I ask you to consider it from my point of view, because if you approve of it, you will be enjoined to carry out all I say. It will be a great responsibility. There are people who ask me whether I am the same man that I was in 1920, or whether there has been any change in me. You are right in asking that question.

Let me; however, hasten to assure that I am the same Gandhi as I was in 1920. I have not changed in any fundamental respect. I attach the same importance to non-violence that I did then. If at all, my emphasis on it has grown stronger. There is no real contradiction between the present resolution and my previous writings and utterances. Occasions like the present do not occur in everybody's and but rarely in anybody's life. I want you to know and feel that there is nothing but purest Ahimsa1 in all that I am saying and doing today. The draft resolution of the Working Committee is based on Ahimsa; the contemplated struggle similarly has its roots in Ahimsa. If, therefore, there is any among you who has lost faith in Ahimsa or is wearied of it, let him not vote for this resolution.

317

Let me explain my position clearly. God has vouchsafed to me a priceless gift in the weapon of Ahimsa. I and my Ahimsa are on our trail today. If in the present crisis, when the earth is being scorched by the flames of Himsa2 and crying for deliverance, I failed to make use of the God given talent, God will not forgive me and I shall be judged unwrongly of the great gift. I must act now. I may not hesitate and merely look on, when Russia and China are threatened.

Ours is not a drive for power, but purely a non-violent fight for India's independence. In a violent struggle, a successful general has been often known to affect a military coup and to set up a dictatorship. But under the Congress scheme of things, essentially non-violent as it is, there can be no room for dictatorship. A non-violent soldier of freedom will covet nothing for himself; he fights only for the freedom of his country. The Congress is unconcerned as to who will rule, when freedom is attained. The power, when it comes, will belong to the people of India, and it will be for them to decide to whom it placed in the entrusted. May be that the reins will be placed in the hands of the Parsis, for instance-as I would love to see happen-or they may be handed to some others whose names are not heard in the Congress today. It will not be for you then to object saying, 'This community is microscopic. That party did not play its due part in the freedom's struggle; why should it have all the power?' Ever since its inception the Congress has kept itself meticulously free of the communal taint. It has thought always in terms of the whole nation and has acted accordingly...

I know how imperfect our Ahimsa is and how far away we are still from the ideal, but in Ahimsa there is no final failure or defeat. I have faith, therefore, that if, in spite of our shortcomings, the big thing does happen, it will be because God wanted to help us by crowning with success our silent, unremitting Sadhana1 for the last twenty-two years. I believe that in the history of the world, there has not been a more genuinely democratic struggle for freedom than ours. I read Carlyle's French Resolution while I was in prison, and Pandit Jawaharlal has told me something about the Russian revolution. But it is my conviction that inasmuch as these struggles were fought with the

318

weapon of violence they failed to realize the democratic ideal. In the democracy which I have envisaged, a democracy established by non-violence, there will be equal freedom for all. Everybody will be his own master. It is to join a struggle for such democracy that I invite you today. Once you realize this you will forget the differences between the Hindus and Muslims, and think of yourselves as Indians only, engaged in the common struggle for independence.

Then, there is the question of your attitude towards the British. I have noticed that there is hatred towards the British among the people. The people say they are disgusted with their behaviour. The people make no distinction between British imperialism and the British people. To them, the two are one this hatred would even make them welcome the Japanese. It is most dangerous. It means that they will exchange one slavery for another. We must get rid of this feeling. Our quarrel is not with the British people, we fight their imperialism. The proposal for the withdrawal of British power did not come out of anger. It came to enable India to play its due part at the present critical juncture It is not a happy position for a big country like India to be merely helping with money and material obtained willy-nilly from her while the United Nations are conducting the war. We cannot evoke the true spirit of sacrifice and velour, so long as we are not free. I know the British Government will not be able to withhold freedom from us, when we have made enough self-sacrifice. We must, therefore, purge ourselves of hatred. Speaking for myself, I can say that I have never felt any hatred. As a matter of fact, I feel myself to be a greater friend of the British now than ever before. One reason is that they are today in distress. My very friendship, therefore, demands that I should try to save them from their mistakes. As I view the situation, they are on the brink of an abyss. It, therefore, becomes my duty to warn them of their danger even though it may, for the time being, anger them to the point of cutting off the friendly hand that is stretched out to help them. People may laugh, nevertheless that is my claim. At a time when I may have to launch the biggest struggle of my life, I may not harbour hatred against anybody.

319

Chapter Seventeen

C L R JAMES
Trinidadian political activist, writer and journalist

C L R James 4 January
1901 – 19 May 1989

C.L.R. James, political thinker and scholar (1901-1989)

C. L. R. James's seminal book *At the Rendezvous of Victory* first alerted
me to the Socialist case for Black self-organisation. Although he was a

Trotskyist, Communists not usually linked with support for such things because they said that Black groups would divide the working class movement, James was a brilliant, independent-minded political thinker, writer and scholar prepared to rock the boat. In 1984, when the book was published in Britain, I was an activist in the unofficial Labour Party Black Section campaign which was being bitterly resisted by an unholy alliance of the Labour leadership, right-wing trade union barons and the Trotskyist *Militant Tendency*. James's politics had a massive influence on the Black movement throughout the world. The Times described him as "The black Plato of our generation…the founding father of African emancipation."

Cyril Lionel Robert James was born in Tunapuna, Trinidad in 1901. His childhood home backed onto a cricket ground. Indeed, as he was to later observe, an umpire could have watched a match from the bedroom. So began James's lifelong passion for the English game associated with the notion of 'fair play'. As a boy he knew the great Pan-Africanist George Padmore.

He was also friend with the famous West Indian cricketer Learie Constantine for whom he left Trinidad, aged 31, to join him in England. James, determined to be a novelist, made money by writing cricket reports for the *Manchester Guardian* and the *Glasgow Herald*.

From childhood, his two loves were literature and cricket. His great affection for literature encouraged him to read European literature deeply and critically, whilst the drama and techniques of cricket kept him in contact with the lives and hopes of ordinary working people. James felt fated to be a novelist, but also trained himself to become a journalist. He was a Caribbean nationalist. The First World War, the Russian Revolution and the Garvey movement were key events during James' formative years, but had little impact on him at the time.

When he moved from Constantine's home in Nelson, Lancashire, to London, James joined the Independent Labour Party

(ILP) becoming the Chair of the Finchley branch. But, disenchanted by the ILP's lack of full-blooded Socialism, he split from it with other Marxists to form the Revolutionary Socialist League. He edited the party's paper, *Fight*. Black Communists, including James, had to square several contradictions. Senegal's legendary President Leopold Senghor put it well when he said, at the first Congress of Negro Writers and Artists: "Many of us are Marxists. But Marx was not an African. His doctrine was born from the situation of men in Western Europe. And he said himself that his theory of Capital was only valid for Western Europe."

So James, whose discussion with Trotsky on such questions formed the basis of his *At the Rendezvous of Victory,* saw it as vital that he should not only involve himself with a White left party but also work with Black community groups. He was on the executive of the League of Coloured Peoples, an organisation set up by the south London-based Jamaican medical doctor, Harold Moody. And he was a leading light in the more radical International African Service Bureau, forerunner of the Pan-African Federation. James wrote a play about Toussaint Louverture, the leader of the successful Haitian slave rebellion against the French.

James himself acted in the drama, alongside Paul Robeson, at the Westminster Theatre. The play was the precursor to James's acclaimed book *The Black Jacobins,* a work that stands as a monument to Black political writing. James said: "I was tired of reading and hearing about Africans being persecuted and oppressed in Africa, in the Middle Passage, in the USA and all over the Caribbean. I made up my mind that would write a book in which Africans and people of African descent instead of constantly being the object of other people's exploitation and ferocity would themselves be taking action on a grand scale and shaping other people to their own needs."

The book succeeded in impressing the pundits. It 'contains some of the finest and most deeply felt polemical writing against slavery and racism ever to be published and it locates the Caribbean and Caribbean society firmly on the world stage," said *Time Out*.

The book provides a brave insight into the complex, often troubled relations between "the blacks" and so-called "mulattos" in Haiti. James's first novel, *Minty Alley,* was published in 1936. It is a semi-autobiographical account of a West Indian childhood. James's Classic history of the 'rise and fall of the Communist International, *World Revolution 1917-1936,* became, in the publisher's words, 'a kind of bible of Trotskyism'.

In 1938, James went to lecture in the United States and stayed there illegally for 15 years as an activist in working class struggles, providing them with a hugely significant Black perspective. It was James who pioneered 'the idea of an autonomous black movement that would be socialist but not subject to controls by the leaderships of white-majority parties and trade unions'.

James's visionary stance was expressed long before the Black Power movements of the 1960s and 1970s. Like Eric Williams, who was to become Prime Minister of Trinidad, James caused controversy by arguing that slavery was abolished in the English-speaking world because it was no longer economically viable. In other words, capitalists rather than the William Wilberforce humanitarians were mainly responsible for abolition. James wrote: 'Those who see in abolition the gradually awakening conscience of mankind should spend a few minutes asking themselves why it is that man's conscience, which had slept peacefully for so many centuries, should awake just at the time that men began to see the unprofitableness of slavery.' *State Capitalism and World Revolution (1950)* completed his break with 'orthodox' Trotskyism. Going back to his beloved cricket, *Beyond the Boundary (1963)* was partly a book on his favourite sport and partly autobiographical.

In *Nkrumah and the Ghana Revolution (1977)*, James espoused 'a sequence of political responses to an extreme political situation, the African situation as it has developed during the last thirty years'. Along with Padmore, James was among a gifted group of West Indian intellectuals who met with and supported fellow Pan-Africanists like Ghana's Kwame Nkrumah and Jomo Kenyatta, of Kenya.

This political collaboration included the holding of Pan-Africanist Congresses in Europe that laid the foundation for the liberation of Africa from colonialism, starting with Ghana in 1957. James said: "We had no idea that things we were fighting for would come with such rapidity. Naturally we back Nkrumah and Padmore worked with him to the end. I did what I could also. But we had not the faintest idea that after it had taken place in Ghana, before ten years passed, seven eighths of Africa would be independent."

James's last years were spent in a small room on a road off the "frontline" in Brixton, south London. He died in May 1989. Academic Anna Grimshaw, who had worked for James, wrote: "His death coincided with the explosion of popular forces across China and eastern Europe which shook some of the most oppressive political regimes in human history. These momentous events, calling into question the structure of the modern world order, throw into sharp relief the life and work of one of this century's most outstanding figures."

Now there is an archive and research institute and a foundation in C.L.R. James's memory in the United States and a library named after him in Hackney, London. C.L.R. James became one of the most influential thinkers of the twentieth century. He made outstanding and original contributions across a number of areas, from history and political theory to literature and cultural studies. He was brought up to believe that education was a way out of poverty and into security.

In 1938, James left England for America and spent a few years there working with many different political groups, writing and lecturing on political philosophy, socialist politics, Pan-Africanism and Caribbean nationalism. He became a key figure in Marxist thinking after the second world war with the publication of a number of important books, such as 'Notes on Dialectics', and he attended the 1945 Pan-African Congress in Manchester. He was, because of his radical views, deported from the U.S., and spent a few years in Europe. In 1958 he was invited to return to Trinidad to help his friend and former pupil, the Prime Minister, Eric Williams. However, James did not spare his friend's feelings when he believed that Williams was betraying the Trinidadian people and his own principles. James was obliged to leave Trinidad in 1961.

James spent the rest of his life moving between England and the United States. However, his age did not limit the range of his interests or involvements. He had a central role in the discussions about political theory, Black Power, Pan-Africanism and Caribbean nationalism. He died in 1989, leaving a vast amount of work which is still analysed and debated the world over.

Chapter Eighteen

MUHAMMAD ALI
The people's champion

Born 17 January 1942 and still going strong Jim Thakoordin, meeting the great Champion in 1984

Muhammad Ali was born Cassius Clay, on. 17th January 1942, in Louisville, Kentucky, USA. In 1960 he won the light heavyweight gold medal at the Olympics and began his ascent to the world heavyweight boxing championship, which he won in 1964, by beating the previously indomitable Sonny Liston.

Though Ali won the gold medal at the Rome Olympics in 1960, at the time the experts didn't think much of his boxing skills. His head, eyes wide, seemed to float above the action. Rather than slip a punch, the traditional defensive move, it was his habit to sway back, bending at the waist - a tactic that appalled the experts.

His fight for the heavyweight championship in Miami against Sonny Liston was not very well attended. Lots of Black as well as white people supported Liston who was seen as a thug who would take care of the lippy upstart. Liston promised that he was going to put his fist so far down his opponent's throat; he was going to have trouble removing it. Ali rapidly proved to the world that he was a serious and great champion.

Ali was the greatest heavyweight champion ever. He was more than a boxer - he helped to define what a Black man could and should be in America and elsewhere. Ali took inspiration from past and present Black activists during his boxing career. He drew on the influence and strength of Marcus Garvey, Malcolm X, Kwame Nkrumah and other Black leaders who challenged the stereotypical image of African American men. Ali took an interest in the Black struggle in America even when he was at High School. He surprised his English teacher when he told her that he wanted to write his term paper on the Black Muslims. She refused to let him do so, but his interest in the Nation of Islam increased. He attended a number of meetings organised by the Congress of Racial Equality and the National Association for the Advancement of Coloured People during the early 1960s. His wit, charm, humour and his love for life and humanity won him admiration across the world. Ali is one of the most powerful icons of the 20th century that inspired hundreds of millions of Black, white and brown people around the world.

Ali has always from an early age shown an interest in Black power and politics. He was once a close friend of Malcolm X before he fell out with him because of the internal feud between Malcolm and the Nation of Islam. Ali refused to join the American army and to fight in Vietnam during the early 1960s. He commented "why should I go 10,000 miles from home and drop bombs on brown people in Vietnam while so-called Negro people in Louisville are treated like dogs". He refused to fight the Vietnamese claiming that "I ain't got no quarrel with them Vietcong". "Ali showed his commitment to Black power when he stated in "If I thought going to war would bring freedom and equality to 22 million of my people, they wouldn't have to draft me, I'd join tomorrow. But I either have to obey the laws of the land or the laws of Allah. I have nothing to lose by standing up and following my beliefs. We've been in jail for 400 years". Ali was kept out of boxing for three and a half years because of his refusal to fight the Vietnamese until the Supreme Court ruled in 1971 that the government had acted illegally in banning him from boxing.

During his career as a heavyweight boxer he won 56 of his 61 bouts; with 37 knockouts. He lost 5 bouts and became the first boxer to win the heavyweight title three times. Muhammad Ali revolutionised boxing and has maintained to this day strong worldwide support.

The greatest heavyweight ever

For many people Muhammad Ali was the greatest heavyweight boxer in the history of the sport. He is the most famous person in the world despite the fact that he fought his last fight in 1981 after being defeated by Trevor Berbick at the end of 10 rounds.

Ali took on the greatest boxers during his nearly 20 year's career including the British heavyweight Henry Cooper. For white

328

America black boxing champions should use their fists in the ring and kept their mouth shut outside it. Ali certainly changed the stereotypical image of the heavyweight champion. Muhammad Ali had not only the most powerful fist during his career but also a brilliant mind. In 1967, Ali refused to join the American army and fight in the Vietnam War. He cited his religious beliefs as a Black Muslim, and his refusal to kill foreigners who had never harmed him as his reasons for not fighting the "white man's war". Ali was arrested and his boxing licence suspended. He was also stripped of his heavyweight title.

Ali refused to allow the establishment to intimidate him and he took his case to the people of America. Between 22 March 1967 and 26 October 1970, a period when he was probably at the peak of his career he was forced out of the ring. So he took his case to the people by giving talks at universities, conventions and meetings across America.

The people's champion

Ali remained the people's champion even though he was barred from the ring. He regained his heavyweight crown in 1974 when he defeated the unbeaten champion George Foreman, at the age of 32. Ali has been a great fighter of human and civil rights and was very close to people like Malcolm X and others in the struggles for civil and human rights during the 1960's and 1970's.

Many Americans did not approve of Ali's personal behaviour: the self-promotions ("I am the greatest!"), his affiliation with the Black Muslims and giving up his "slave name" for Muhammad Ali ("I don't have to be what you want me to be; I'm free to be what I want"), the poetry (his ability to compose rhymes on the run could very well qualify him as the first rapper). At the press conferences, the reporters were often sullen. Ali would turn on them. "Why ain't you taking notice?" or "Why ain't you laughing?"

Amongst his most memorable fights were the two battles against Sonny Liston; the fight in 1974 when he defeated George Foreman in the "Rumble in the Jungle" in Zaire, and in 1975 when he defeated Joe
329

Frazier in the "Thrilla in Manila" in the Philippines. Ali was one of the most courageous fighters of his time inside and outside the ring.

A challenge for the white racists

For many white Americans he was the most arrogant and conceited boxer because he was not afraid to challenge white racists and so called "white supremacy" which was prevalent in America, and still is to a fair extent. Ali refused to play along with the white establishment. Instead he stood by his principles, people and supporters and played a major part in transforming the level of racial awareness, especially amongst white and Black people around the world. Ali knew that white Americans would only support and reward a Black champion in the absence of and "white hope", so he and his supporters were delighted when he defeated the best of the white hopefuls from around the world.

A fearless fighter inside and outside the ring

Ali was not afraid of the racist media and the racist organisations, which tried to intimidate him. He showed the world that a black man can be the world heavyweight champion and exercise his civil, human and moral rights to express himself condemn institutional, cultural and economic exploitation and racism.

Encouraged to fight long after he should have retired, and perhaps because he loved the sport too much to leave it, Ali ended up being beaten by a couple of black fighters who themselves took little pleasure in their victory over the great man.

Despite his retirement from the ring after being defeated by Larry Holmes in 1980 and Trevor Berbeick in 1981 and his subsequent poor health Ali remains the most famous champion of all time. He is truly the people's champion who gave pleasure, hope and inspiration to billions of people around the world. In 1996, Ali opened the Olympic Games in Atlanta. He also visited Britain on several occasions. I met him twice, once in Birmingham when he opened the Muhammad Ali

Centre, and on the other occasion at an Awards Dinner in London, organised by Arif Ali and Hansib Publications.

Ali also toured the London Borough of Lambeth, which has a majority Black population. Ali was not only the greatest; he was double greatest. Not only did he knock them out, he picked the round when he knocked them out.

Ali has always been full of humour and fun below the surface of a tough person. He would sometimes joke about serious and even difficult issues. When reporters asked about his affiliation with Islam, he joked that he was going to have four wives: one to shine his shoes, one to feed him grapes, one to rub oil on his muscles and one named Peaches. In his boyhood he was ever the prankster and the practical joker. His idea of fun was to frighten his parents by putting a sheet over his head and jumping out at them from a closet, or tying a string to a bedroom curtain and making it move after his parents had gone to bed.

Ali was asked on a television show what he would have done with his life, given a choice. After an awkward pause--a rare thing, indeed--he admitted he couldn't think of anything other than boxing. That is all he had ever wanted or wished for. He couldn't imagine anything else. He defended boxing as a sport: "You don't have to be hit in boxing. People don't understand that."

Ali was wrong. Joe Frazier, speaking of their fight, said he had hit Ali with punches that would have brought down a building. The very sport, which brought Ali to world fame also, helped to severely damage his health. Ali is a person of many talents and would have succeeded in any profession he had chosen. He once said "I'm not only the greatest; I'm the double greatest. Not only do I knock 'em out, I pick the round".

More than 25 years after leaving the ring he is still the greatest.

Peace, love and happiness always Muhammad.

Chapter Nineteen

DR. MARTIN LUTHER KING JR
Civil Rights Leader

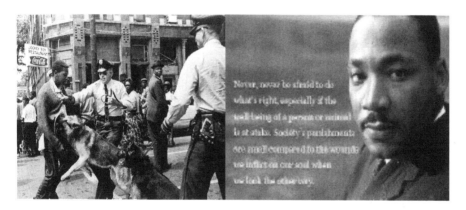

Dr. Martin Luther King Jr. 15 January 1929 - 4 April 1968.
He was killed by gunshot, age 39. Very little has changed in America for
African or native Americans since the murder of Dr King Jr.

Dr. Martin Luther King Jr. had more impact upon the consciousness of
the world than any other civil rights leader in the 20th century. Without
his support the struggle for equal rights for Black Americans might
have taken much longer to achieve. Black Americans today owe a great
deal to the freedom fighters over the centuries. From Frederick
Douglas, and those engaged in the struggles during the centuries of
slavery and racism, to people like George Jackson, Huey Newton,
Bobby Seale, Eldridge Cleaver, Malcolm X, Angela Davis, Paul

Robeson, Muhammad Ali, Martin Luther King, Marcus Garvey and others who have openly and without any fear for their own safety, challenged institutional racism in America.

A great man, a great leader and a great American

Dr. Martin Luther King Jr. had his own ideology and strategy on how to challenge centuries of racism, even though he took a great deal strength from people like Mahatma Gandhi the father of the theory on non-violence and other Black liberators. He combined his great gift for oratory with his commitment to non-violence. Martin Luther King did not invent a new philosophy, tactic or strategy to change hearts and minds; he relied on what other Black activists had done in the past. He used his great ability to manipulate the power and sound of words enabled him to create and develop a formidable weapon of offence and defence in the struggle for civil rights. Martin Luther King was fascinated by words from a young age. He saw his father King Sr. Pastor of Ebenezer Baptist Church in Atlanta and other ministers controlling audiences with skilfully chosen words and longed to follow their footsteps.

Twenty years after King Jr. uttered the following words Public Law 98 - 144 was enacted in America to designate the third Monday in January as a Federal holiday to commemorate King's birthday on 15 January 1929:

"I have a dream that one day this nation will rise up, live out the true meaning
Of its creed, we hold these truths to be self evident, that all men are created equal."

Despite his obvious greatness his contribution to the emancipation of Black people from institutional, social, economic and cultural racism was relatively modest. Racism still pervades American society despite the increasing number of Black politicians, statesmen and women,

333

Mayors, Police Chiefs and national role models. America is still largely a segregated, unequal and oppressive society for Black people even though the Secretary of State for Defence, Colin Powell is the son of Black Jamaican immigrants.

Printed below is brief review of this great man, who helped to shape race relations and civil rights laws not only in America, but worldwide. He is remembered as one of the greatest persons in the American civil rights movement. Dr Martin Luther King, Jr. was the youngest person to win the Nobel Peace Prize. His birthday is now a national holiday in America only the second American to have his birthday designated a Federal holiday. The other American is George Washington.

Family background

Martin Luther King, Jr. was born on Tuesday, January 15, 1929, at the family home, 501 Auburn Avenue, N.E., Atlanta, Georgia. Dr. Charles Johnson was the attending physician. Martin Luther King, Jr., was the first son and second child born to the Reverend Martin Luther King, Sr., and Alberta Williams King. Other children born to the Kings were Christine King Farris and the late Reverend Alfred Daniel Williams King. Martin Luther King's maternal grandparents were the Reverend Adam Daniel Williams, second pastor of the Ebenezer Baptist Church and Jenny Parks Williams. His paternal grandparents, James Albert and Delia King, were sharecroppers on a farm in Stockbridge, Georgia.

He married Coretta Scott, younger daughter of Obadiah and Bernice McMurray Scott of Marion, Alabama on June 18, 1953. They had four children.

Education

Martin Luther King, Jr. began his education at the Yonge Street Elementary School in Atlanta, Georgia. Following Yonge School, he was enrolled in David T. Howard Elementary School. He also attended the Atlanta University Laboratory School and Booker T. Washington High School. Because of his high score on the college entrance
334

examinations in his junior year of high school, he advanced to Morehouse College without formal graduation from Booker T. Washington. Dr. King entered Morehouse at the age of fifteen.

In 1948, he graduated from Morehouse College with a B.A. degree in Sociology. He then enrolled in Crozer Theological Seminary in Chester, Pennsylvania. While attending Crozer, he also studied at the University of Pennsylvania. He was awarded a Bachelor of Divinity degree from Crozer in 1951.

In September of 1951, at the young age of 22 Martin Luther King began doctoral studies in Systematic Theology at Boston University. He also studied at Harvard University. His dissertation, *"A Comparison of God in the Thinking of Paul Tillich and Henry Wieman,"* was completed in 1955, and the Ph.D. degree from Boston, a Doctorate of Philosophy in Systematic Theology, was awarded on June 5, 1955. King was very much inspired by Dr Benjamin Mays the President of Morehouse College. Mays challenged the traditional view of education for Black people who focussed on a mixture of compromise within the American culture and the power of protest. Instead Mays saw education as means to liberation and intellectual freedom for the Negroes through knowledge and organisation.

The power of non-violence

Dr. King was able to, from his appointment as a Baptist Minister combine the spiritual, intellectual, social and moral messages, which stimulated Black people across America. Much to the annoyance of many Black radicals King argued that the moral power of non-violence developed by Mahatma Ghandi could transform race relations in America and elsewhere and create a powerful vehicle for social change. Dr. King followed the path laid by Gandhi which meant non-co-operation with evil through civil disobedience, protests, marches, boycotts and mass gatherings which also included white supporters. His philosophy was designed not to create hate and bitterness between Black and white Americans but to win over white Americans through love, logic and rational thinking and action. Dr. King's dreams for civil and human rights were not a great deal dissimilar from that of Malcolm X, but their journeys to justice, rights and freedom took different routes. Dr. King preached racial harmony and tolerance, he did not preach revolution or encourage Negroes to challenge the social values of America. He was not interested in the defeat of white America but in reforming America's moral and social thinking and behaviour. He was not a threat to the establishment in America and other powerful white nations and naturally enjoyed the support of The Kennedy administration and many white liberals, academics and famous people around the world.

The influence of Gandhi on the Civil Rights Movement

In 1929 the year of Dr. King. birth Gandhi told a group of African Americans:

"Let not the 12 million Negroes be ashamed of the fact that they are the grandchildren of slaves. There is no dishonour of being slaves. There is dishonour of being slave owners.

Honorary Degree

Dr. King was awarded honorary degrees from numerous colleges and universities in the United States and several foreign countries.

Dr. Martin Luther King entered the Christian ministry and was ordained in February 1948 at the age of nineteen at Ebenezer Baptist Church, Atlanta, Georgia. Following his ordination, he became Assistant Pastor of Ebenezer. From 1960 until his death in 1968, he was co-pastor with his father at Ebenezer Baptist Church and President of the Southern Christian Leadership Conference.

Bus boycott

In 1954, Dr. King Jr. became the Pastor of the Dexter Avenue Baptist Church in Montgomery Alabama. It was in Montgomery on 1 December 1955 where a Negro seamstress, Rosa Park was arrested,

336

charged and convicted in the City Court for violating a state law mandating segregation of Black and white passengers on the busses. Mrs Park refused to move from the seat in the bus which she occupied to allow a white person to sit instead. She was fined $10. This incident provided Dr. King Jr with an opportunity to organise a major campaign against segregation. He was elected President of the Montgomery Improvement Association (MIA) and arranged for a one-day boycott of the buses by the Black community in Montgomery on the day of Rosa's trial.

Dr. King was a pivotal figure in the Civil Rights Movement. The MIA was responsible for the successful Montgomery Bus Boycott in 1955 and 1956, which lasted 381 days. Dr. King told his supporters:

"We have no alternative but to protest. For many years we have shown an amazing patience. We have sometimes given our white brothers the feeling that we liked the way we were being treated. But we came here tonight to be saved from that patience that makes us patient with anything less than freedom and justice".

The protest was vicious and violent from the law and order and enforcement agencies. Despite the police brutality and violence from white racists the protesters remained non-violent. Dr. King stated that:

"One of the great glories of American democracy is that we have the right to protest for rights... This is a non-violent protest. We are depending on moral and spiritual forces, using the method of passive resistance. And this is resistance, he [Gandhi] would insist, it is not a stagnant passivity, a do-nothing method. It is not passive non-resistance to evil. And it is not a method for cowards. Gandhi said that if somebody uses it because he is afraid, he's not truly non-violent. Really non-violence is the way of the strong".

After the boycott the buses were de-segregated and Dr King and Rosa Parks were the first passengers to take their seats anywhere in the bus. Dr. King advised his supporters to return to using the buses with humility and meekness, and not to brag that the Negroes had won a victory over the white people. He advised his people to seek integration based on mutual respect and to move from protest to reconciliation. King and his supporters across the southern states of America then proceeded to ensure Black voter registration, desegregation of educational institutions, shops and food outlets in many Southern town and cities. Black and white people including students joined the "sit-ins" and the freedom riders that took to the buses throughout the South despite opposition from hardened white racists. Organised gangs from the white supremacists Klu Klux Klan used all sorts of weapons in full view of the law to attack the protesters who went on to form the Student Non-violent Co-ordinating Committee (SNCC) and achieved many victories in desegregating services.

Dr. King Jr. was arrested thirty times for his participation in civil rights activities. He was a founder and president of Southern Christian Leadership Conference from 1957 to 1968. Dr. King was elected to membership in several learned societies including the prestigious American Academy of Arts and Sciences. He received several hundred awards for his leadership in the Civil Rights Movement.

A famous orator

Dr. Martin Luther King, Jr. was a vital and persuasive personality with the ability to put together words which brought out immense emotions from people of all races and status. His lectures and remarks stirred the concern and sparked the conscience of a generation; the movements and marches he led brought significant changes in the fabric of American life. His courage and devotion to his cause gave direction to the Civil Rights movement during the 1960's. Dr King was well known for his charismatic leadership that inspired men and women, young and old, Black and white America and abroad.

Dr. King and the Civil Rights Movement to which many people subscribed, gave Black and poor people a new sense of worth, pride, respect and dignity.

Dr. King's speech at the march on Washington on 28 August 1963 which was attended by over 250,000 people, Black and white will always be remembers as one of his finest. The world watched the march as it gathered momentum and heard extracts from the speeches from people from many spheres of life. Dr King delivered his speech which outlined his dream with passion, clarity, integrity and humility. After the march President John F Kennedy invited the organisers to a reception at the White House. After the assassination of President Kennedy on 22 November 1963 President Lyndon Johnson successfully introduced the Civil Rights Act in 1964 which brought in the most far-reaching civil rights legislation in American history.

Dr. King's acceptance speech of the Nobel Peace Prize, his last sermon at Ebenezer Baptist Church, and his final speech in Memphis are among his most famous utterances (I've Been to the Mountaintop). The Letter from Birmingham Jail ranks among the most important of American documents.

The Voting Rights Act of 1965, for example, went to Congress as a result of the march from Selma to Montgomery Alabama, which was led by Dr King and other civil rights leaders. The march exposed police brutality as well as white racism. Many white anti-racists joined the march and suffered the brutality and taunts from the police and racists.

Living in fear

Despite his massive support amongst the blacks, and certain sections of the white population Dr King was constantly being attacked. His house was fire bombed and he received over 30 hate letters each day. Many contained threats to him and his family. Dr King was determined that the racists should not put him off his mission. He was prepared to engage the racists in the streets on a non-violent basis. He joined the
339

black students in their sit-in protests against the café owners who refused to serve them refreshments because of their skin colour. He was arrested and received 4 months hard labour. The President of the United States assisted in his release from prison. The segregation in America, especially in the Southern States was more profound; it extended to housing, education, transport, jobs and careers. The protests and the resulting brutality of the police and the white racists had a massive impact on the public in America and other parts of the world. Many white people joined in the various protests and demands for civil rights which improved during the late 1950's and 1960's.

Assassination of Dr King

James Earl Ray shot Dr. King while he was standing on the balcony of the Lorraine Motel in Memphis, Tennessee on April 4, 1968. Ray was arrested in London, England on June 8, 1968 and returned to Memphis, Tennessee to stand trial for the assassination of Dr. King. On March 9, 1969, before coming to trial, he entered a guilty plea and was sentenced to ninety-nine years in the Tennessee State Penitentiary. Dr. King had been in Memphis to help lead sanitation workers in a protest against low wages and intolerable conditions. His funeral services were held April 9, 1968, in Atlanta at Ebenezer Church and on the campus of Morehouse College, with the President of the United States proclaiming a day of mourning. The area where Dr. King was entombed is located on Freedom Plaza and surrounded by the Freedom Hall Complex of the Martin Luther King, Jr. Centre for Non-violent Social Change, Inc. The Martin Luther King, Jr. Historic Site, a 23 acre area was listed as a National Historic Landmark on May 5, 1977, and was made a National Historic Site on October 10, 1980 by the U.S. Department of the Interior.

Dr. King was assassinated on April 4, 1968, in Memphis, Tennessee. He was posthumously awarded the Presidential Medal of Freedom in 1977 and Congressional Gold Medal in 2004; Martin Luther King, Jr. Day was established as a U.S. federal holiday in 1986.

340

Editor's update:

America is far from being a post racial society

Racism and ethnic discrimination in the United States has been a major issue since the colonial and slave era. Legally sanctioned racism, sanctioned privileges and rights for white Americans have not been granted to Native Americans, African Americans Asian and Chinese Americans and Latin Americans. European Americans, especially those whose ancestors were from Britain and Western Europe were privileged by law in matters of education, immigration, voting rights, citizenship, land acquisition, and criminal procedure from the 17th century to the start of the Civil Rights Movement in the 1960s. Other white groups from Europe including Jews, Irish, Poles, Italians and others from Eastern Europe suffered from some discrimination and exclusion and other forms of ethnicity-based discrimination in American society.

Racially and ethnically structured institutions were created by white European settlers who declared themselves superior to all non-whites. These institutions and structures included slavery, Indian Wars, ethnic cleansing, genocide against Native Americans, reservations for Native Americans, segregation, internment camps, apartheid and racism. Such practices were common in America for centuries. It was not until the late 19th century before there were a few changes, but American society remained deeply racist until some more changes were made starting in the mid-20th century and the struggles around the bitter and divisive struggles for Civil Rights in the 1960s.

Despite the limited success of the latter part of the 20th century, America remains a highly stratified society in the 21st century, with a massive non-white underclass. Racial politics remains a major phenomenon, Racism continues to be reflected in all areas of American society from socio-economic issues to politics, education, housing, employment, the judiciary and access to power, despite the fact that a mixed race Black man - Barak Obama - has been President since 2012.

Poverty, rising inequality police harassment and brutality continue to affect non-white people in America even though it remains the richest and most powerful country in the world.

The recent uprising in Ferguson, Missouri where an African American teenager, Michael Brown was gunned down by a white police officer Daren Wilson, on 9 August 2014, it attracted world attention for nearly three weeks. Brown was shot at least six times: twice in the head, he was unarmed and according to witnesses had both his hands above his head. A few days later another African American male was shot dead by a white police officer, just a few miles from Ferguson. According to various reports, at least 2 black men are killed by police officers every week in America. .Black men are seven times more likely to be in prison than white men. Over 60 per cent of the population in Ferguson are black, yet of the 53 police officers only 3 are black. Like the rest of America the majority of the black population in Ferguson are either living in poverty, or very near poverty. Unemployment, poor housing, high crime rates and criminalisation of the black population are major concerns for generations of black men and women.

The black community in Ferguson took to the streets in growing numbers after the killing of Michael Brown. The demonstrations and picketing were also supported by many local white residents and others from outside the area. Demonstrations against police brutality and in support of "Justice for Michael Brown" took place in many cities and States in America.

The police responded to the demonstrators in Ferguson with the same show of strength, arrogance, insensitivity and equipment they had displayed and used against those campaigning for civil and human rights 50 years ago. Except in 2014, the police were equipped with more lethal weapons and were armed as though were in a war zone in a foreign country. The police were equipped with automatic weapons, tear gas, rubber bullets, live bullets, flash bombs and armoured vehicles, which they deployed against unarmed and almost totally peaceful demonstrators. The white Governor of Missouri, kept quiet for days after the demonstrators demanding action against the police and for answers to the shooting and police brutality.

Many journalists covering the discontent in Ferguson were caught up in police action that forced them to limit their coverage of their stories by segregating them and restricting their movement. They were told to keep moving but only within a confined space and several were arrested along with hundreds of peaceful demonstrators mainly black. Parts of Ferguson resembled the scene of a war zone, especially at night when grenades and flash bombs were deployed by the heavily armed police during weeks of demonstrations. The armed police used the armoured vehicles to seal off certain areas and to contain the demonstrators and journalists in the full view of the world media. The local black people stopped the few incidents of looting which took place by removing the criminals from the demonstration.

Several black people interviewed by the media locally and nationally highlighted the fact that the non-white population of America has been suffering from severe racism, poverty, inequality, prejudice, police brutality and neglect by the state for generations and life has hardly changed relatively, for the non-white population for generations. African Americans were particularly suffering as part of a large underclass for centuries. Many black people feel imprisoned in a society that has condemned them to a life of poverty, criminalisation and institutional racism. Over 50 per cent of young people age 16-24 years in America, are either unemployed, imprisoned or have criminal records. Racism is pervasive and systematic in America.

Chapter Twenty

MALCOLM X
Civil Rights Leader

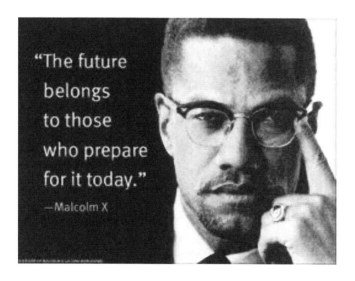

"The future belongs to those who prepare for it today."
—Malcolm X

EL-Hajj Malik EL Malcolm X. 19May 1925
– 21 February 1965. Died by gunshot, age 39

MALCOLM X

Malcolm Little was born on May 19, 1925, the son of Louise and Earl Little of Omaha, Nebraska. Louise Little was born on the Island of Grenada in the British West Indies where she was the unacknowledged offspring of a white Scot and a Black Grenadian woman. Earl Little was born in Georgia in 1890 and was a Baptist minister and organizer for Marcus Garvey's Universal Negro Improvement Association (UNIA). He was the President of the Omaha Branch of the UNIA. From humble beginnings Malcolm managed to change forever the way "Negroes" in America thought about themselves and one another. Before Malcolm X many Blacks and white people in 20th century America never really questioned the loyalty of African Americans towards the American state. Malcolm penetrated the conscience and re-awakened the deep-rooted resentment of Black people towards the ruling elite and institutions in America, which denied them their civil, and human rights and liberties. His analysis of the conditions of African Americans and other Black people around the world was built influenced by people like Marcus Garvey, Kwame Nkrumah and other Black radicals in America, Africa and Europe.

Malcolm X influenced and inspired tens of millions of Black and white anti-racists and radicals around the world. Malcolm was a brilliant speaker, debater, organiser and challenger of the status quo. He was indeed a revolutionary who was seen by people either as a Prophet, a Messenger, the Black Prince or the people's champion. Malcolm lived and died for the liberation of Black people. He was one of the most determined crusaders for justice, freedom and emancipation from the slave mentality which so many Black people in America and elsewhere were infected. Malcolm X opened up the debate about racism which threatened white institutions in America and around the world. He brought racism out into the open from the deep shadow of American

345

society. Malcolm exposed the hypocrisy of American religious leaders, politicians, business people and law and order enforcement agencies.

He shifted the debates about racism and oppression from gentle disagreements about prejudice and civil rights to human and universal rights. Malcolm placed the historical situation of enslavement, exploitation, oppression and degradation of African Americans for centuries fully in the domain of corporate America. He placed the ideology and practice of racism within the heart of American institutions from the political, education, social and economic structures to the religious, cultural and judicial structures. Whilst Malcolm shared may of the values of Martin Luther King Jr. his philosophy was distinct from that of King in many ways.

Family background

Louise Little Earl's second wife, bore him six children and they lived with the three other children by Earl's first wife. Malcolm was always a lively child who would often get up to all sorts of mischief as well as playing tricks on people around him. As a child Malcolm experienced poverty especially after his father died.

In 1929 the family house was burned down, allegedly by white supremacists because they bought a house in a white neighbourhood. After Earl Little died in 1931 in a streetcar accident, Malcolm's mother eventually had a mental breakdown and entered an asylum. The siblings were dispersed to other families. Malcolm lived with a foster family before moving to Roxbury, a mainly black neighbourhood in Boston, Massachusetts, in 1941 to live with a half sister. Malcolm was born in a society characterised by white supremacy and Black inferiority. The America of Malcolm's childhood and most of his adult life was known for segregation, racial tensions, inequality and oppression of Black

346

people. It was and still is in many ways a land in which people are not judged by their character or beliefs but by the colour of their skin.

Petty crimes

A few months after his arrival in Roxbury, Malcolm dropped out of school and took a job as a shoeshine boy at the Roseland Ballroom. A career as a hustler seemed a more tempting option, and he was soon peddling drugs and engaging in petty crimes. Roxbury proved to be too small for him, and in 1942 he took a job as a railroad dining-car porter, working out of Roxbury and Harlem. Settling in Harlem, he became involved in criminal activities (robbery, prostitution, and narcotics).

Malcolm soon learned to survive in hustler society. His nickname was "Red" because of his red skin colour, his quick temper and his capacity to engage in anti-social behaviour. After a year in Harlem Malcolm returned to Boston in 1945 after a falling out with another hustler, and continued a life of crime, forming his gang. He was arrested for robbery in February 1946, and convicted and sentenced to prison in Charlestown, for seven years when he was 19 years old. .

Prison experience

While in prison, Malcolm educated himself and became a follower of Elijah Muhammad, the leader of the Nation of Islam, with branches in Detroit, Chicago, and New York. Malcolm and Elijah Muhammad corresponded by mail. Malcolm's brother Reginald and half sister Ella, visiting him in prison, urged him to join Muhammad's cult, and while still in prison he did.

Malcolm's association with the Nation of Islam had a profound impact on his life. He changed his "slave name," Little, and renamed himself "X". His conversion let him to greater literacy, immersion in the Qur'an and strict adherence to the Nation of Islam. Malcolm developed politically during his time in prison. He also gave a lot of attention to the Black struggles and the fight against racism. After his parole in 1952, Malcolm X worked for the Nation of Islam under the guidance of Elijah Muhammad. Malcolm founded mosques in Boston, Philadelphia, Harlem, and elsewhere and was credited with the national expansion of the movement, the membership of which evidently reached around 30,000 by 1963.

National recognition

Malcolm X came to broad public notice as the result of a television special in 1959 which told the story of him emerging as one of the most important leaders of the Nation of Islam. The programme also brought the Nation of Islam (also known as the Black Muslim Movement) to the attention of the wider American public. Malcolm's militant radical vision was expressed in speeches, newspaper articles, radio and television interviews. He also helped found the Black Muslim newspaper, *Muhammad Speaks* Partly because of tensions within the Black Muslim movement, Malcolm became critical of Elijah Muhammad. He was eventually "silenced," for 90 days after commenting on the assassination of Pres. John F. Kennedy with the phrase "chickens come home to roost." But before his silence was lifted, Malcolm X left the Nation of Islam in March 1964 to form the Muslim Mosque, Inc.

Malcolm was a person who would tell things as he sees them even if it meant that the very people whose liberation he is fighting for would condemn him. He was always fearless in his criticisms of those African Americans who colluded with the institutions, politicians and structures that only paid lip service to tackling racism. Many middle class and aspiring middle class Black in America and Europe were opposed to declaring their support for Malcolm because they felt that their own cosy relationship with the white institutions may suffer if Black people started to challenge institutional racism. Malcolm's message had great impact on Blacks whose lives were damaged by racism, oppression and powerlessness.

Malcolm then began to tour several cities and made speeches on the position of Black people in America and the rest of the world. He advocated the need for a Black revolution and encouraged the formation of a more secular Black nationalism, arguing that blacks should control the politics within their own community and, through his speeches, encouraging his followers to use the ballot to effect change. Malcolm encouraged Black people to combine and to organise; to take responsibility for their liberation and to use any means necessary to achieve their goals. He emphasized the power of collective strength of organised communities.

Friend of Muhammad

Malcolm X was a close friend of Muhammed Ali who joined the Black Muslims and remained with them until his expulsion in 1969. Malcolm was regarded as Ali's mentor for many years and they shared a lot of thoughts and ideas with each other until Malcolm left the Nation of Islam.

Global fight against racism

Malcolm advocated global action against racism through unity and solidarity of African and other countries populated by non-white people. At the height of his powers Malcolm X was one of Black America's most compelling voices at home and abroad much to the annoyance of the white establishment in North America and Europe. He had enormous influence among Black youth especially those who have suffered from harassment and brutality from law enforcement agencies and under achievement due to racism. Malcolm was also admired by progressive intellectual circles across America, Europe and in other countries. He travelled widely in Europe, and Africa, and the Middle East modelling his Organisation of African-American Unity after the Organisation of African Unity. He saw the Black American struggle partly as an extension of the effort of third world nations for human and civil rights, freedom and justice.

Malcolm X described the next stage of his personal evolution in a speech entitled "The Bullet or the Ballot," in which he attempted to stake out a role for himself in the civil rights movement. With other Black nationalists, he added "Black is beautiful" themes to his rhetoric. He continued to stress self-reliance as one of the core values of the Nation of Islam. Malcolm encouraged Black people to help shape their destiny and environment through unity, pride, assertiveness and ideology. He wanted Black people to believe in themselves to have a vision for their future and to maximise every opportunity through political, community and business involvement to improve their status and procure the advancement of their people.

Malcolm X went on a pilgrimage to Mecca in 1964 and there began to consider changing his views toward integration. Afterward he was, if anything, more ambiguous about the outcome of the race struggle in the United States, and he left open the possibility that some whites could contribute to the struggle. He took the view that what a man says and does is more important than the colour of his skin. This was different to the earlier years when he argued for black self-organisation. The pilgrimage had a profound impact on Malcolm's thinking on racial supremacy and the struggle by black people to secure justice, freedom and civil rights. He genuinely felt that to achieve his aims like-minded people of all colours would have to join the struggle. When asked whether he would let white people join his organisation, he replied that he "would if John Brown was around today". (John Brown was a white American, born in 1800, who took up arms against the slave owners, and helped black slaves to gain their freedom. He was captured and hanged for his activities in 1859). After the pilgrimage Malcolm adopted the name El-Hajj Malik El-Shabazz.

The Queens, N.Y., home Malcolm X shared with his wife, Betty (whom he had married in January 1958) and his six children was fire bombed in early February 1965, as he addressed 400 supporters at the Audubon Ballroom in the Washington Heights section of upper Manhattan.

Death and place in history

Two weeks before Malcolm's death on 21 February 1965 at the Audubon Ballroom in New York, he visited London to address the first Congress of the Council of African Organisations. Malcolm had a lot of support amongst the rising Black organisations supported by young Blacks who were often the victims of racist policing and institutional prejudice. Many of the older Back people in Britain were reluctant to support Malcolm's approach to racial liberation because of the highly political and militant aspects associated with it. Malcolm will always be remembered because of his tremendous personality, and the massive impact, which he has had on the identity of America and Black people around the world. Malcolm's life and thinking was shaped by his experience of living in a racist, oppressive, unequal, unfair and unjust environment.

Malcolm X has inspired millions of black people around the world through his political speeches and his writings. I have followed his politics and his life carefully and with great admiration for his courage and commitment towards liberating black people worldwide, from white racist oppression, which lasted for centuries under slavery, imperialism, colonialism and capitalism. Both Martin Luther King Jr. and Malcolm X failed to reach their 40th birthdays and were both assassinated by men using guns.

Chapter Twenty One

Marcus Garvey
Civil Rights Leader and entrepreneur

Marcus Mosiah Garvey Jr.
17 August 1887 – 10 June 1940

Marcus Garvey 1887 – 1940

Marcus Garvey is best remembered as pivotal figure in the struggle for racial equality throughout the world. He founded the UNIA (Universal

352

Negro Improvement Association) and championed the 'back to Africa' movement of the 1920s. His legacy makes him an inspirational figure for many civil rights leaders and politicians today, and in his lifetime Black people everywhere hailed him as a prophet and redeemer. Garvey was the first Black leader to inspire millions of African Americans with pride in their race. He was a well known political thinker, journalist, entrepreneur and civil rights leader.

The youngest of 11 children, Marcus Mosiah Garvey was born in St Ann's Bay, Jamaica in 1887. Garvey inherited a keen interest in books from his father and made full use of the extensive family library.

At the age of 14 he left school and worked in a print shop. In 1908 he participated in Jamaica's first Printers' Union strike which came as a result of major earthquake in Kingston a year earlier. Around this time he also published a small newspaper, called *The Watchman*.

Seeking funding for future projects, Marcus Garvey left Jamaica to work as a timekeeper in Costa Rica. It was while working in Central America that he experienced the harsh realities of racial discrimination, amassing evidence that black people were victims of prejudice on a worldwide scale.

Garvey encouraged workers to form unions to negotiate for better terms and started newspapers in Costa Rica and Panama complaining about poor conditions. His activities were soon brought to the attention of the Costa Rican government and he was promptly expelled from the country. Garvey's political thinking was widely supported by African Americans and African Caribbeans. The British administration which managed the Caribbean colonies was petrified at the impact Garvey was having on the consciousness of African Caribbeans under colonial rule. Garvey was a prolific writer of articles and editor of several and publications always championing the cause of Black Africans.

After returning to Jamaica distressed by what he had seen in Central America, he began to lay foundations for the Universal Negro Improvement Association, to which he would later devote his life.

African pride

Marcus Garvey moved to England to live with his sister who was a governess. While in London, Garvey worked on a newspaper called *The African and Orient Review*. In 1914 he founded the Universal Negro Improvement Association, whose motto was 'One God, One Aim, One Destiny'. The UNIA set up the Negro Factories Corporation (NFC) to help promote economic self-reliance. Garvey supported self-determination of Black Africans and the need for African Americans to achieve independence through economic development and enterprise. Many publications referred to Garvey as the "Black Moses" who will lead his people back to the promise land in Africa.

Then in 1916 he moved the UNIA headquarters to Harlem in New York and set up branches in other countries with large black populations. By now Garvey had become a formidable public speaker and his political agenda demanded radical reforms. Hundreds would listen to him speak, inspired by his speeches encouraging them to have pride in themselves as Africans. Garvey's message was clear, 'Up you mighty race, you can accomplish what you will'.

He was not ready to pursue his most ambitious plans. The UNIA negotiated with the government of Liberia for land which would be made available to repatriate Black people from the USA, Caribbean, South and Central America. At first the Liberian government agreed but soon changed its mind before any settlers could arrive.

Under Marcus Garvey's leadership the UNIA did enjoy some success and in 1920 held a month-long international conference in New York which was attended by delegates from all over the world. The conference was a huge success and seven more were held in Garvey's lifetime.

In 1919 he attempted to set up a steamship company called the Black Star Line, hoping to trade goods from Africa and the West Indies back to the USA, but the plan failed.

In August 1920 Garvey organised an event in Madison Square Garden, New York under the auspices of UNIA in which some 25,000 Black people of all shades of Black and Brown from 25 countries attended the First International Convention of the Negro Peoples of the World.

Back in Jamaica, Marcus Garvey continued his work with the UNIA, dabbling in local politics with limited success. In 1935 the UNIA moved its headquarters to London and Marcus Garvey continued his work in relative obscurity before dying in 1940. During his work in London Garvey played a major role in organising the struggle against fascism, imperialism and colonialism. He work with Jomo Kenyatta, the first President of independent Kenya, Kwame Nkrumah, Sylvia Pankhurst, CLR James, Fenner Brockway and others in the anti-colonialism struggles which spanned several decades in the first half of the 20th century. His strong leadership and commitment to justice for people of Black African descent made him a prominent target for the British ruling class.

Garvey's writings influenced two generations of African and African American leaders. Numerous books have been written by well known authors on issues associated with Black liberation and freedom from colonialism during the 20th century which acknowledged the enormous contributions made by Garvey in the struggle for Black liberation. Many activists associated with the Civil Rights Movement in America during the 1950s, 1960s and beyond acknowledged the influence Garvey has had on their thinking.

Chapter Twenty Two

SHAPURJI SAKLATVALA MP
Socialist and political activist

Shapurji Saklatvala MP for
North Battersea (1874-1936)

Marc Wadsworth – The Legacy of Shapurji Saklatvala MP

When Shapurji Saklatvala was alive, his residence, Number 2 St Albans Villas in Highgate Road, was the unofficial London home of the Indian independence movement. People like B. G. Tilak, known as the "father of Indian unrest", and key Congress Party member Mohammed Ali were guests. Despite the tactical differences that Saklatvala, a Communist, had with them, the Congress Party described him as "India's greatest fighter for Indian independence abroad". He seized every opportunity to wage his struggle at the heart of imperialism. From his earliest days in Britain, there was a dossier on Saklatvala compiled by the secret service. In 1911 they noted that he kept in touch with radical Indian nationalists like fellow Parsi Madam Bhikaji Rustom Cama and Bipin Chandra Pal. The secret service named him as "one of the most violent anti-British agitators in England".

Born in Bombay, India, in 1874, Saklatvala moved to England as a young man to recover from malaria. Though a member of the fabulously rich Tata family, he fell in love with and married a working class woman, Sally Marsh. Before he was elected MP for the solidly working class constituency of North Battersea in 1922, he attended a meeting of Indians at Caxton Hall in Central London to explain why they must support the Labour Party. He said prophetically: "In this country no political progress can be made except through the channel of one of the existing parties..." Indians, he insisted, must stand for parliament because: "The first thing that a member can do is to advertise better from the House of Commons than anywhere else."

Although he made the struggle for Indian freedom his main focus, Saklatvala was always concerned to put this into the widest international focus. He said Indians must stop asking "what have other people done for us?" They must begin to ask: "What have we done for the Irish, the Egyptians, the Russians?" and throw themselves into the "world movement of the Labour classes".

I first became acquainted with Saklatvala on the eve of the 1983 General Election when a Labour Party Black Section comrade of mine, Russell Profitt, was selected to fight the 'safe' Labour constituency of Battersea North. Saklatvala's name cropped up as the former MP for the same seat (then known as North Battersea, the words having been switched round). Perversely, the Boundary Commission stepped in and merged North and South into one Battersea seat. And, true to form, Labour dumped Profitt for Alf Dubs, the White MP for Battersea South. Dubs won the seat but then lost it to a Conservative and was given a peerage by a Labour leadership keen to keep him in parliament. Later they made him a government minister.

It could be said that, with John Archer, the Black Liverpudlian ex-Mayor of Battersea, Saklatvala formed the first Labour Party 'Black Section' when the two joined forces in 1921. That year Archer took Saklatvala, Battersea's prospective parliamentary candidate, to the second Pan Africanist Congress, held in London.

Saklatvala gave the delegates greetings from the Indian people stating that India was 'very proud to be a part of the coloured world', and that 'coloured people ought to be proud of themselves'.

African-Asian unity was one of the themes taken up by Saklatvala in an article criticising Mahatma Gandhi in 1930. He said that when Gandhi was in South Africa: 'He never made the slightest attempt socially and politically to unite Negroes and Indians together for the overthrow of the white man's tyranny...Whenever some vulgar favour was shown by the British master towards a few rich Indians in South Africa, Gandhi would burst out into a song like the Empire's nightingale...He ignored the fact that South Africa belongs to the Negroes and that the white tyrants were a small minority, and were the worst type of exploiters, gold hunters and diamond diggers.' Such rhetoric would have given Saklatvala notoriety as a dangerous Black militant today.

Saklatvala brought a forthright anti-imperialist dimension to British politics. But his love affair with the left was not always an immediate meeting of minds. Saklatvala's devotion to his family and the Zoroastrian customs instilled in him by them caused conflicts which exposed the Euro-centric limitations of the Communist Party.

The left are just as guilty today of failing to understand that cultural and religious differences need not necessarily be counter-posed to Socialist politics. For instance, there is a knee-jerk rejection of the adherents of so-called 'fundamentalism' in the Muslim faith. In France this Euro-centric intolerance reared its head in the divisive row about women wearing the customary 'hijab' scarf and in Britain there was the Rushdie affair which saw the on-set of 'Islamaphobia'.

Both controversies saw White liberals equating Islam to barbarism and marginalising its believers. Fortunately, a fight-back has resulted in which Muslims have forced a debate about the widespread religious and racial discrimination they face. Britain's increasingly confident Muslim community is demanding that their faith be afforded the same respect and protection as Christianity. Ironically, Saklatvala hung on to his Zoroastrian religion despite belonging to the atheist Communist Party – one of his several contradictions. It gave him a grounding among a section of the oppressed firmly rooted in the non-Western world.

Some people might argue that Saklatvala's commitment to Communism sprang from the longing of a highborn twentieth century intellectual for a radical, charitable cause to which he could dedicate his life. He yearned for a vaguely conceived new world. Some might argue that Saklatvala's ploughshare of anti-imperialism was fashioned from his sword of Communism, an emotional response to his passionate support for Indian Home Rule, the first acid test he applied to any political party. Therefore the Independent Labour Party's lukewarm attitude to self-government was the main reason he left them, after flirting with the Liberals, and became a Communist.

At one point he had a dramatic exchange with the great Indian nationalist Mohandas Karamchand Gandhi. Saklatvala's dispute with the 'Mahatma' is particularly revealing.

They exchanged several letters. What emerged from the correspondence was that Saklatvala was more at home on British parliamentary terrain than dealing with domestic Indian politics. Gandhi won the debate. But a major contribution Saklatvala made was to soften the Communist Party of Great Britain's attitude to the newly emerging Indian nationalist movement. Moscow, under the hardline influence of fellow Indian M.N. Roy, viewed Gandhi and his Congress supporters as impossibly bourgeois and therefore not potential allies. They viewed Gandhi solely through the optic of class. Guided by Saklatvala, the party had a more sophisticated approach and dared to disagree. It reminds one of the 'U' turn forced on Jamaican Communists by a reassessment of the Pan-Africanist leader Marcus Garvey who is now considered a 'revolutionary', thanks to his popularity among Black workers and left intellectuals.

There were perhaps two turning points in Saklatvala's life, first when he was sent away from a White man's club in India, one of the rare occasions he documented a personal experience of racism. Then, once he was settled in England, his rejection of liberalism as a vehicle for emancipation. In a statement reminiscent of a key contemporary debate on the left, Saklatvala urged a vigorous fight against Labour ideology which he dubbed as 'Labouralism'.

Today 'New' Labour prime minister Tony Blair has gone even further by reshaping the Social Democratic space in British politics to the extent that his particular brand is no longer Labour and many commentators believe is located to the right of even the Liberal-Democrats. Saklatvala's politics sprang from Communist ideals that rejected this drift to the right. As an MP, he had a platform from which he eloquently espoused his view of Socialism. It was an uncompromisingly anti-imperialist perspective. The two Indian MPs in the Commons before Saklatvala, themselves also Parsis, were Dadabhai Naoroji, a Liberal, and the Conservative Sir Mancherjee Bhownagree — neither making as much of an impact as him but all of them facing racism and marginalisation during their political career.

Saklatvala bridged the class and cultural barriers with his powerful commitment to the revolutionary cause. One of his celebrated statements was: 'I am out for a revolution and am quite willing to be shot down.'
From Saklatvala's first days in the Commons, his biting wit was unleashed. The Times of 28 February 1923 reported: 'As to the Indian Civil Service', Saklatvala said, 'it was not Indian, it was not civil, and it was a domination and a usurpation. Barring those three great defects, the Service was all right.'

According to the Manchester Guardian: `No contribution to the debate had such a stirring and stimulating effect as Mr Saklatvala's, and for some hours afterwards the enquiry was everywhere made when two persons met within the walls of Parliament, `Did you hear Saklatvala?'

Such was Saklatvala's enthusiasm to get back to the Commons after he lost his south London seat in 1929, he fought a by-election in Glasgow a year later. But, even though he stood in Battersea again in 1931, never again was he returned to the Commons. He died five years later.

The tide had turned against his brand of left-wing politics. It was to be more than half a century before another Black person became an MP, and then only after a bitter struggle waged by `Black Section' activists in the Labour Party.

Editor's note: Shapurji Saklatvala (March 28, 1874 – January 16, 1936) was a British politician of Indian Parsi heritage. He was the third Indian Member of Parliament (MP) in the Parliament of the

United Kingdom after fellow Parsis Dadabhai Naoroji and Mancherjee Bhownagree.

Saklatvala was born in Bombay (now Mumbai), India, the son of a merchant. He worked briefly as an iron and coal prospector for Jamsetji Tata before moving to England in 1905 where he worked for British Westinghouse. It was at this time that he joined Lincoln's Inn and qualified as a barrister. [2] He joined the Independent Labour Party, the Labour Party and on its formation the Communist Party of Great Britain (Labour allowed joint membership at the time). At the 1922 general election he was elected as the Communist candidate for the constituency of Battersea North, with the support of the Labour Party.

Chapter Twenty Three

CLAUDIA JONES

Feminist, political activist and community leader

**Claudia Jones 15 February 1915
– 24 December 1964, age 49**

Claudia Jones, feminist, Black nationalist, political activist, community leader, communist and journalist, has been described as the mother of the Notting Hill carnival. The diversity of her political affiliations clearly illustrates her multifaceted approach to the struggle for equal rights in the 20th century. Claudia was a fearless person with a political perspective, which regarded the human race as a single race of people

363

with equal rights. She fought for the Black immigrants who had to endure enormous suffering due to racial prejudice and stereotyping.

She was born in Belmont, Port-of-Spain, Trinidad in 1915 and at the age of eight moved to Harlem, New York with her parents and three sisters. Her education was cut short by Tuberculosis and the damage to her lungs as well as severe heart disease plagued Claudia for the rest of her life.

For over 30 years she lived in New York and during this time became an active member of the American Communist party, an organisation in which her journalistic and community leadership skills were maximised. By 1948 she had become the editor of Nergo Affairs for the Party's paper the Daily Worker and had evolved into an accomplished speaker on human and civil rights.

In 1955 she was deported from the US and given asylum in England, where she spent her remaining years working with London's African-Caribbean community. Claudia started campaigning against racism as soon as she had arrived in London. She helped to bring Black people and white anti-racists together and to encourage them to form cohesive and supportive community organisations to promote race equality in all areas of life in London. She founded and edited the *The West Indian Gazette* which despite financial problems remained crucial in her fight for equal opportunities for black people.

Claudia Jones lasting legacy is undoubtedly the Notting Hill carnival, which she helped launch in 1959 as an annual showcase for Caribbean talent. These early celebrations were held in halls and were epitomised by the slogan, "A people's art is the genesis of their freedom".

The ant-racism work carried out by Claudia and other Black and white activists encouraged the Labour Government in the 1960s and 1970s to introduce positive Race Relations legislation.

Chapter twenty four

KWAME NKRUMAH

Statesman, liberator and Advocate for African Unity

Kwame Nkrumah 21 September, 1909 – 27 April 1972

Childhood

Kwame Nkrumah considered to be the father-figure of Pan-Africanism and the liberator of Ghana from British colonial rule. He was born in Nkruful in the Western Region in the country known at Ngonloma the time as the Gold Coast and later renamed Ghana. Nkrumah was first named Francis Nwia-Kofi but later changed his name to Kwame Nkrumah in 1945 when he visited the UK as he was born on a Saturday. Nkrumah attended Elementary School at Half Assini where his father worked as a goldsmith. He later attended the Government Training College in Accra and in 1930 obtained a Teacher's Certificate from the College which was renamed Achimota School.

Education

Nkrumah was determined to maximise his education and after becoming a Head teacher of a Roman Catholic junior school he went back to learning as a student in a Roman Catholic Seminary in Amisano before enrolling at Lincoln University in America. Having graduated from Lincoln with a BA in Theology he went on to the University of Pennsylvania where he completed an MSc in Education and an MA in Philosophy a year later. Whilst studying in America Nkrumah helped to found the African Students Association of America and Canada and became their President. During his studies he did part-time lecturing in Negro History. Before arriving in England in 1945 to study law he was voted "Most Outstanding Professor of the Year" by Lincoln. Nkrumah was a brilliant Scholar with a strong interest in politics.

Political philosophy

Nkrumah's experience in America led him to think that a united landmass of African countries, similar to the United States of America would be the best way to build a powerful economic entity which would be prosperous because of the abundance of natural resources available. This would ensure political and economic prosperity for Africa and would deny the Europeans opportunities to exploit the continent as they have done for centuries. To ensure his vision for Africa Nkrumah recognised that first of all Africa would have to be free from colonial rule. Nkrumah devoted the rest of his life towards the liberation of Africa. Soon after arriving in London in May 1945 he completed his thesis for a Doctorate and became involved with international political movements. Influenced by books he had read by Marx and Lenin and Black thinkers like George Padmore, he helped to organise the Sixth Pan-African Congress in Manchester. For the first time the Congress demanded 'autonomy and independence' for Africa as well as the right for all colonial people to control their own destiny. Whilst he was in London he became the Vice-President of West African Students Union and leader of the "Circle" the secret organisation dedicated to the unity and independence of West Africa.

Imprisonment

Before returning to Ghana Nkrumah wrote his first book "Towards Colonial Freedom". Nkrumah returned to Ghana in December 1947 and became General Secretary of the United Gold Coast Convention (UGCC) and began to organise a mass base for the UGCC. Like other anti-colonial leaders such as Mahatma Gandhi, Jawaharlal Nehru, Jomo Kenyatta, Chedi Jagan and others, he was imprisoned by the British. In September 1948 he was dismissed as General Secretary of the UGCC following disturbances and the detention of himself and his Executive Members. In 1949 Nkrumah launched a new radical party - the Convention Peoples Party (CPP) committed to a programme of immediate self-government. In 1950 he initiated a 'positive action' campaign which involved strikes, protests and non-co-operation with British rule. He was arrested in January 1950 and sentenced to imprisonment. Nkrumah, like so many aspiring political leaders was greatly inspired by the philosophy of non-violence practised by Gandhi.

In February 1951, whist still in prison, he won a seat in the Parliamentary elections securing 22,780 of the 23,122 votes cast to become the Member for Accra Central. He was released from prison within a few days and took a position in Government. In 1952 he became Prime Minister of the Gold Coast. His Party the CPP won the 1956 elections which led the way for independence from Britain. The territory became independent as Ghana in March 1957 and Nkrumah was the nation's first Prime Minister.

Commitment to African unity

In 1958 Nkrumah organised an All-African Peoples Conference in Accra. In the same year he married Helena Ritz Fathia an Egyptian and relative of Gamal Abdul Nasser, President of Egypt and they had three children. In 1960 when the country became a republic, he became its first President. He first began to build up the infrastructure of the country for its people and to carry out an Africanisation policy that allowed Ghanaians into jobs, which only Europeans had had before. In 1962 he survived an assassination attempt at Kulunguga in the Northern Region.

He then began to concentrate on campaigning for the political unity of Black Africa. In 1962 the First International Congress of Africans was held in Accra, the capital of Ghana. It marked the formal launching of the Pan-African Movement on African soil.

International Statesman

Nkrumah's ideas on Black Nationalism, independence and unity were to influence the Black movement throughout the world. Many people, from Herman Edwards who built up the British self-help movement, to Amilcar Cabral who led the African struggle against Portuguese colonialism, have acknowledged their debt to the example and writings of Nkrumah. He was at one time the most respected leader of independence movements and the person who spoke out loudest against apartheid in South Africa. Under Nkrumah's leadership Ghana was prosperous and many projects were implemented to improve education, transport, health and living standards. Nkrumah had to transform the economy which was built around a single product cocoa, during colonial rule. The government invested heavily in the infrastructure of the country but ran into difficulties due to the manipulation of the price of cocoa on the international market.

Collapse of the cocoa economy

Once the cocoa prices fell in the early 1960's the currency also suffered and inflation escalated. Food prices increased by over 250 per cent over 1957 levels and the economic growth declined from 9 per cent to 2 per cent in the space of five years. As the economy declined dissatisfaction with Nkrumah's rule began to take effect. The government commitment to a socialist economy also meant the introduction of high levels of taxation upon an increasingly disgruntled middle class. Opposition to the government increased as the capitalist control of the economies of Africa tightened and cocoa prices slumped on the world markets.

In addition the international financial markets and speculators supported by America, Britain and many European governments ensured that Nkrumah was taught a lesson because of his commitment to socialism and his association with radical socialist countries. During this period Ghana became a victim of the "Cold War" which characterised the antagonistic relationship between western democracies and socialist/communist oriented economies. Nkrumah responded to the internal dis-satisfaction by declaring himself President for life in 1965 and implementing legislation which eroded many of the democratic and traditional processes, including either reducing or suspending the powers of the traditional Chiefs who had helped the British to rule the country during colonialism. Nkrumah also alienated himself from sections of the law enforcement agencies and the army which proved to be fatal for his rule.

The fall of Nkrumah

On 24 February 1966 whilst on a visit to North Vietnam the Army along with the National Police staged a coup and announced over the

369

radio that the government had been taken over by the National Liberal Council. Parliament was suspended, the CPP was banned and President Nkrumah dismissed from office. The coup was welcomed by Britain, America and the capitalist nations as many British politicians and the Western media portrayed Nkrumah as one of the most evil and despotic ruler in Africa.

Nkrumah was a pain in the side of those with ambitions to sustain colonialism in Africa and to continue to exploit Africa's resources to benefit the Western economies. Nkrumah found himself on the wrong side of the world order between capitalism and socialism/communism. Western countries were prepared to tolerate apartheid in South Africa which denied the overwhelming majority of the population who happened to be Black their civil, democratic and human rights whilst condemning an African government which was seeking to break the stranglehold of foreign colonial domination over its economy for centuries.

It has been suggested that the U.S.A. and Britain helped to stage the coup against Nkrumah. Whilst this may be true there were other reasons why Nkrumah was brought down. Nkrumah was defeated because of the economic depression caused by the slump in the world markets for cocoa which was under the control and direction of Western buyers of the product; the country's dependence on a single product for its prosperity; the legacy of centuries of colonialism and exploitation; Nkrumah's antagonism towards capitalist America and Europe; his support for liberation movements in Africa and elsewhere; his leanings towards socialism; the corruption and mis-management which characterised the government; and the formation of a one-Party state.

The legacy of Nkrumah

Nkrumah spent the last six years of his life in Romania. He died on 27 April 1972 from natural causes and was later reburied in Ghana on 7 July 1972. Despite the failings of Nkrumah his personal standing remains high in Ghana and elsewhere. His vision for Africa is still shared by many people in Africa and the rest of the world. Europeans have exploited the continent of Africa for centuries until they were forced out of occupation by liberating forces. Nkrumah's vision for Africa gave many Africans and others the inspiration, which enabled many countries in Africa, the Caribbean, and Asia and elsewhere to liberate themselves from foreign domination. He will always be remembers for his enormous contributions in the eradication of colonialism in Africa.

Over his lifetime, Nkrumah was awarded honorary doctorates by Lincoln University, Moscow State University; Cairo University in Cairo, Egypt; Jagiellonian University in Kraków, Poland; Humboldt University in the former East Berlin; and many other universities.

In 2000, he was voted Africa's man of the millennium by listeners to the BBC World Service

Nkrumah's advocacy of industrial development at any cost, led to the construction of a hydroelectric power plant, the Akosombo Dam on the Volta River in eastern Ghana. Kaiser Aluminum agreed to build the dam for Nkrumah, but restricted what could be produced using the power generated. Nkrumah borrowed money to build the dam, and placed Ghana in debt. To finance the debt, he raised taxes on the cocoa farmers in the south. This accentuated regional differences and jealousy. The dam was completed and opened by Nkrumah amidst world publicity on 22 January 1966.

Nkrumah wanted Ghana to have modern armed forces, so he acquired aircraft and ships, and introduced conscription. He also gave military support to anti-British Empire backed government guerrillas in Rhodesia (now Zimbabwe). In February 1966, while Nkrumah was on a state visit to North Vietnam and China, his government was overthrown in a military coup led by Emmanuel Kwasi Kotoka and the National Liberation Council. Several commentators claimed the

371

coup received support from the British secret service and the American Central Intelligence Agency (CIA).

Kwame Nkrumah: I Speak of Freedom, 1961

Kwame Nkrumah was the leader of Ghana, the former British colony of the Gold Coast and the first of the European colonies in Africa to gain independence with majority rule. Until he was deposed by a coup d'état in 1966, he was a major spokesman for modern Africa.

"For centuries, Europeans dominated the African continent. The white man arrogated to himself the right to rule and to be obeyed by the non-white; his mission, he claimed, was to modernise Africa. Under this cloak, the Europeans robbed the continent of vast riches and inflicted unimaginable suffering on the African people. They manipulated the country's economy and supported internal and external opposition.

All this makes a sad story, but now we must be prepared to bury the past with its unpleasant memories and look to the future. All we ask of the former colonial powers is their goodwill and co-operation to remedy past mistakes and injustices and to grant independence to the colonies in Africa....

It is clear that we must find an African solution to our problems, and that this can only be found in African unity. Divided we are weak; united, Africa could become one of the greatest forces for good in the world.

Although most Africans are poor, our continent is potentially extremely rich. Our mineral resources, which are being exploited with foreign capital only to enrich foreign investors, range from gold and diamonds to uranium and petroleum. Our forests contain some of the finest woods to be grown anywhere. Our cash crops include cocoa, coffee, rubber, tobacco and cotton. As for power, which is an important factor in any economic development, Africa contains over 40% of the

*potential water power of the world, as compared with about
10% in Europe and 13% in North America. Yet so far, less than
1% has been developed. This is one of the reasons why we have
in Africa the paradox of poverty in the midst of plenty, and
scarcity in the midst of abundance.*

*Never before have a people had within their grasp so great an
opportunity for developing a continent endowed with so much
wealth. Individually, the independent states of Africa, some of
them potentially rich, others poor, can do little for their people.
Together, by mutual help, they can achieve much. But the
economic development of the continent must be planned and
pursued as a whole. A loose confederation designed only for
economic co-operation would not provide the necessary unity of
purpose. Only a strong political union can bring about full and
effective development of our natural resources for the benefit of
our people.*

*The political situation in Africa today is heartening and at the
same time disturbing. It is heartening to see so many new flags
hoisted in place of the old; it is disturbing to see so many
countries of varying sizes and at different levels of development,
weak and, in some cases, almost helpless. If this terrible state of
fragmentation is allowed to continue it may well be disastrous
for us all.*

*There are at present some 28 states in Africa, excluding the
Union of South Africa, and those countries not yet free. No less
than nine of these states have a population of less than three
million. Can we seriously believe that the colonial powers meant
these countries to be independent, viable states? The example of
South America, which has as much wealth, if not more than
North America, and yet remains weak and dependent on outside
interests, is one which every African would do well to study.*

*Critics of African unity often refer to the wide differences in
culture, language and ideas in various parts of Africa. This is*

true, but the essential fact remains that we are all Africans, and have a common interest in the independence of Africa. The difficulties presented by questions of language, culture and different political systems are not insuperable. If the need for political union is agreed by us all, then the will to create it is born; and where there's a will there's a way.

The present leaders of Africa have already shown a remarkable willingness to consult and seek advice among themselves. Africans have, indeed, begun to think continentally. They realise that they have much in common, both in their past history, in their present problems and in their future hopes. To suggest that the time is not yet ripe for considering a political union of Africa is to evade the facts and ignore realities in Africa today.

The greatest contribution that Africa can make to the peace of the world is to avoid all the dangers inherent in disunity, by creating a political union which will also by its success, stand as an example to a divided world. A Union of African states will project more effectively the African personality. It will command respect from a world that has regard only for size and influence. The scant attention paid to African opposition to the French atomic tests in the Sahara, and the ignominious spectacle of the U.N.in the Congo quibbling about constitutional niceties while the Republic was tottering into anarchy, are evidence of the callous disregard of African Independence by the Great Powers.

We have to prove that greatness is not to be measured in stockpiles of atom bombs. I believe strongly and sincerely that with the deep-rooted wisdom and dignity, the innate respect for human lives, the intense humanity that is our heritage, the African race, unite under one federal government, will emerge not as just another world bloc to flaunt its wealth and strength, but as a Great Power whose greatness is indestructible because it is built not on fear, envy and suspicion, nor won at the

374

expense of others, but founded on hope, trust, friendship and directed to the good of all mankind.

The emergence of such a mighty stabilising force in this strife-worn world should be regarded not as the shadowy dream of a visionary, but as a practical proposition, which the peoples of Africa can, and should, translate into reality. There is a tide in the affairs of every people when the moment strikes for political action. Such was the moment in the history of the United States of America when the Founding Fathers saw beyond the petty wrangling of the separate states and created a Union. This is our chance. We must act now. Tomorrow may be too late and the opportunity will have passed, and with it the hope of free Africa's survival.

From: Kwame Nkrumah, I Speak of Freedom: A Statement of African Ideology (London: William Heinemann Ltd., 1961), pp. xi-xiv

Chapter Twenty Five

GAMAL ABDAL NASSER

Egyptian leader, statesman and anti-colonialist

**Gamal Abdal Nasser, 15 January
1918 – 28 September 1970**

A place in history

Gamal Abdal Nasser was one of the most important Arab leaders of the
20th Century. He was President of the Republic of Egypt from 1954 to
1970. Nasser was born in 1918 in Alexandria. His father, who was a

post office administrator and moved around the country, sent him to school in Cairo. As a boy he joined demonstrations against the British who then ruled Egypt with the help of Egyptian kings. As a young man he was a great reader, deeply concerned about the political future of his country. Nasser was a Pan-Arabist and advocated Third-World unity. He was particularly keen to lead his country away from political corruption and decades of Western domination and to establish unity amongst Arab nations. Nasser established a political system in Egypt which promoted economic and social development including land reform and centralised control which described as "Arab socialism".

Rebellious teenager

As a teenager he was involved in student demonstrations which led to violent clashes with local and British police forces. He was expelled from secondary school in Cairo for leading an anti-British student demonstration in 1935. In 1937, at his second attempt, he got into the Military Academy. He was not particularly attracted to military life as such, but he saw the army as the only way of ridding Egypt of British power and corrupt local rulers. Nasser's education was completed during his time in the Army. He graduated from the Royal Military Academy in 1938 as a lawyer. At the time in question King Farouk was the Head of the Egyptian nation which was dominated by British rule. King Farouk was popular with the British establishment and he tolerated their presence much to the anger of Egyptian nationalists like Nasser.

Military experience

During his time in the army, Nasser founded the secret Society of Free Officers who were fiercely opposed to the occupation of their country by a foreign power. The Free Officers also wanted to depose the monarchy, reduced the power of the landlords and foreign influence and rid their country of political corruption and dependence on the Western nations. In 1948 Nasser was a Major in the Army and took part against the 1948 Arab-Israeli war. By July 1952 Nasser led a group of army officers against King Farouk and staged a coup d'Etat to get rid of him and the British troops.

In 1956 Nasser became President of the country and he decided to nationalise the Suez Canal. He also negotiated an agreement, which terminated 72-year presence of the British in Egypt. The Canal had been opened in 1869 and, because it linked Western Europe with the Indian Ocean, it shortened the journey from England to India by over 5,000 miles. Since this saved so much time and money, ships were prepared to pay for the privilege of using the Canal. But all those payments were going to the foreign company that 'owned' the Canal. In 1956 America and Britain withdrew their promised support to build a new Aswan Dam to provide power for the Egyptian economy. On 26 July, Nasser declared the Canal belonged to Egypt and that he would build a dam with the revenues. After all, he said, Egypt had built the Canal but had never benefited from it. Imperialists, he said, could "choke in their rage". The Aswan Dam was eventually built with support from the Soviet Union, which provided Egypt with economic and military aid. This relationship drew Egypt closer to the Soviet Union much to the annoyance of the Western powers such as America and Britain.

Nationalisation of the Suez Canal

Britain, France and Israel were furious with Nasser and decided to invade Egypt to retain foreign control of the Canal. The invasion was short-lived and the foreigners retreated. Most of the world's countries opposed the invasion, including the two super-powers – U.S.A. and the Soviet Union. It was a victory for Egypt which won complete control of the Canal and got rid of the British military base in the Canal zone and confiscated its stores.

The Western powers then retaliated with an economic boycott, which America joined, but this did not bring down the government or people of Egypt. Instead Nasser enjoyed massive popularity at home, in the Middle East region and among other Third World countries which tried to copy his ideas. Nasser was seen as a hero in the Arab world. Cairo was already the headquarters of the Arab League, set up in 1945. Now Nasser's picture appeared in shops, taxis and cafes from Aden to Tripoli. Everyone saw him as the leader who would stand up to the imperialist powers, return Palestine to the Arabs and restore them to ancient glories by uniting them into one single state.

The impact of Nasser's leadership

After the expulsion of the foreign powers from Egypt one by one Iraq, Syria, Algeria and Yemen began to try to get rid of foreign Western influences and regarded themselves as 'liberated Arab states'. Nasser was opposed to monarchical governments in the Middle East and he provided troops to support the Yemenite revolutionaries against the Saudi Arabian backed royalists. There was an attempt by Nasser to create a United Arab Republic to unite all Arab states but Syria departed from the pact following a coup in Syria1961.

In 1967 Nasser precipitated war with Israel by dissolving the United Nations peacekeeping forces in the Sinai and blockading the Israeli port of Elat. The war with Israel went against Egypt and Nasser resigned as President. He returned as Prime Minister after massive popular demonstrations supporting his involvement in government.

Because of its geographical position, Egypt is as much part of Africa as it is of the Arab world. Under Nasser, Cairo provided a refuge for anti-colonial leaders from North Africa, the Cameroon and Uganda. As a centre for radical anti-imperialist ideas, Nasser's Egypt played a key role in the independence struggles of Africa between 1954 and 1970.

Chapter Twenty Six

ANGELA DAVIS

Political activist, scholar, writer and civil rights campaigner

Angela Davis 26 January 1944

Angela Davis

Early years

Angela Davis was born on 26 January 1944, and grew up in Birmingham, Alabama, an area where racial tension between Black and white gad been rife since the days of slavery. Her parents were schoolteachers. Angela Davis inspired many anti-racist people from within and outside America towards the struggle for racial and social equality and against imperialism, which condemns hundreds of millions of people to poverty, exploitation and misery. As a Black woman Angela has been a role model for the many Black women who participated in the Civil Rights Movement and the fight for emancipation of Black people around the world from economic enslavement and political domination.

Education

Davis like so many Black activists has herself been inspired by great African leaders like Kwame Nkrumah, Marcus Garvey, Du Bois, Malcolm X, Paul Robeson, Franz Frantz and others. Angela Davis was well aware of the humiliation, and degradation of African Americans during her early years. She witnessed at first hand the suffering of people because of the colour of their skin and she was contemptuous of the ruling political elite and law enforcement agencies, which sustained the marginalisation of Black and poor people in America.

In 1965, Angela Davis studied at the University of California, where she became the protégé of the Marxist philosopher. Herbert Marcuse. She also lectured in philosophy at the university's Los Angeles campus. Angela was deeply committed to the Civil Rights Movement and supported many campaigns and protests in favour of civil and human rights for African Americans from an early age. During her time at college, Angela spent a year in Paris where she became acquainted with Algerian student revolutionaries who believed that Marxism held the solution to the United States' racial and social problems.

Black struggles

However, it was the callous bombing of a Black church in Birmingham, Alabama in 1963 in which 4 children were killed that cemented her political commitment. When Angela returned to the US in 1968 to complete her degree she joined the Communist Party. She was also an active member of the Black Panther Party and the Student Non-Violent Co-ordinating Committee. In 1969 she was appointed a lecturer in Philosophy at the University of California in Los Angeles (UCLA). But, because of her membership of the Communist Party, the university governors refused to confirm her position. So a long campaign began for Angela to keep her post. Angela also became active in various campaigns on campus and in the community. Most notably, she was active in the movement to release the Soledad Brothers – one of whom was George Jackson – and in 1969, she was dismissed from UCLA for her 'radical' views and activities on behalf of the Soledad Brothers. Davis also championed the cause of Black prisoners especially those who regarded themselves as political prisoners because of their commitment to anti-racism.

A wanted woman

After being refused permission to visit George Jackson in prison, Angela became friendly with his younger brother, Jonathan. This relationship had far-reaching consequences for Angela. It was after Jonathan's failed attempt to secure the release of the Soledad Brothers that Angela Davis became a household name. Jonathan was one of the four persons killed - including the trial Judge - in the abortive escape and kidnapping attempt from the Hall of Justice, in Marine County in California on 7 August 1970. The guns used in the kidnapping had been registered in Angela's name. She became the woman most wanted by the Federal Bureau of Investigation (FBI) in its clampdown on the Black Panther Party, and a nation-wide hunt for her was launched.

Angela was found two months later in New York. She was charged with conspiracy, murder and kidnap. Angela had become a victim of the system she had been fighting. In 1972, after a 13-week trial, she was acquitted of all charges. Angela was also active in organisations such as the national alliance against Racist and Political Repression and the Black Women's Health Project. In 1980 and 1984 she stood as the Communist Party's vice-presidential candidate.

Since the 1970s, Angela has travelled all over the world to speak and teach. Based in California she is a Professor at the University of California, Santa Cruz where she lectures to university students on Black philosophy and aesthetics as well as running courses in women's studies. Her *"Women, Race & Class"* published in 1981, and *"Women, Culture and Politics"* published in 1989 are regarded as two of the most important books to examine the triple oppression facing Black women.

For Angela when answering a question on the role of the Black middle class in the continuing struggle for Black liberation;

> *"...the quest of for the emancipation of Black people in the US has always been a quest for economic liberation which means to a certain extent that the rise of Black middle class would be inevitable. What I think is different today is the lack of political connection between the Black middle class and the increasing numbers of Black people who are more impoverished than ever before".*

Angela is still a prolific campaigner and political activist, scholar, and author. She is a retired professor, with the History of Consciousness Department at the University of California, Santa Cruz and is the former director of the university's Feminist Studies department. Her research interests are in feminism, African American studies, critical theory, Marxism, popular music and social consciousness, and the philosophy and history of punishment and prisons.

There is no doubt that Angela will continue to inspire students and others with her passion and commitment for justice, equality and liberation.

Chapter Twenty Seven

BOB MARLEY

Musician, singer and peace maker

Bob Marley 1945 - 1981

Early years

Robert Nesta Marley was a legendry musician and singer who impressed, inspired and entertained hundreds of millions of people of

384

all ethnic, social, cultural and political backgrounds for over four decades. Bob's music and songs will continue to entertain people and to remind them of a range of social issues for decades to come. Bob Marley born on 6 February 1945, at his grandfather's house at two thirty in the morning, in the rural area of St Ann, Jamaica. His father, middle aged Englishman, Captain Norval Marley married his mother Cedalla Booker in 1944. Soon after Bob was born his father left his mother. During the late of 1950s he, like many others, moved to the capital, Kingston, settling in Trench Town, one of the shanty towns in the west of the city. Whilst in Trenchtown Bob and his friend Bunny received extensive tuition from the great vocalist Joe Higgs who was one of Trentchtown's most famous residents and a well known Rasta. Higgs was a committed Rastafarian and publicly preached the philosophy of Rastafarian which took roots in the ghettos of Kingston and elsewhere.

Interest in music and the Rastafarian faith

Marley was working, learning the welding trade in Kingston when he formed his first harmony group in 1961. Jimmy Cliff a young musician who had already a few hit records by the time he was 14 years old introduced Marley to a local producer Leslie Kong and Marley made his first single "Judge Not" in 1961. In Trenchtown Marley also met fellow musicians Bunny Wailer and Peter Tosh. After cutting his first record in 1961, he teamed up with Bunny and Peter to form the 'Wailing Wailers'. Their first single, Simmer Down, went to number 1 in the Jamaican charts in 1963.

Over the next few years they put out almost 30 records that established their reputation. Bob became increasingly drawn towards Rastafarianism, and used its language in his lyrics to express the yearnings of Jamaica's shantytown poor. Conflicts with producers led the group to set-up their own, short-lived, record label, Wail 'N' Soul. But perhaps their most memorable music dates from the early 1970s and their collaboration with Lee Perry. With the release, in 1973, of the 'Catch A Fire' album followed by 'Burning', Marley began to make an

385

impact outside the Caribbean. The albums 'Natty Dread' (1975) and 'Rastaman Vibrations' (1976) contained some of Marley's most committed songs, like 'Rebel Music', 'Them Belly Full (But We Hungry)' and 'War' – the lyrics for the latter came from a speech by Emperor Haile Selassie of Ethiopia, the Rastafarians figurehead.

Bob's message to the world

By now Marley's message was reaching the Jamaican political scene. His Rastafarianism and calls for an end to the violence that marked the December 1976 general election found strong echoes with young people in the Jamaican ghettos. It was probably his condemnation of violence, expressed in a free concert at Kingston National Heroes Park shortly before the election that led to an assassination attempt. Despite being wounded he did not stop playing. Much of the next two years were spent on the road, although two new albums came, 'Exodus' and 'Kaya'. In April 1978 he returned to Jamaica to play the One Love Peace Concert, which brought together opposing politicians Prime Minister Michael Manley and opposition leader Edward Seaga. Marley's contribution through his music and songs helped towards the anti-racism struggles in America and around the world was very inspiring. His songs of freedom, liberation, love, peace and harmony won the hearts and minds of many people and in turn influenced their attitudes and behaviour towards their fellow human beings.

Bob toured the world and shared his thoughts for a more fair, just and peaceful world. He was a genuine fighter for peace, love and respect and did his very best through his music to express his feelings. He visited Africa for the first time, travelling from Kenya to Ethiopia, the spiritual homeland of Rastafari. In April 1980 he and his group performed at the Independence Day celebrations of the recently liberated Zimbabwe. The release of the albums, 'Survival' (1979) and 'Uprising' (1980) were followed by groundbreaking tours of Europe (where a 100,000 crowd saw the Milan performance) and the United States. On the U.S. tour, Bob was taken ill with cancer. He died in

Miami on May 11, 1981 aged 36. The people of Jamaica gave him a state funeral.

Bob Marley's legacy

Bob Marley will be remembered as one of the greatest songwriter, singer and musician for many decades to come.

He was the rhythm guitarist and lead singer for the ska, rocksteady and reggae band Bob Marley & The Wailers (1963–1981). Marley remains the most widely known and revered performer of reggae music in the world. He is credited with helping to spread both Jamaican music and the Rastafari movement to a worldwide audience.

Marley's music was heavily influenced by the social issues of his homeland, and he is considered to have given voice to the specific political and cultural nexus of Jamaica. His best-known hits include "I Shot the Sheriff", "No Woman, No Cry", "Could You Be Loved", "Stir It Up", "Get Up Stand Up", "Jamming", "Redemption Song", "One Love" and, "Three Little Birds",[3] as well as the posthumous releases "Buffalo Soldier" and "Iron Lion Zion". The compilation album Legend (1984), released three years after his death, was reggae's best-selling album, going ten times Platinum which is also known as one Diamond in the U.S., and selling 25 million copies worldwide.

Bob Marley was the Third World's first pop superstar. He was the man who introduced the world to the mystic power of reggae. In 1999 Time magazine chose Bob Marley & The Wailers' Exodus as the greatest album of the 20th century. In 2001, he was posthumously awarded the Grammy Lifetime Achievement Award, and a feature-length documentary about his life, Rebel Music, won various awards at the Grammys. With contributions from Rita, The Wailers, and Marley's lovers and children, it also tells much of the story in his own words. A statue was inaugurated, next to the national stadium on Arthur Wint Drive in Kingston to commemorate him. In 2006, the State of New

York renamed a portion of Church Avenue from Remsen Avenue to East 98th Street in Brooklyn "Bob Marley Boulevard". In 2008, a statue of Marley was inaugurated in Banatski Sokolac, Serbia.

Internationally, Marley's message also continues to reverberate amongst various indigenous communities. For instance, the Aboriginal people of Australia continue to burn a sacred flame to honour his memory in Sydney's Victoria Park, while members of the Native American Hopi and Havasupai tribe revere his work. There are also many tributes to Bob Marley throughout India, including restaurants, hotels, and cultural festivals.

Bob Marley had a number of children: three with his wife Rita, two adopted from Rita's previous relationships, and several others with different women. The Bob Marley official website acknowledges eleven children.

Chapter Twenty Eight

FRANTZ FANON
Revolutionary, philosopher and writer

**Frantz Fanon 20 July1925 –
6 December 1961**

Early opposition to fascism and racism

Frantz Fanon was born to a middle class family in what was then the French colony of Martinique on June 20 1925. His parents worked hard so that their children could go to school. At school Fanon became conscious of identity as a Black person. Because of his schooling and culture Fanon considered himself as French, and the encounter he later experienced with racism in France left him somewhat dis-orientated and helped to shape his psychological theories about race and culture. For Fanon, a racist culture alienates Black people and prevents them from breaking away from a mentality of inferiority and independence. In a racist society Black people are alienated from themselves as many of them aspire to be like the white person and behave accordingly in order to progress.

For Fanon, speaking French meant that one accepts, or is coerced into accepting, the collective consciousness of the French, which identifies blackness with evil, sin and inferiority. In an attempt to deny the association of blackness and all things undesirable, the Black person dons a white mask, or thinks of himself as a universal subject equally participating in a society that advocates an equality supposedly abstracted from personal appearance. Cultural values are therefore internalised into consciousness, creating a fundamental disjuncture between the Black person's consciousness and his/her body. Under these conditions the Black person is necessarily alienated from himself/herself.

This analysis could equally apply to Black people who were brought up under English speaking colonial rule. It is not easy to follow Fanon's work and thinking although much of it is about fighting colonialism, racism, fascism, inequality, poverty and exploitation.

When he was 17, Fanon's island was occupied by the Nazis and he escaped in 1943 to volunteer his services to the allied forces fighting fascism in North Africa and Europe during World War II. After the War, Fanon remained in France to study medicine and psychiatry on a scholarship to Lyon. He married a French woman Jose Duble and started to write political essays and plays. He was regarded as a Black intellectual and wrote on issues around racism and colonialism.

390

Joining the Algerian liberation struggle

Whilst in the French army, Fanon and other Black troops experienced the racism of the other troops and the European people they had been fighting for. After a few years in France, Fanon left for Algeria to take up a post as head of the Blida-Joinville Hospital in Algiers. Algeria was in great political turmoil at the time as the Algerian people were fighting a bloody war to drive the French occupiers out of their country. Here he threw himself into his work and also used his skills as a psychiatrist and a soldier to train and aid the guerrilla fighters. Eventually he resigned from his job, and began to work full time for the revolution. Through his efforts he became one of the main thinkers behind the struggle for freedom and wrote a number of books about it. The most famous of these, 'The Wretched of the Earth', was written after Fanon was diagnosed as having leukaemia. This book became a worldwide best seller. Not only did Fanon present a picture of the connections between colonialism and mental illness, both among the colonisers and the colonised, but also showed how important it was for the colonised to free themselves from their psychological, cultural, social and economic chains.

After becoming Head of the Psychiatry Department at the Bilda-Joinville Hospital in Algeria in 1953, Fanon introduced several reforms, which benefited his patients. Whilst he was at Bilda the war between France and Algeria broke out and many of Fanon's patients related to him the torture they had suffered at the hands of the French. In 1956 he resigned his post at Bilda with the French government to work for the Algerian cause. Fanon was horrified at the fact that foreigners who occupied their land persecuted the Algerians in their own country.

Living in Tunisia

After fleeing Algeria, Fanon settled in Tunisia where he worked openly with the Algerian Independence Movement. He also helped many patients and wrote many articles denouncing colonialism and racism.

He was also designated the Ambassador to Ghana by the Provisional Algerian Government.

His final work

While in Ghana, Fanon developed leukaemia. He refused to accept the advice of people close to him and continued to work tirelessly for justice. Most of all he completed his final book *"The Wretched of the Earth"*, which was the most his final and most damning indictment of colonial rule.

For Fanon, the true liberation from colonial rule in Africa can only come from the peasants. He put the peasants at the vanguard of any revolution for overthrowing colonial rule. In his view the urban middle classes with their nationalist views are not genuine revolutionaries, as their main strategy is to substitute themselves in the place of the colonial masters. Fanon warned against simply replacing people with white skins by Black people with masks.

Shortly after *"The Wretched of the Earth"* was finished, Fanon's health got a lot worse and he eventually had to be taken to the United States for treatment. However, the American authorities did not allow him to be treated until they had questioned him for ten days. He died from pneumonia a short while afterwards on 6 December 1961. A few days before his death, he summed up the meaning of his life in a letter: *"We are nothing on earth if we are not in the first place the slaves of the cause, the cause of the people, the cause of liberty and justice."*

Chapter Twenty Nine

REV JESSIE JACKSON
Civil Rights Leader

Speech, 18 July *1984 Democratic National Convention*

8 October 1941

Thank you very much.

Tonight we come together bound by our faith in a mighty God, with genuine respect and love for our country, and inheriting the legacy of a great Party, the Democratic Party, which is the best hope for redirecting our nation on a more humane, just, and peaceful course.

This is not a perfect party. We are not a perfect people. Yet, we are called to a perfect mission. Our mission: to feed the hungry; to clothe the naked; to house the homeless; to teach the illiterate; to provide jobs for the jobless; and to choose the human race over the nuclear race.

We are gathered here this week to nominate a candidate and adopt a platform which will expand, unify, direct, and inspire our Party and the nation to fulfill this mission. My constituency is the desperate, the damned, the disinherited, the disrespected, and the despised. They are restless and seek relief. They have voted in record numbers. They have invested the faith, hope, and trust that they have in us. The Democratic Party must send them a signal that we care. I pledge my best not to let them down. There is the call of conscience, redemption, expansion, healing, and unity. Leadership must heed the call of conscience, redemption, expansion, healing, and unity, for they are the key to achieving our mission. Time is neutral and does not change things. With courage and initiative, leaders change things.

No generation can choose the age or circumstance in which it is born, but through leadership it can choose to make the age in which it is born an age of enlightenment, an age of jobs, and peace, and justice. Only leadership -- that intangible combination of gifts, the discipline, information, circumstance, courage, timing, will and divine inspiration -- can lead us out of the crisis in which we find ourselves. Leadership can mitigate the misery of our nation. Leadership can part the waters and lead our nation in the direction of the Promised Land. Leadership can lift the boats stuck at the bottom.

I have had the rare opportunity to watch seven men, and then two, pour out their souls, offer their service, and heal and heed the call of duty to direct the course of our nation. There is a proper season for everything. There is a time to sow and a time to reap. There's a time to compete and a time to cooperate.

394

I ask for your vote on the first ballot as a vote for a new direction for this Party and this nation -- a vote of conviction, a vote of conscience. But I will be proud to support the nominee of this convention for the Presidency of the United States of America. Thank you.

I have watched the leadership of our party develop and grow. My respect for both Mr. Mondale and Mr. Hart is great. I have watched them struggle with the crosswinds and crossfires of being public servants, and I believe they will both continue to try to serve us faithfully.

I am elated by the knowledge that for the first time in our history a woman, Geraldine Ferraro, will be recommended to share out ticket. Throughout this campaign, I've tried to offer leadership to the Democratic Party and the nation. If, in my high moments, I have done some good, offered some service, shed some light, healed some wounds, rekindled some hope, or stirred someone from apathy and indifference, or in any way along the way helped somebody, then this campaign has not been in vain.

For friends who loved and cared for me, and for a God who spared me, and for a family who understood, I am eternally grateful.

If, in my low moments, in word, deed or attitude, through some error of temper, taste, or tone, I have caused anyone discomfort, created pain, or revived someone's fears, that was not my truest self. If there were occasions when my grape turned into a raisin and my joy bell lost its resonance, please forgive me. Charge it to my head and not to my heart. My head - so limited in its finitude; my heart, which is boundless in its love for the human family. I am not a perfect servant. I am a public servant doing my best against the odds. As I develop and serve, be patient: God is not finished with me yet.

This campaign has taught me much; that leaders must be tough enough to fight, tender enough to cry, human enough to make mistakes,

395

humble enough to admit them, strong enough to absorb the pain, and resilient enough to bounce back and keep on moving. For leaders, the pain is often intense. But you must smile through your tears and keep moving with the faith that there is a brighter side somewhere.

I went to see Hubert Humphrey three days before he died. He had just called Richard Nixon from his dying bed, and many people wondered why. And I asked him. He said, "Jesse, from this vantage point, the sun is setting in my life, all of the speeches, the political conventions, the crowds, and the great fights are behind me now. At a time like this you are forced to deal with your irreducible essence, forced to grapple with that which is really important to you. And what I've concluded about life," Hubert Humphrey said, "When all is said and done, we must forgive each other, and redeem each other, and move on."

Our party is emerging from one of its most hard fought battles for the Democratic Party's presidential nomination in our history. But our healthy competition should make us better, not bitter. We must use the insight, wisdom, and experience of the late Hubert Humphrey as a balm for the wounds in our Party, this nation, and the world.

We must forgive each other, redeem each other, regroup, and move one. Our flag is red, white and blue, but our nation is a rainbow - red, yellow, brown, black and white - and we're all precious in God's sight. America is not like a blanket -- one piece of unbroken cloth, the same color, the same texture, the same size. America is more like a quilt: many patches, many pieces, many colors, many sizes, all woven and held together by a common thread. The white, the Hispanic, the black, the Arab, the Jew, the woman, the native American, the small farmer, the businessperson, the environmentalist, the peace activist, the young, the old, the lesbian, the gay, and the disabled make up the American quilt. Even in our fractured state, all of us count and fit somewhere. We have proven that we can survive without each other. But we have not proven that we can win and make progress without each other, we must come together. From Fannie Lou Hamer in Atlantic

City in 1964 to the Rainbow Coalition in San Francisco today; from the Atlantic to the Pacific, we have experienced pain but progress, as we ended American apartheid laws. We got public accommodations. We secured voting rights. We obtained open housing, as young people got the right to vote. We lost Malcolm, Martin, Medgar, Bobby, John, and Viola. The team that got us here must be expanded not abandoned.

Twenty years ago, tears welled up in our eyes as the bodies of Schwerner, Goodman, and Chaney were dredged from the depths of a river in Mississippi. Twenty years later, our communities, black and Jewish, are in anguish, anger, and pain. Feelings have been hurt on both sides. There is a crisis in communications. Confusion is in the air. But we cannot afford to lose our way. We may agree to agree; or agree to disagree on issues; we must bring back civility to these tensions.

We are co-partners in a long and rich religious history -- the Judeo-Christian traditions. Many blacks and Jews have a shared passion for social justice at home and peace abroad. We must seek a revival of the spirit, inspired by a new vision and new possibilities. We must return to higher ground. We are bound by Moses and Jesus, but also connected with Islam and Mohammed. These three great religions, Judaism, Christianity, and Islam, were all born in the revered and holy city   of   Jerusalem.

We are bound by Dr. Martin Luther King Jr. and Rabbi Abraham Heschel, crying out from their graves for us to reach common ground. We are bound by shared blood and shared sacrifices. We are much too intelligent, much too bound by our Judeo-Christian heritage, much too victimized by racism, sexism, militarism, and anti-Semitism, much too threatened as historical scapegoats to go on divided one from another. We must turn from finger pointing to clasped hands. We must share our burdens and our joys with each other once again. We must turn to each other and not on each other and choose higher ground.

Twenty years later, we cannot be satisfied by just restoring the old coalition. Old wine skins must make room for new wine. We must

397

heal and expand. The Rainbow Coalition is making room for Arab Americans. They, too, know the pain and hurt of racial and religious rejection. They must not continue to be made pariahs. The Rainbow Coalition is making room for Hispanic Americans who this very night are living under the threat of the Simpson-Mazzoli bill; and farm workers from Ohio who are fighting the Campbell Soup Company with a boycott to achieve legitimate worker's rights.

The Rainbow is making room for the Native American, the most exploited people of all, a people with the greatest moral claim amongst us. We support them as they seek the restoration of their ancient land and claim amongst us. We support them as they seek the restoration of land and water rights, as they seek to preserve their ancestral homeland and the beauty of a land that was once all theirs. They can never receive a fair share for all they have given us. They must finally have a fair chance to develop their great resources and to preserve their people and their culture.

The Rainbow Coalition includes Asian Americans, now being killed in our streets - scapegoats for the failures of corporate, industrial, and economic policies. The Rainbow is making room for the young Americans. Twenty years ago, our young people were dying in a war for which they could not even vote. Twenty years later, young America has the power to stop a war in Central America and the responsibility to vote in great numbers. Young America must be politically active in 1984. The choice is war or peace. We must make room for young America.

The Rainbow includes disabled veterans. The color scheme fits in the Rainbow. The disabled have their handicap revealed and their genius concealed; while the able-bodied have their genius revealed and their disability concealed. But ultimately, we must judge people by their values and their contribution. Don't leave anybody out. I would rather have Roosevelt in a wheelchair than Reagan on a horse.

The Rainbow is making room for small farmers. They have suffered tremendously under the Reagan regime. They will either
398

receive 90 percent parity or 100 percent charity. We must address their concerns and make room for them. The Rainbow includes lesbians and gays. No American citizen ought be denied equal protection from the law. We must be unusually committed and caring as we expand our family to include new members. All of us must be tolerant and understanding as the fears and anxieties of the rejected and the party leadership express themselves in many different ways. Too often what we call hate -- as if it were some deeply-rooted philosophy or strategy -- is simply ignorance, anxiety, paranoia, fear, and insecurity.

To be strong leaders, we must be long-suffering as we seek to right the wrongs of our Party and our nation. We must expand our Party, heal our Party, and unify our Party. That is our mission in 1984.

We are often reminded that we live in a great nation -- and we do. But it can be greater still. The Rainbow is mandating a new definition of greatness. We must not measure greatness from the mansion down, but the manger up. Jesus said that we should not be judged by the bark we wear but by the fruit that we bear. Jesus said that we must measure greatness by how we treat the least of these.

President Reagan says the nation is in recovery. Those 90,000 corporations that made a profit last year but paid no federal taxes are recovering. The 37,000 military contractors who have benefited from Reagan's more than doubling of the military budget in peacetime, surely they are recovering. The big corporations and rich individuals who received the bulk of a three-year, multibillion tax cut from Mr. Reagan are recovering. But no such recovery is under way for the least of these.

Rising tides don't lift all boats, particularly those stuck at the bottom. For the boats stuck at the bottom there's a misery index. This Administration has made life more miserable for the poor. Its attitude has been contemptuous. Its policies and programs have been cruel and unfair to working people. They must be held accountable in November for increasing infant mortality among the poor. In Detroit one of the great cities of the western world, babies are dying at the same rate as Honduras, the most underdeveloped nation in our hemisphere. This
399

Administration must be held accountable for policies that have contributed to the growing poverty in America. There are now 34 million people in poverty, 15 percent of our nation. 23 million are White; 11 million Black, Hispanic, Asian, and others -- mostly women and children. By the end of this year, there will be 41 million people in poverty. We cannot stand idly by. We must fight for a change now.

Under this regime we look at Social Security. The '81 budget cuts included nine permanent Social Security benefit cuts totaling 20 billion over five years. Small businesses have suffered under Reagan tax cuts. Only 18 percent of total business tax cuts went to them; 82 percent to big businesses. Health care under Mr. Reagan has already been sharply cut. Education under Mr. Reagan has been cut 25 percent. Under Mr. Reagan there are now 9.7 million female head families. They represent 16 percent of all families. Half of all of them are poor. 70 percent of all poor children live in a house headed by a woman, where there is no man. Under Mr. Reagan, the Administration has cleaned up only 6 of 546 priority toxic waste dumps. Farmers' real net income was only about half its level in 1979.

Many say that the race in November will be decided in the South. President Reagan is depending on the conservative South to return him to office. But the South, I tell you, is unnaturally conservative. The South is the poorest region in our nation and, therefore, [has] the least to conserve. In his appeal to the South, Mr. Reagan is trying to substitute flags and prayer cloths for food, and clothing, and education, health care, and housing.

Mr. Reagan will ask us to pray, and I believe in prayer. I have come to this way by the power of prayer. But then, we must watch false prophecy. He cuts energy assistance to the poor, cuts breakfast programs from children, cuts lunch programs from children, cuts job training from children, and then says to an empty table, "Let us pray." Apparently, he is not familiar with the structure of a prayer. You thank the Lord for the food that you are about to receive, not the food that just left. I think that we should pray, but don't pray for the food that left.

Pray for the man that took the food to leave. We need a change. We need a change in November.

Under Mr. Reagan, the misery index has risen for the poor. The danger index has risen for everybody. Under this administration, we've lost the lives of our boys in Central America and Honduras, in Grenada, in Lebanon, in nuclear standoff in Europe. Under this Administration, one-third of our children believe they will die in a nuclear war. The danger index is increasing in this world. All the talk about the defense against Russia; the Russian submarines are closer, and their missiles are more accurate. We live in a world tonight more miserable and a world more dangerous.

While Reaganomics and Reaganism is talked about often, so often we miss the real meaning. Reaganism is a spirit, and Reaganomics represents the real economic facts of life. In 1980, Mr. George Bush, a man with reasonable access to Mr. Reagan, did an analysis of Mr. Reagan's economic plan. Mr. George Bush concluded that Reagan's plan was "voodoo economics." He was right. Third-party candidate John Anderson said "a combination of military spending, tax cuts, and a balanced budget by '84 would be accomplished with blue smoke and mirrors." They were both right.

Mr. Reagan talks about a dynamic recovery. There's some measure of recovery. Three and a half years later, unemployment has inched just below where it was when he took office in 1981. There are still 8.1 million people officially unemployed; 11 million working only part-time. Inflation has come down, but let's analyze for a moment who has paid the price for this superficial economic recovery.

Mr. Reagan curbed inflation by cutting consumer demand. He cut consumer demand with conscious and callous fiscal and monetary policies. He used the Federal budget to deliberately induce unemployment and curb social spending. He then weighed and supported tight monetary policies of the Federal Reserve Board to deliberately drive up interest rates, again to curb consumer demand created through borrowing. Unemployment reached 10.7 percent. We
401

experienced skyrocketing interest rates. Our dollar inflated abroad. There were record bank failures, record farm foreclosures, record business bankruptcies, record budget deficits and record trade deficits.

Mr. Reagan brought inflation down by destabilizing our economy and disrupting family life. He promised -- he promised in 1980 a balanced budget. But instead we now have a record 200 billion dollar budget deficit. Under Mr. Reagan, the cumulative budget deficit for his four years is more than the sum total of deficits from George Washington to Jimmy Carter combined. I tell you, we need a change.

How is he paying for these short-term jobs? Reagan's economic recovery is being financed by deficit spending -- 200 billion dollars a year. Military spending, a major cause of this deficit, is projected over the next five years to be nearly 2 trillion dollars, and will cost about 40,000 dollars for every taxpaying family. When the Government borrows 200 billion dollars annually to finance the deficit, this encourages the private sector to make its money off of interest rates as opposed to development and economic growth. Even money abroad, we don't have enough money domestically to finance the debt, so we are now borrowing money abroad, from foreign banks, governments and financial institutions: 40 billion dollars in 1983; 70-80 billion dollars in 1984 -- 40 percent of our total; over 100 billion dollars -- 50 percent of our total -- in 1985. By 1989, it is projected that 50 percent of all individual income taxes will be going just to pay for interest on that debt.

The United States used to be the largest exporter of capital, but under Mr. Reagan we will quite likely become the largest debtor nation. About two weeks ago, on July the 4th, we celebrated our Declaration of Independence, yet every day supply-side economics is making our nation more economically dependent and less economically free. Five to six percent of our Gross National Product is now being eaten up with President Reagan's budget deficits. To depend on foreign military powers to protect our national security would be foolish, making us

402

dependent and less secure. Yet, Reaganomics has us increasingly dependent on foreign economic sources.

This consumer-led but deficit-financed recovery is unbalanced and artificial. We have a challenge as Democrats to point a way out. Democracy guarantees opportunity not success.

Democracy guarantees the right to participate, not a license for either a majority or a minority to dominate.

The victory for the Rainbow Coalition in the Platform debates today was not whether we won or lost, but that we raised the right issues. We could afford to lose the vote; issues are non-negotiable. We could not afford to avoid raising the right questions. Our self-respect and our moral integrity were at stake. Our heads are perhaps bloody, but not bowed. Our back is straight. We can go home and face our people. Our vision is clear.

When we think, on this journey from slave-ship to championship, that we have gone from the planks of the Boardwalk in Atlantic City in 1964 to fighting to help write the planks in the platform in San Francisco in '84, there is a deep and abiding sense of joy in our souls in spite of the tears in our eyes. Though there are missing planks, there is a solid foundation upon which to build. Our party can win, but we must provide hope which will inspire people to struggle and achieve; provide a plan that shows a way out of our dilemma and then lead the way.

In 1984, my heart is made to feel glad because I know there is a way out -- justice. The requirement for rebuilding America is justice. The linchpin of progressive politics in our nation will not come from the North; they, in fact, will come from the South. That is why I argue over and over again. We look from Virginia around to Texas, there's only one black Congressperson out of 115. Nineteen years later, we're locked out of the Congress, the Senate and the Governor's mansion. What does this large black vote mean? Why do I fight to win second primaries and fight gerrymandering and annexation and at-large

403

[elections]. Why do we fight over that? Because I tell you, you cannot hold someone in the ditch unless you linger there with them. If you want a change in this nation, you enforce that Voting Rights Act. We'll get 12 to 20 Black, Hispanics, female and progressive congresspersons from the South. We can save the cotton, but we've got to fight the boll weevils. We've got to make a judgment. We've got to make a judgment. It is not enough to hope ERA will pass. How can we pass ERA? If Blacks vote in great numbers, progressive Whites win. It's the only way progressive Whites win. If Blacks vote in great numbers, Hispanics win. When Blacks, Hispanics, and progressive Whites vote, women win. When women win, children win. When women and children win, workers win we must all come up together.

Thank you.

For all of our joy and excitement, we must not save the world and lose our souls. We should never short-circuit enforcing the Voting Rights Act at every level. When one of us rise[s], all of us will rise. Justice is the way out. Peace is the way out. We should not act as if nuclear weaponry is negotiable and debatable.

In this world in which we live, we dropped the bomb on Japan and felt guilty, but in 1984 other folks [have] also got bombs. This time, if we drop the bomb, six minutes later we, too, will be destroyed. It's not about dropping the bomb on somebody. It is about dropping the bomb on everybody. We must choose to develop minds over guided missiles, and think it out and not fight it out. It's time for a change.

Our foreign policy must be characterized by mutual respect, not by gunboat diplomacy, big stick diplomacy, and threats. Our nation at its best feeds the hungry. Our nation at its worst, at its worst, will mine the harbors of Nicaragua, at its worst will try to overthrow their government, at its worst will cut aid to American education and increase the aid to El Salvador; at its worst, our nation will have partnerships with South Africa. That's a moral disgrace. It's a moral disgrace. It's a moral disgrace.

We look at Africa. We cannot just focus on Apartheid in Southern Africa. We must fight for trade with Africa, and not just aid to Africa. We cannot stand idly by and say we will not relate to Nicaragua unless they have elections there, and then embrace military regimes in Africa overthrowing democratic governments in Nigeria and Liberia and Ghana. We must fight for democracy all around the world and play the game by one set of rules.

Peace in this world. Our present formula for peace in the Middle East is inadequate. It will not work. There are 22 nations in the Middle East. Our nation must be able to talk and act and influence all of them. We must build upon Camp David, and measure human rights by one yard stick. In that region we have too many interests and too few friends.

There is a way out -- jobs. Put America back to work. When I was a child growing up in Greenville, South Carolina, the Reverend Sample used to preach every so often a sermon relating to Jesus. And he said, "If I be lifted up, I'll draw all men unto me." I didn't quite understand what he meant as a child growing up, but I understand a little better now. If you raise up truth, it's magnetic. It has a way of drawing people.

With all this confusion in this Convention, the bright lights and parties and big fun, we must raise up the simple proposition: If we lift up a program to feed the hungry, they'll come running; if we lift up a program to study war no more, our youth will come running; if we lift up a program to put America back to work, and an alternative to welfare and despair, they will come working.

If we cut that military budget without cutting our defense, and use that money to rebuild bridges and put steel workers back to work, and use that money and provide jobs for our cities, and use that money to build schools and pay teachers and educate our children and build hospitals and train doctors and train nurses, the whole nation will come

405

running to us.

As I leave you now, we vote in this convention and get ready to go back across this nation in a couple of days. In this campaign, I've tried to be faithful to my promise. I lived in old barrios, ghettos, and reservations and housing projects. I have a message for our youth. I challenge them to put hope in their brains and not dope in their veins. I told them that like Jesus, I, too, was born in the slum. But just because you're born in the slum does not mean the slum is born in you, and you can rise above it if your mind is made up. I told them in every slum there are two sides. When I see a broken window -- that's the slummy side. Train some youth to become a glazier -- that's the sunny side. When I see a missing brick -- that's the slummy side. Let that child in the union and become a brick mason and build -- that's the sunny side. When I see a missing door -- that's the slummy side. Train some youth to become a carpenter -- that's the sunny side. And when I see the vulgar words and hieroglyphics of destitution on the walls -- that's the slummy side. Train some youth to become a painter, an artist -- that's the sunny side.

We leave this place looking for the sunny side because there's a brighter side somewhere. I'm more convinced than ever that we can win. We will vault up the rough side of the mountain. We can win. I just want young America to do me one favour, just one favour. Exercise the right to dream. You must face reality -- that which is. But then dream of a reality that ought to be -- that must be. Live beyond the pain of reality with the dream of a bright tomorrow. Use hope and imagination as weapons of survival and progress. Use love to motivate you and obligate you to serve the human family.

Young America, dream. Choose the human race over the nuclear race. Bury the weapons and don't burn the people. Dream -- dream of a new value system. Teachers who teach for life and not just for a living; teach because they can't help it. Dream of lawyers more concerned about justice than a judgeship. Dream of doctors more concerned about public health than personal wealth. Dream of preachers and priests who

406

will prophesy and not just profiteer. Preach and dream!

Our time has come. Our time has come. Suffering breeds character. Character breeds faith. In the end, faith will not disappoint. Our time has come. Our faith, hope, and dreams will prevail. Our time has come. Weeping has endured for nights, but now joy cometh in the morning. Our time has come. No grave can hold our body down. Our time has come. No lie can live forever. Our time has come. We must leave racial battle ground and come to economic common ground and moral higher ground. America, our time has come. We come from disgrace to amazing grace. Our time has come. Give me your tired, give me your poor, your huddled masses who yearn to breathe free and come November, there will be a change because our time has come.

PART 4

Conclusion and
Useful information

Chapter Thirty

Conclusion -Looking back, looking forward

"Nobody in the world, nobody in history, has ever gotten their freedom by appealing to the moral sense of the people who were oppressing them."

The topics covered in this book include a wide variety of issues on history, race and racism, trade unions, politics, culture and black struggles against colonialism, imperialism and capitalism. The purpose of this chapter is to pull some of these issues together so that having explored so much about the past we can look at the ways in which we can move forward in building a united, strategic and successful anti-racism future for the present and future generations. Learning about the past helps us to assess and understand who we are and how we can build a future that is free from the prejudices, injustices, brutality inequality, exploitation and racism from the past.

For over 400 years black people -meaning those people of African, Asian, Caribbean and South East Asian and mixed race descent-, have been attacked, brutalised and demonised by white people of European descent, through imperialism, colonialism and enslavement and capitalism. The enslavement demonization, genocides and mass murders by the Europeans took place in Africa, North and South America, the Caribbean, Asia, Australia, and the Middle East and indeed every corner of the world saw the destruction of hundreds of millions of lives. Although the natives of North, Central and South America suffered the most savage and inhuman cruelty for over about the same duration as the natives of Africa, the genocide against the natives in the Americas was the biggest and most prolonged holocaust in the history of human experience. Had the Europeans not invaded and exterminated around 95 per cent of the native population over 400 years, the native population would have exceeded well over 150 million people. Similarly, the genocide in Africa over the same period would have seen the population almost doubled today.

This period of colonialism, enslavement, occupation and genocide provided the Europeans with the resources in human and physical capital, goods, commodities, raw materials and wealth to start and build the industrial revolution and the economies of Europe, whilst at the same time enabling them to settle hundreds of millions of Europeans in the Americas, Africa, Australia, New Zealand, India and elsewhere. The prosperity of Western Europe was built on the blood, sweat, tears and genocide of hundreds of millions of black people not only during the hundreds of years of colonisation, but in many cases around the world today. Especially in Africa where over 20 million people in the Congo have suffered from cruel death over the last 50 years and are continuing to do so, due to the exploitation of the people and the natural resources of the Congo by the Western capitalists. These capitalists are set on a course to re-colonise Africa through land grabs, wars and corruption of the leaders and political structures across the African continent.

I hope that by defining the term "black" the way I did will not cause any offence or, cause different groups to feel marginalise or excluded. I know that many Asians would not describe themselves as "black" and this may also apply to some people of mixed race. I also know that the term "black" evokes the specific historical experience of people of African descent. Given the fact that there are over 2.3 people of African descent living in Britain today and over 25 per cent of relationships in Britain especially in urban areas in England involves someone from an African or non-white background and another person from a white background. This means that there is considerable inter-relationships between black and white people. Hence a growing number of children from mixed ethnic and racial backgrounds.

There will always be problems over how the non-white population is defined, especially as their number and diversity continue to increase in Britain and Europe. There are over 12 million non-white people in Britain today, mainly Asians and over 40 million in Europe with a number of people defining themselves by their ethnicity, race, or culture, such as British Asians, British Muslims, Black Londoners, Black British and so on. The reason for a common term in defining all non-white people in Britain is a political one, due to the nature of the British society, culture, history and institutions. For most white people in Britain today, if you are not white you are broadly categorised as black, Pakistanis, Caribbeans or Africans. The fact is that you are not white in Britain, Europe, America, Australia, New Zealand, Canada and parts of South America you are more likely to suffer from racism; exploitation; poverty; and inequality in health, education, housing, employment and opportunities.

Unity is strength

In order to counteract such a situation it makes sense for the non-white population to UNITE and work together in every area of activity including economic, political, social and cultural areas to combat the oppression of racism and marginalisation by the white dominated structures and institutions that are controlled by white people. Uniting with other non-white groups that are part of the underclass and victims of racism and oppression can only make sense. It does not mean that groups and organisations involving, organising and representing specific groups on the basis of ethnic, racial, national, cultural or religious identities should discontinue such actions, which are aimed at strengthening their particular interests, but it would be a major advancement if all these groups would UNITE under a wider umbrella to share their common experience of racism and oppression. In many trade unions and in political parties there are sections that have been created for specific groups such as women, black and ethnic minorities, gays and lesbians, disabled people and young people, in order to bring people with common interests and concerns together, whilst also seeking to involve them in the wider key decision making structure of the organisation. People from all these categories have made substantial progress in achieving power and influence within these organisations as well as using these organisations to change not only the organisation they are attached to, but have created change within the wider economic, political and social systems. Black people will never be able to challenge racism and oppression effectively without building the essential UNITY through co-operation, understanding and compromises.

One of the most successful campaigns in Britain in recent decades has been the campaign around the racist murder of Stephen Lawrence, who was killed by a bunch of racist thugs in London in 1993. The huge success of this campaign which included the appointment of Doreen Lawrence – mother of Stephen Lawrence- to the House of Lords, where she is promoting anti-racism policies; the production of the McPherson Report on the Murder of Stephen Lawrence; the changes in the Race Relations Act in 2000 and the many changes within local government and public bodies, especially the Police Service have changed Britain in many ways. What is interesting is that the Lawrence Campaign was a united Campaign from the start. Doreen and Neville Lawrence were supported by professional people and well known anti-racist activists such as Marc Wadsworth, Lawyer Imran Khan, Kamaljeet Jandu, Diane Abbott MP, Suresh Grover, The Labour Party Black Sections, Black

Trades Union Solidarity Movement, the unions and the TUC. Many white trade union leaders, politicians, white activists and others joined the Campaign, which is black led to secure justice not only for Stephen Lawrence, but for ALL victims of police incompetence, racism and corruption. The Campaign has also been built on justice for all victims of racism and has benefitted both black and white people. My trade union, during my time as a member of the National Executive Committee gave the Campaign office facilities within its headquarters in Kings Cross free of cost, to continue its work.

Sadiq Khan MP, Michael Mansfield QC, Baroness

Doreen Lawrence and Jim Thakoordin in London,

2014, at the Lawrence Memorial Lecture

Clearly, some people may say "so what" despite the Lawrence Campaign; racism still pervades British society, institutions and life as a whole. As black people are still being killed by the police; unemployment, poverty and inequality is still rising amongst black people; racial attacks and stop and search amongst black people is still taking place. I would agree with some of this criticism and that is why I spend a lot of my time writing, organising, campaigning and fighting against racism and inequality not only within black organisations, but

413

mainly within the wider mainstream economic, political and social structures. It is relatively easy to sit back amongst like minded black people discussing black history and oppression, racism and the conditions of black people in Britain, Africa, Europe and America, and declaring racism a problem for white people. It is far more difficult, but at the same time more important to stand up against racism in mainstream institutions, such as unions, political parties, health and school boards and at meetings with the police, councillors and people with power over black people.

Just imagine if the black people in each town and city with over say, between 10 and 15 per cent of non-white population were organised and worked together in a UNITED way to elect local government councillors, members of Parliament, trustees on health and school boards, Crime and Police Commissioners and take part in local campaigns, how effective we could be! There are over 170 Parliamentary seats in the United Kingdom where black voters have the power to elect a black Member of Parliament if only they were united and worked together. Instead, what we get is individual black careerist and opportunist individuals, with very little or no involvement in the black community attaching themselves to political parties, get themselves elected and hardly, if ever, raise issues of race and racism in Parliament or in local government. Black disunity is a big problem for black people living in Britain. Black organisations that preach and practice exclusivity, Black Nationalism or, seeking the "black business route" through which that can defeat racism needs to look at this model again. There are well over 40,000 Asian millionaires and several billionaires, including the two richest people in Britain who happen to be Indians, but such personal wealth has done nothing in uplifting the 65 per cent of Asians, mainly Muslim people in Britain who are below or near the official poverty level. The capitalist system will always ensure that a few people get rich at the expense of the poor. The black middle class and millionaires are no different in their treatment of workers than white entrepreneurs.

Racism is personal and institutional and to change this evil system of oppression black people must stand together and also with the white working class through organisation within the unions and radical political parties that are positively opposed to racism, oppression and inequality. Not all white workers and institutions are equally racist, anti-racist or neutral on race and racism. Neither are all white people enemies of black people. Many white people over the centuries have been in the forefront of anti-racism struggles since colonialism, slavery and the arrival of the Windrush generation. When we look at the resistance against the racist, fascist and anti-immigration extremist organisations in Britain and Europe, we see white people, especially white working class people standing up in much greater numbers than the proportion of black people in the area where the fascists choose to make their presence felt. Opposing institutional racism and building the struggle to create equal opportunities to housing, jobs, education, public services, living standards and freedom from harassment, bullying, police brutality and discrimination will not just happen for black or white working class people. Rights, justice and freedom will only come about through conscious struggles, involving ALL victims of the institutionally racist and rotten class system.

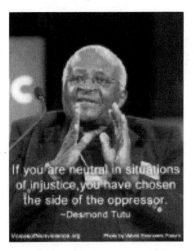

Black people must be part of the wider economic, political and social class struggles to secure equality, fairness, justice and freedom that will benefit society as a whole. Racism, sectarianism and nationalism are often seen as a populist approach to resolving conflicts over power and resources, but in reality such ideologies are destructive, dysfunctional and destructive for society as a whole. Injustice, oppression, inequality, discrimination and racism are all parts of the same evil that has ensured black people being an underclass in Britain, Europe and America. The political, economic and social structures operating in all these countries and supported by the media, large businesses and corporations, the rich and the ruling elites depends on inequality, conflicts, wars, oppression, discrimination injustice and racism for its survival. That is why they have been attacking the trade unions, public services, funding of community organisations, cutting benefits, dismantling the welfare state and privatising the National Health Service and public assets. Black people and black led organisations must decide what and whose purpose they serve, what is their role in defending the welfare state, the NHS, job opportunities, and to secure decent education, housing and living standards for ourselves, our children and for future generations.

Black people have suffered most under the austerity measures which imposed severe cuts in public services, living standards and the ability of trade unions to defend and promote the interests of workers without breaking the law. Both Labour and Conservative governments have imposed harsh measures against working class people which affected black people far more than they did the rest of the population. Unemployment amongst black people stands at twice and three times that of the rest of the population, with young blacks suffering up to 60 per cent unemployment in parts of the country. Black people are more than five times likely to be stopped and searched, incarcerated in prisons and mental institutions, three times more likely to be expelled from school, have a criminal record and drop out of the education system before completing university.

The black population in Britain live and work in the most deprived areas, earning over £7,000 less than the average worker each year, dies on average eight to 10 years before the average population and suffers greater inequality in health, housing and the environment. A few black people huddling together in relatively small numbers at meetings or, turning out when there is a crisis situation, such as a death in police custody; a black person killed by the police, or at individual events with a racist undertone will not seriously change the many issues facing black people, even though it is very important for black people to show solidarity with victims of racism.

The most successful demonstrations against the racists and fascists groups have been in the areas where local black people themselves have turned out in large numbers as they did in Tower Hamlets. This is in contrast to the two large demonstrations in Luton in 2011 and 2012 when the racist EDL and their thousand or so supporters descended on the town. Those opposing the EDL on both occasions were three times the size of the EDL mob, but it was noticeable that less than 2 per cent of the anti-EDL demonstrators were black in a town with over 35 per cent non-white population. The overwhelming majority of the anti-EDL people were from outside Luton and as far away as London, Bradford, Leeds, Cardiff, and other cities many miles away. This has been the same story across the UK where the racist EDL and the other racist and fascist parties have sought to intimidate, bully and abuse the local black communities.

The Black population in Britain exceeds 9 million people with the many large towns and cities having in excess of 30 per of the population and between 40 and sixty per cent of school children being non-white. This population is likely to double within the next 20 years and many towns and cities may have between 40 and 55 per cent non white population as the proportion of the white population declines and the black population rises. Given this situation, are we going to allow the situation to become similar to the situation in America where over 65 per cent of black population of African, Caribbean and indigenous descent suffering from the legacy of racism, systematic discrimination, marginalisation, poverty, and distress, whilst the minority being integrated within the prosperous white dominated class that controls the economic, political and social systems? The same system that exploits black people more than it exploits white is no answer to equality and

417

justice for black people who have suffered under white rule in America, Britain and Europe for centuries. Becoming capitalists and propping up the system will not liberate black people; it will ensure they remain as the dominant underclass. Some black people like black Americans have turned to the Black Churches for support and comradeship as well as the opportunity to save their souls, but as history has taught us, simply going to places of worship, accepting Christ and the teachings of the Bible has not saved black people from chattel slavery, economic slavery or being the most deprived underclass in America or Europe. People need basic things each day in order to survive, such as food, shelter, clothing, somewhere to live, healthcare and a supportive environment.

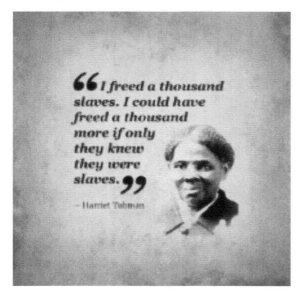

Too many black middle class people who have joined the ruling elite and have adopted the values and life styles of the dominant culture are not prepared to challenge the system which is institutionally racist. Many of them are proud of the sought after high positions they occupy in employment and in society and are very proud of their honours such as being a Member of the British Empire (MBE, CBE, Knighthood, Barons and Baronesses and other titles reserved for those loyal to the Queen, country and its institutions as well as the fame and fortune that goes with being a "successful" person. A sizeable number of blacks are prepared to deny any experience of racism, historical association with slavery or colonialism, and some are even convinced that they would be better off if they were living under colonial rule. Others have adopted the strategy of survival at any cost, by being self centred and self serving and even adopting what is often described by some black people as the "crab mentality." This strategy includes serving oneself, serving and propping up the dominant institutions and values, being loyal to the system even when they know the system is corrupt, unequal and racist. It also means not participating in challenging the system, pulling fellow colleagues down if they seek to escape from the system hence the "crab mentality" and even being prepared to join Her Majesty's armed forces and kill others including blacks to defend the very system that is institutionally racist.

So despite all the claims of the so-called black "community", which gives the impression that we are basically in the same boat, this is far from the truth, as the black community is as divided and in many ways more so that the white community because of the massive diversity in social and economic backgrounds, culture, religion, lifestyle, geographical and historical experiences. As a consequence many black groups generally associate with people from their ethnic, national, geographical, cultural, religious or socio-economic backgrounds, which make UNITY amongst black people extremely difficult. The dominant system relies on this diversity and differences in all the areas identified above to maintain the dominant values and culture, which are often defined as Britishness, democracy, rule of law, fairness, equality, human rights, justice and freedom. These values are of course far from being British values, as they are all also universal values to which every country would subscribe to. The fact that none of these so-called values are in practice free from prejudice, racism, and mis-application, and that Britain, America and other Western countries are institutionally racist; profoundly unequal; far from being democratic, free, or fair; fail to treat everyone equally in the eyes of the law; are sexist; disrespect the human rights of some immigrants, refugees, asylum seekers and minorities; and seek to control the actions and minds of the people, by

419

all means necessary, does not prevent the ruling elite and the media to frequently repeat them.

Our lives, our history our future

The main purpose of this book is to give the reader an opportunity to reflect and review their thinking and attitudes towards the issues and concerns facing us in Britain and in countries where we are in the minority and are faced with racism and oppression. We can choose to exercise a number of ways forward to overcome racism through the knowledge and experience we have of the past. The choices we have include the following:

Organise in small self support ethnic, racial, national or cultural groups and broadly internalise the problems we are faced with as black people and stay out of the dynamics that are taking place in the wider community and society that impacts on our daily lives, such as jobs, education, housing, health, the environment, pensions, living standards and justice, or we can do both. Black groups and communities can organise internally and at the same time establish strong links and alliances with groups, campaigns and institutions in which we have common interests, such as trade unions, political organisations and specific campaigns. It is in all of our interests to support the NHS and defend it from privatisation; participate in campaigns against racism and fascism; participating in the struggle to defend the welfare state, the education system and public services; campaign for better housing, employment opportunities and improvements in living standards; as well as joining in the campaigns to improve our environment and save our planet from global warming, famine, poverty, wars and exploitation.

Some people may choose to give up and accept whatever the system decides to do. Others may choose to withdraw from political actions and discussions and rely entirely on what the future holds for them either in a fatalistic way or by relying on God or some supernatural being or force to save them if not during their lifetime, but after they have died. A number may be prepared to become extremists and engage

420

in wars, terrorism as is the case in the Middle East with Islamists, Jihadists and terrorists, or take part in violence and crimes at home.

Most law abiding, caring and peaceful people who are opposed to racism, exploitation, oppression, poverty and violent conflicts would seek to work with and through organisations and institutions that are seeking the change they want. They are prepared to stand up and to demonstrate and campaign against wrong doing by the state; corporations; institutions; racist and fascist groups; those responsible for damaging our environment; corrupt politicians; abuse of power; discrimination and policies that would reduce our living standards and human rights. The only problem is that too many people who consider themselves in the categories mentioned above are not prepared to stand up and fight in numbers that would force those in power to do what is best for everyone, and not to put profits before people, or greed before need.

Black people must become an essential part of the struggle with the white working class to secure justice for all, especially since black people are more vulnerable due to racism and oppression.

We cannot afford to be spectators at a time when the world is changing so fast and is moving into situations that are causing more conflicts and damage to the environment as well as threatening the survival of the planet through global warming, pollution and climate change. In addition we are living in a world that has become more unequal, the rich getting richer and the poor, poorer; the number of conflicts and wars increasing; greater proportion of the world's resources being spent on weapons of destruction, instead of attacking poverty, famine, hunger, inequality in health and job opportunities; greater access to housing, education and a better life for ALL.

I believe that we can achieve all these qualities and a better and happier life for all if the majority of victims of racism, oppression and injustice are prepared to get up, stand up, and fight for their rights.

421

Chapter Thirty One

Useful information

TIME LINE OF KEY DATES, EVENTS AND FACTS IN CRONOLOGICAL ORDER

800-1500AD
Africa and parts of the Americas was as developed as Europe in agriculture, trade, arts, architecture
Industry and education. The slave trade existed in Africa. Conquered people and criminals were bought and sold as common transitions. The Arabs were regular purchasers of African slaves long before the Europeans entered the trade following the journeys by Christopher Columbus in 1492. Europeans, Arabs and Africans bought and sold slaves before 1492 and after.
1450 –1900
At least 40 million Africans were forcibly removed from Africa as slaves.
1502 First reported African slaves in the New World.
1505 First baby born to a Black couple was born in 1505 to the King of Scotland's African drummer and his wife.
1540 It is estimated that 1,000,000 Indians lived in Cuba before the arrival of the Europeans. Twenty-five years later only 2,000 survived. Most died from disease, starvation, genocide, forced labour or suicide.

423

In 1540 the Europeans imported 10,000 slaves each year to replace Indians.

1562 Britain entered the African slave trade. Spain started in 1479, Holland 1625, Sweden 1647 and Denmark 1697.

1562 First English slaving expedition by Sir John Hawkins.

1596 Queen Elizabeth I objecting to the presence of Blacks in Britain and arranged for their departure to Africa

1600 Blacks and Asians have been part of the standing British army since it was formed in 1600.

1619 The Dutch landed the first cargo of slaves from Africa in British America.

1619 First recorded cargo of Africans landed in Virginia.

1625 First English settlement on Barbados.

1626 First boatload of enslaved Africans to St. Kitts.

1631 Charles 1 granted monopoly on Guinea trade to a group of London merchants.

1640-1680 Beginning of large- scale introduction of African slave labour in the British Caribbean for sugar production.

1649 King Charles was beheaded in England.

1655 British capture of Jamaica

1672 Royal Africa company granted charter to carry Africans to Americas.

1740-1790 Between 1740 and 1790 hundreds of Black slaves emancipated themselves by running away from their masters.

1765-1946 Britain ruled India for nearly 200 years against constant rebellion by a minority of Indians. India gained independence from Britain in 1947.

1768 20,000 Black servants in London

1770 Captain James Cook ship Endeavour landed in Australia

1772 Slavery declared illegal in England, Wales & Ireland (the Somerset case).

1772 200 Blacks had a party in Westminster after the Lord Mansfield Judgement, which declared that Blacks should not be stripped out of Britain against their will.

424

1773 2 Black men imprisoned in Bridewell Prison, London for begging. 300 Black people visited them.

1776-1783 American War Of Independence

1778 Slavery declared illegal in Scotland.

1780 Asians in Britain. 1,000 Asian men are down and outs in London. East India Company is responsible for their presence. A Black woman called Charlotte Gardener was hanged on Tower Hill, London for her past in the Gordon Riots in which working class people rebelled against poverty.

1781 Over 100 enslaved Africans thrown overboard from the ship Zong.

1782 The first Black prose writer, Ignatius Sancho Had his letters published in England in 1782, two years after his death. He was born on a slave ship.

1783 Committee on a slave trade established by Quakers for sufferings.

1784 At least 4,00 Blacks arrived in England following the end of the American Civil War- (War of Independence) 20% of soldiers on both sides were Black.

1787 600 ex-slaves and servants deported to Sierra Leone in Africa. Most of them died within a short period. White Londoners were dancing to Black dance music at "Black Hopes" in 1787.

The first abolitionist to demand publicly for the total abolition of the slave trade and emancipation of slaves was Ottobah Cugoano, a Ghanaian whose book was published in 1787.

1787 Society for the abolition of the slave trade founded:Sharp as a president of a mostly Quaker committee

1788.First boatload of English prisoners deported to Australia where the Black Aborigines lived for 100,000 years.

14 July 1789 French Revolution started in France.

1789 George Washington elected the first President of the USA.

1788-1870 William Cuffy, a Black man was a prominent activist in the Chartist movement. He was deported to Tasmania after being convicted of insurrection. Black soldiers served under Admiral Nelson in the naval battles with the French.

1791 23 August - St.Dominique (Haiti) slave revolt.

425

1791 The Haitian Revolution begins as a slave uprising near Le Cap in the French West Indian colony of Santo Domingo and leads to establishment of black nation of Haiti in 1801.

1792 Resolution for gradual abolition of the slave trade

1793 King Louis XVI and his wife Marie Antoine were guillotined in France.

1793 Waves of white refugees pour into U.S. ports, fleeing the insurrection in Santo Domingo.

1794 The French National Convention emancipates all slaves in the French Colonies.

1794 March 22: U.S. Congress passes legislation prohibiting the manufacture, fitting, equipping loading or dispatching of any vessel to be employed in the slave trade.

1795 Pinckney's Treaty establishes commercial relations between U.S. and Spain.

1800 May 10: U.S. enacts stiff penalties for American citizens serving voluntarily on slavers trading between two foreign countries.

1804 January 1: The Republic of Haiti is proclaimed. The hemisphere's second Republic is declared on January 1, 1804 by General Jean-Jacques Dessalines. Haiti, or Ayiti in Creole, is the name given to the land by the former Taino-Arawak peoples, meaning "mountainous country."

1805 Bill for abolition passed in Commons, rejected in House of Lords.

1807 25 March – Slave Trade Abolition Bill passed in the British Parliament.

1807 British Parliament bans the Atlantic Slave Trade.

1808 US abolished the slave trade.

1817-1820 William Davidson and Robert Wedderburn both Black Jamaicans living in England were members of the revolutionary socialist organisations during working class rebellions between 1817 and 1820.

1820 Davidson a Black Jamaican who was elected as secretary of the newly formed shoemakers union was hanged 1st May 1920 with four of his white comrades for conspiracy.

1833 Abolition of slavery British Empire Bill passed, with effect from1834 and providing for up to six year apprentice transition. £20m voted as compensation to slave owners.

1838 1 August – enslaved men, women and children in Britain became free.

1842 Britain & US signed Webster-Ashburton Treaty, banning the slave trade on high seas.

1845 –1856 Mary Seacole, part Jamaican, part Scottish nursed soldiers in the Crimean War 1854-6.

1848 Emancipation by the French of their slaves.

1850 The fugitive slave law passed in the United States.

1861-1865 American Civil War between Southern and Northern states. It started on 12 April 1865. Blacks fought on both sides.

1865 Slavery finally abolished in United States Territory.

1873 Black spirituals were first sung in Britain by Fisk Jubilee singers in 1873.

1888 Slavery abolished in Brazil.

1889 Ernest Goffe a Black man from Jamaica arrived in Britain to study medicine. He was a doctor for many years. He was a member of the Fabian Society, a radical socialist movement which supported the Labour Party.

1890 Britain's first Black editor was Dominican- born, Samuel Jules Celestine Edwards who edited "Lux and Fraternity".

1890-1926 Africans were classified as a race that had not made any contribution to human civilisation despite their many achievements in language, medicine, architecture, scientists, artists and inventors.

1892-1895 The first Asian Member of Parliament was Dadabhai Naoroji who sat as Liberal MP for Finsbury in London.

1906 Two men, one Black and one white planted the American flag on the North Pole. Matthew A. Henson, a Black man, was the first American to reach the top of the world.

1912 The first political journal produced for Black people in Britain was the African Times and the Orient Review in 1912.

1913 John Archer Major of Battersea elected. John Archer a Black man born in Liverpool was elected to Battersea Council in London and served as Major in the same year 1913-14. He was the first British born Councillor in Britain to become an Alderman and an election agent for a constituency labour party.

1914-1918 War over. 2,068,665 Black and Asian soldiers died. Over 1,000 Black seamen from Cardiff in Wales were killed at sea during the 1914-18 war supporting Britain. 16 members of the West African Rifles were awarded the DCM during the 1914-18 World War. The British West Indies Regiment was awarded 5 D50s, 9 MCs, 8 DCMs, 37 MMs and 49 mentions in dispatches.

1917 The United States entered the Second World War (1914-18). Over 2,000,000 American Blacks registered to fight. 31% were accepted compared to only 26% of white men.

1921-27 **Gospel music started in America in the 1920's under the leadership of Thomas A> Dorsey.**

1922 Shapurji Saklatava, first Black MP in Britain. He was elected as a *communist.*

Marcus Garvey famous Black Nationalist died a lonely man in Fulham, London.

1923-1937 African German women were regularly forced to accept sterilisation as a means of keeping the numbers of Blacks in Germany down. The Society for Racial Hygiene founded in 1905 started to conduct sterilisation operations for so-called eugenic reasons and elimination of racial disease. This practice was regularly conducted against white German women who had Black male partners.

1927 The commissioner for the Palestine (state) informed the Imperial Bureau of concerns regarding Black children in Germany as the mature into adulthood.

15 January 1929 Birth of Martin Luther King in Atlanta Georgia. He was assassinated in Memphis on 4 April 1968.

1939-45 Around 6 million Jews were sent to death camps in Germany and Poland by the Nazis. Many thousands of Blacks living in Germany perished in forced labour and extermination camps by the Nazis. Germany colonised several African countries including Cameroon, South West Africa, Tanganyika, Togo and Rwanda up to the First World War.

1942 Congress of Racial Equality (CORE) founded in America.

1944 Famous West Indian Cricketer Sir Learie Constantine won a case against a top London hotel for refusing him accommodation.

1945 One of the first liberators of the Nazi death camp was an all Black Tank Regiment of the segregated USA army.

1960 The Royal Navy regularly arrested slave-trading crafts between Africa and some Arab states.

1962 Slavery outlawed in Saudi Arabia in 1962.

Immigration Act terminating entry to Britain from the Commonwealth

1963 Four Black children murdered in their Baptist church by racists in Birmingham, Alabama.

28 August 1963 Over 250,000 people marched on Washington to support civil rights.

22 November 1963 President Kennedy assassinated.

1964 Three Civil Rights workers murdered in America.

2 July 1964 Civil Rights Act 1964 passed in USA.

1964-1968 Riots took place in several American cities because of racism and poverty involving Black people. There were over 150 riots between 1965 and 1968. 83 people, mainly Blacks were killed and 1,800 seriously injured by police and white racists in 1967 alone.

1965 Two whites and one Black murdered in Selma, Alabama during a civil rights demonstration.

1970 Muskat and Oman stopped the slave trade in 1970.

1975 Race Relations Act making it unlawful to discriminate in jobs and services

1983 Establishment of a natural holiday in America to honour Dr. Martin Luther King.

1984 It was estimated that up to 250,000 slaves were held by slave owners in the Sahel, which is part of the Sahara desert.

1987 The Anti-Slavery Society found evidence of slavery in India, South America, Africa, the Philippines and Yugoslavia.